WORD TRAPS

Other books by Jordan L. Linfield and Joseph Krevisky

The Bad Speller's Dictionary
The Awful Speller's Dictionary
Guide to Films on Jobs, Training and the Ghetto

WORD TRAPS

A Dictionary of the 5,000 Most Confusing Sound-Alike and Look-Alike Words

Jordan L. Linfield
Joseph Krevisky

AN INNOVATION PRESS BOOK

Collier Books
Macmillan Publishing Company
New York

Maxwell Macmillan Canada
Toronto

Maxwell Macmillan International
New York   Oxford   Singapore   Sydney

Collier Books
Macmillan Publishing Company
866 Third Avenue
New York, NY 10022

Maxwell Macmillan Canada, Inc.
1200 Eglinton Avenue East
Suite 200
Don Mills, Ontario M3C 3N1

Macmillan Publishing Company is part of the Maxwell Communication Group of Companies.

Library of Congress Cataloging-in-Publication Data
Linfield, Jordan L.
    Word traps: a dictionary of the 5,000 most confusing sound-alike and look-alike words / Jordan L. Linfield, Joseph Krevisky.—1st Collier Books ed.
        p. cm.
    ISBN 0-02-052751-9
        1. English language—Homonyms—Dictionaries.   I. Krevisky, Joseph.   II. Title.
PE1595.L56   1993
423'.1—dc20
                                                    92-25760
                                                        CIP

Macmillan books are available at special discounts for bulk purchases for sales promotions, premiums, fund-raising, or educational use. For details, contact:

Special Sales Director
Macmillan Publishing Company
866 Third Avenue
New York, NY 10022

FIRST COLLIER BOOKS EDITION 1993
10 9 8 7 6 5 4 3 2 1
Printed in the United States of America

Introduction

"Wondrous the English language . . ."

Walt Whitman was right in 1856 when he penned this line, and he'd be even more so today. English is the language of commerce and trade, of diplomacy and science. It is the language used to land airplanes in Tokyo and Berlin, in Rio and Moscow. And its more than 500,000 words serve us well.

But spelling many of those words is a real problem.

There are only twenty-six letters in our alphabet but more than forty distinct sounds. And each of those sounds can be spelled as many as five or six different ways. For example, the sound *ch* as the word *church* can also be spelled as:

c as in *c*ello
che as in ni*che*
cz as in *Cz*ech
tch as in ma*tch*
te as in righ*te*ous
ti as in ques*ti*on
t as in na*t*ure

The sound of the letter *n* at the beginning of words such as *no* can be spelled as *gn* (gnat), *kn* (know), *mn* (mnemonic), and *pn* (pneumonia). And in some words we use one *n* (inane), while in others we have to use *nn* (manner).

Vowels give us even more trouble, causing us to ask: Why doesn't *break* rhyme with *freak?* Why do we say *sew*, but also *few?* Why isn't *enough* spelled like *bluff?*

This would be bad enough ... but there is more to come. For starters, let's go back to the word *manner.* There is another that sounds the same but is spelled *manor.* There are several thousand such sound-alike words. Works like *its* and *it's; there* and *their; affect* and *effect; to, too,* and *two.* It can all get very confusing, especially with sound-alikes like: *ewe, hew, hue, whew, yew, you,* and even *yu.*

Then there are look-alikes, words that look the same but are pronounced differently. Words like: *wind* (the wind that blows) and *wind* (wind the clock), or *row* (with an oar) and *row* (a fight). In order to pick out the correct member of these groups, you have to understand the context in which the word is being used.

Word Traps is the largest and most complete compilation of words that sound alike or look alike. This book has been designed to take up where your desk dictionary or computer spelling checker is of little help. *Word Traps* will save you time and effort in needless searches for these troublesome combinations. It will also reduce such embarrassments as the one that occurred recently at the United States Naval Academy graduation, where diplomas were presented to the graduates with the word *Naval* spelled *Navel.* All the diplomas had to be recalled when the error was discovered.

Such mistakes can happen to anyone. *Word Traps* will reduce the chance of it happening to you.

How to Use *Word Traps*

First, look over the book. Browse through it and enjoy the wealth of words contained in it. Then go searching for your demons. The look-alikes and sound-alikes are arranged in alphabetical order. For example, the sound-alikes **centaur, center, scenter** appear in the letter **C** in alphabetical order, along with definitions and examples of their use. They are also cross-referenced in the letter **S,** as "*scenter* See centaur." Thus you can easily locate this sound-alike combination either under the letter *C* or under the letter *S.*

You might want to keep a list or notebook of your personal

spelling and pronunciation demons. You will note that several blank pages have been left at the back of the book for such use.

Pronunciation Because some words have different meanings depending on how they're pronounced (for example, *bow* means one thing when it's pronounced like *cow* and another thing when it's pronounced like *so*), *Word Traps* uses a simple phonetic pronunciation guide to distinguish between sound-alike, look-alike, and spelled-alike words. The pronunciation is bracketed and follows the word entry. For example: access *[ak'* • *sess]*. There is a dot to show how the word is broken into syllables, and a short accent mark (') right after the syllable that is stressed. In some cases, the pronunciation of the entire word is spelled out; in others, the entry might indicate that the word rhymes with a more commonly used word by *"[rhymes w.]."* Vowel sounds are represented phonetically. The unaccented vowel sound (the "schwa") is shown as *[u]*, *[uh]*, or *[i]*.

For example: area *[air'* • *ee* • *uh]*.

We have only included a pronunciation entry for those words whose pronunication is confusing, since the pronunciation of many of the words in *Word Traps* is quite clear.

Abbreviations The following abbreviations are used in *Word Traps:*

adj.	adjective
adv.	adverb
aux.	auxiliary
conj.	conjunction
contr.	contraction
interj.	interjection
n.	noun
pl.	plural
prep.	preposition
pron.	pronoun
sing.	singular
v.	verb
w.	with

If we have left out any sound-alikes or look-alikes that you feel ought to appear in the next edition, please write us at Innovation Press, 373 Broadway, Suite F-4, New York, NY 10013. We would also appreciate receiving any clippings or citations where misuse of a look-alike or sound-alike appears.

Acknowledgments We thank Natalie Chapman for her support and advice, and Nancy Cooperman for her superior editing.

WORD
TRAPS

A

abac, abac
>abac *n.* a diagram used in mathematical calculations
>aback *adv.* backward; surprised: 'We were taken aback by his sudden hostility'

abbé, abbey
>abbé *n.* a French clergyman; a courtesy title for an ecclesiast or priest
>abbey *n.* a monastery or convent

abject, object
>abject *n.* an outcast
>abject *adj.* wretched; hopelessly downcast; oppressed by superior power
>object *[ob'•ject] n.* a goal, an aim: 'The object of the game is to win'; a material thing
>object *[ob•ject'] v.* to oppose a person, idea, or action: 'I object to that ugly object in the middle of my room'

abjure, adjure
>abjure *v.* to reject or recant under oath: 'The prisoner will abjure his coerced confession'
>adjure *v.* to put under oath, solemnly command; to advise or urge earnestly: 'I adjure you to tell the truth'

abrogate, arrogate
>abrogate, *v.* to do away with, to abolish, to annul: 'The enemy will abrogate their nonaggression treaty and attack'

arrogate *v.* to make an unjust or presumptuous claim: 'He likes to arrogate the right to make changes without consultation'

absent, absinth/absinthe

absent *[ab•sent']* *v.* to keep away

absent *[ab'•sent]* *adj.* not present, missing

absinth *or* absinthe *[ab'•sinth]* *n.* a liqueur flavored with anise

absentee, absentia

absentee *[ab•sen•tee']* *n.* one who isn't present

absentia *[ab•sen'•shuh]* *adj.* in the absence of (used in legal papers): 'in absentia'

absorb, adsorb

absorb *v.* to take in an object, substance, or idea and make it part of one's own; to suck up or swallow up

adsorb *v.* to take up onto or adhere to a surface, used to describe chemical reactions: 'The gases will adsorb on the charcoal in this experiment'

abstract, obstruct

abstract *[ab'•stract]* *n.* a condensation; a synopsis

abstract *[ab•stract']* *v.* to condense; to disassociate; to remove or separate

abstract *[ab•stract']* *adj.* theoretical, not easy to understand

obstruct *v.* to block; to impede; to shut out

abstruse, obtuse

abstruse *adj.* hard to understand; deep, profound

obtuse *adj.* dull or slow in understanding; not sharp

abysmal, abyssal

abysmal *adj.* extremely bad: 'That slum provides abysmal housing'; extreme: 'Most people display abysmal ignorance of nuclear fission'

abyssal *adj.* pertaining to the lowest ocean depths

academia, academy

academia *n.* the academic world

academy *n.* a special or advanced school, usually private: 'the U.S. Naval Academy' or 'the Soviet Academy of Sciences'; a society

accede, axseed, exceed

accede *v.* to agree or give approval to a proposal or request: 'I accede to your request that we start earlier'; to take office: 'Prince Charles will accede to the throne'

axseed *n.* a plant

exceed *v.* to go over a limit: 'At seventy miles an hour you exceed the speed limit'

accelerate, exhilarate

accelerate *v.* to speed up or hasten

exhilarate *v.* to make happy or elate

accent, ascend, ascent, assent

accent *[ak'•sent] n.* the distinctive, often regional, pronunciation of words: 'People born in Mississippi usually speak with a Southern accent'; inflection or tone; the emphasis placed on a syllable; any special emphasis: 'The accent in style is on youth'

ascend *[uh•send'] v.* to go up, to climb: 'God instructed Moses to ascend Mount Sinai to receive the Ten Commandments'

ascent *[a•sent'] n.* an upward movement; an upward slope

assent *[uh•sent'] v.* to agree: 'The Iraqis had to assent to a ceasefire'

accept, except, excerpt

accept *v.* to agree; receive; approve; understand

except *v.* to exclude

except *prep.* besides, excluding: 'She invited everybody in the class except him'

except *conj.* only; with the exception: 'I would go around the world on the *QE 2* except it's too expensive'

excerpt *n.* a short extract from something written or filmed

accepter, acceptor

accepter *n.* one who receives something

acceptor *n.* in physics, an atom that receives an electron; one who accepts a bill of exchange

access, excess

access *[ak'•sess] n.* entry: 'You can gain access to the building through the back door'; the right to see or use something: 'His new job gave him access to classified information'

excess *[ek•sess'] n.* overindulgence or immoderation; a surplus: 'An excess of revenues over expenditures'; whatever exceeds an accepted limit: 'The excess of Hitler's regime shocked the world'

See also axes

accessible, assessable

accessible *adj.* unrestricted; practicable; able to be reached: 'The auditorium was quite safe, as all the exits were easily accessible'

assessable *adj.* capable of being taxed or evaluated: 'The city administration decided to increase the number of assessable homes'

accidence, accidents

accidence *n.* a subject of grammar that deals with word inflections

accidents *n.* (pl.) unexpected injuries, events, or mishaps

acclamation, acclimation

acclamation *n.* strong or loud approval or praise; an overwhelming vote by cheers or applause rather than by ballot: 'She was elected to the chair by acclamation'

acclimation *n.* adaptation to new circumstances or surroundings: 'His acclimation to the Arctic weather was very slow'

accrue, ecru

accrue *[uh•crew'] v.* to increase or accumulate: 'Interest will accrue to his account daily'

ecru *[eck'•rue] n.* a very light-brown color

acentric, eccentric
> acentric *[ay•cen'•trik] adj.* off center; having no center
> eccentric *[ek•sen'•trik] n.* a person of unusual or peculiar
> behavior or appearance; one who deviates from the
> norm

acetic, ascetic
> acetic *[a•seat'•ik] adj.* pertaining to the acid in vinegar
> ascetic *[a•set'•ik] n.* one who leads a life of extreme self-
> denial and austerity, often for religious or spiritual
> reasons

acidulous, assiduous
> acidulous *adj.* caustic or acid in taste or manner
> assiduous *adj.* industrious, diligent: 'She is assiduous in
> mastering calculus'

action, auction
> action *n.* initiative or enterprise: 'Let's take action on the
> environment'; a thing done, a deed: 'His action in
> helping her was greatly appreciated'; events in a play; a
> legal process; a military battle; the most exciting area:
> 'where the action is'
> auction *n.* a sale in which people bid against one another for
> an item

activate, actuate
> activate *v.* to rouse to action: 'Her speech will activate you to
> start working'; to stimulate; to make radioactive; to get
> something going
> actuate *v.* to put into motion, often of a mechanical device:
> 'The electronic impulse will actuate the machinery'; to
> act; to motivate

acts, ask, ax/axe
> acts *v.* 3d person, sing., present tense of act, to play a role in
> a play; to perform a duty; to behave: 'He acts like a fool'
> acts *n.* (pl.) enactments or laws: 'the acts of Congress'; deeds
> ask *v.* to question or inquire (often mispronounced as *aks*)
> ax *or* axe *n.* a heavy cutting tool often used to fell trees

ax *or* axe *v.* to cut brutally; to dismiss: 'The commissioner was
forced to axe her deputy for having his fingers in the till'

ad, add

ad *n.* an advertisement

add *v.* to increase; to append; to sum numbers in arithmetic

adapt, adept, adopt

adapt *v.* to adjust: 'I hope she can adapt to her new
surroundings'

adept *[ad'•ept] n.* one who is an expert

adept *[uh•dept'] adj.* very capable or proficient: 'She is very
adept at mathematics'

adopt *v.* to take into one's family legally; to accept; to make
one's own; to accept formally: 'Congress should adopt
the legislation by a close vote'

addable/addible, edible

addable *or* addible *adj.* capable of being increased; able to be
added

edible *adj.* suitable for eating

addict, attic, edict

addict *n.* one who is compulsive or habituated; an aficionado:
'He's an addict of classical music'

attic *n.* a room just beneath the roof; a garret

edict *n.* a proclamation; a decree; an order or command

addition, edition

addition *n.* the result of adding; the part added

edition *n.* the total number of copies printed at one time; the
form or version of a publication: 'The book was revised
and went into its second edition after the first edition
sold out'; a special issue

adds, ads, adz/adze

adds *v.* 3d person, sing., present tense of add, to increase; to
do arithmetical sums

ads *n.* (pl.) more than one advertisement

adz *or* adze *n.* a tool with a thin curved blade for shaping
wood

adept *See* adapt

adherence, adherents

adherence *n.* the act of sticking to a surface, idea, movement, or person

adherents *n.* (pl.) people who support or stick with an idea, sect, person, or movement

adieu, ado, à deux

adieu *interj.* goodbye, so long

ado *n.* a fuss or bother

à deux *adj.* involving two people; intimate

adjoin, adjoint, adjourn, adjunct

adjoin *[uh•join']* *v.* to attach; to be close to or in contact with

adjoint *[uh•joint']* *n.* a mathematical operation

adjourn *[uh•jurn']* *v.* to suspend or recess: 'The meeting is due to adjourn at noon'

adjunct *[aj'•unkt]* *n.* an assistant; a person of lower rank; a part-time college teacher: 'They were hiring another adjunct to save money'

adjure *See* abjure

adjutant, adjuvant

adjutant *n.* an assistant to a commanding officer

adjuvant *n.* a substance added to a drug to enhance its effect

adjuvant *adj.* auxiliary; serving to aid

ado *See* adieu

adolescence, adolescents

adolescence, *n.* the stage or age between childhood and adulthood

adolescents *n.* (pl.) people between the ages of 13 and 19; teenagers

adopt *See* adapt

ads *See* adds

adsorb *See* absorb

adverse, adverts, averse

adverse *adj.* unfavorable; against one's interest: 'The scandal created adverse publicity for the town' adverts *v.* 3d person, sing, present tense of advert, to call attention; refer to

averse *adj.* feeling strongly opposed to an idea or action; disinclined: 'It seems that Mario Cuomo was averse to running for president'

advert, avert, evert

advert *[ad•vurt']* *v.* to allude to; to call attention to; to refer to; to pay attention to

avert *[uh•vurt']* *v.* to ward off; to deflect; to turn away: 'She tried to avert her eyes from the accident'

evert *[ee•vert']* *v.* to turn something inside out; to overturn: 'His article will evert my theory about global warming'

advice, advise

advice *[ad•vise']* *n.* counsel

advise *[ad•vize']* *v.* to counsel or recommend: 'I advise you to take my advice'

adz/adze *See* adds

Aegean, Augean

Aegean *n.* the Aegean Sea

Augean *adj.* filthy; corrupt; distasteful; extremely formidable

aegis, ages

aegis *[ee'•jis]* *n.* sponsorship; protection

ages *n.* a long period of time: 'I haven't seen him in ages'; periods; epochs

ages *v.* 3d person, sing., present tense of age, to mature, mellow, or develop

aerial, ariel

aerial *n.* an antenna for receiving radio waves; a forward pass in football

aerial *adj.* imaginary; of, relating to, or occuring in the air

ariel *n.* a gazelle

aerie, eerie/eery

aerie *[air'•ee]* *n.* a bird's nest on a high cliff or mountain

eerie *or* eery *[ear'•ee]* *adj.* frightening or mysterious; weird or strange

affair, affaire

> affair *n.* a piece of business; a concern; an issue: 'Discuss that affair with your lawyer'; a special event; a controversy: 'the Iran-Contra affair'
>
> affaire *n.* a love affair: 'They have been having an affaire for more than two years'

affect, effect

> affect *n.* a feeling or emotion
>
> affect *v.* to influence: 'That song can affect me so much that I can't help crying'; to pretend or cultivate: 'She likes to affect a French accent'
>
> effect *n.* a result: 'The effect of her efforts was substantial'; the power to bring about results: 'That song has quite an effect on me—it makes me cry'
>
> effect *v.* to bring about or to result in: 'She will effect a big change in the organization if she fires all the men'

affective, effective

> affective *adj.* relating to emotions or feelings
>
> effective *adj.* producing desired results

affluent, effluent

> affluent *adj.* rich, wealthy
>
> effluent *n.* something that flows out, as a river from a lake or garbage from a sewer

afflux, efflux

> afflux *n.* a flowing to, or something that flows: 'an afflux of pain to the arm'
>
> efflux *n.* an ending; a passing away or expiration

Africans, Afrikaans

> Africans *n.* (pl.) inhabitants of Africa
>
> Afrikaans *n.* a language spoken in South Africa

afterward/afterwards, afterword

> afterward *or* afterwards *adv.* after a while; later; subsequently
>
> afterward *n.* hereafter; by and by; the future
>
> afterword *n.* an epilogue; a short concluding section to a literary work

ages *See* aegis

aggression, egression

>aggression *n.* an unwarranted attack: 'The enemy committed an act of aggression'; belligerence: 'The patient displayed aggression in the psychiatrist's office'; self-assertiveness
>
>egression *n.* the act of emerging or of going out

aid, aide

>aid *n.* a helper; the act of helping; tangible assistance, such as money or food
>
>aide *n.* an assistant; one who performs a military, medical, or confidential role

AIDS, aides

>AIDS *n.* acronym, acquired immune deficiency syndrome
>
>aides *n.* (pl.) more than one aide or helper

aigrette, egret

>aigrette *n.* feathers; a spray of gems worn in the hair or on a hat
>
>egret *n.* a heron

ail, ale

>ail *v.* to be sick; to trouble
>
>ale *n.* a drink like beer: 'Too much ale can ail you'

ailment, aliment

>ailment *n.* an illness
>
>aliment *n.* food; material or moral support: 'We have to furnish these refugees with all types of aliments'

air, e'er, ere, err, heir

>air *n.* the mixture of oxygen and nitrogen that we breathe; demeanor: 'an air of dignity'; an artificial manner: 'put on an air'
>
>air *v.* to express views: 'He should air his gripes to me'; to ventilate; to broadcast on TV or radio: 'The program will air at 7 P.M.'
>
>e'er *[air] adv.* ever or forever (poetic use)
>
>ere *[air] prep.* before (poetic use)
>
>err *[ur] v.* to make a mistake
>
>heir *[air] n.* one who will or does inherit property or title
>
>*See also* hair

airless, hairless, heirless

    airless *adj.* having no air; lacking fresh air

    hairless *adj.* without any hair; bald

    heirless *[air' • less] adj.* without an heir

aisle, I'll, isle

    aisle *n.* a narrow indoor passageway

    I'll *contr.* I will or I shall

    isle *n.* a little island

ait, ate, eight

    ait *[ate] n.* a small island

    ate *v.* past tense of eat: 'We ate fish for dinner last night'

    eight *n.* the number between 7 and 9, 8

ala, à la/a la

    ala *n.* a wing or a winglike structure

    à la *or* a la *prep.* according to, in the style of: 'She wrote
        poetry à la Emily Dickinson'

à la mode, alamode

    à la mode *adj.* fashionable; served with ice cream: 'pie à la
        mode'

    alamode *n.* a light, glossy silk

albumen, albumin

    albumen *n.* the white of an egg

    albumin *n.* a protein found in blood and in animal and plant
        tissue

ale *See* ail

aleph, alif

    aleph *n.* the first letter of the Hebrew alphabet

    alif *n.* the first letter of the Arabic alphabet

align, A-line

    align *v.* to place in a line; to ally; to adjust to a proper
        position

    A-line *adj.* having a flared bottom and a fitted top, referring
        to a garment

aliment *See* ailment

alimentary, elementary

alimentary *adj.* relating to nourishment or nutrition: 'The alimentary canal is part of the digestive system'

elementary *adj.* relating to the simplest, basic, or fundamental: 'an elementary school'; 'an elementary particle'

all, awl

all *n.* everything: 'to give one's all'

all *adj.* the entire quantity or group: 'We ate all the cake'; every; to the greatest extent; the whole of

all *adv.* completely: 'I ran all through the town'; 'She's all alone'

all *pron.* totality; everybody and everything, the entire group: 'All of the children got sick from the food'; the entire situation: 'All went well'

awl *n.* a tool used to mark surfaces or pierce small holes

allay, alley

allay *[uh•lay']* *v.* to relieve or to calm; to alleviate: 'She can allay my fears with her quiet voice'

alley *[al'•lee]* *n.* a narrow outdoor passageway between two buildings

allegation, alligation

allegation *n.* something declared or asserted; an unsupported declaration

alligation *n.* the condition of being attached or conjoined

allergenic, allergic, allogeneic

allergenic *adj.* pertaining to the cause of an allergy or the substance which induces the allergy

allergic *adj.* reacting adversely, as to medication; having a negative reaction generally

allogeneic *adj.* referring to biologically related but different structures: 'An allogeneic skin graft might not take'

alliterate, illiterate

alliterate *[uh•lit'•e•rate]* *v.* to repeat an initial consonant sound in two or more words: 'She sells seashells by the seashore' is an example of alliteration (of the initial consonant 's') illiterate [i•lit'•e•rit] n. one who cannot read or write; one who lacks knowledge or understanding of a particular field: 'He's a computer illiterate'

all mighty See almighty

allover, all over

allover adj. ubiquitous; omnipresent; general: 'The allover effect of his speech was nil'

all over adv. finished, ended: 'Having lost the game, they felt that the season was all over'

allow, aloe, alow

allow [rhymes w. cow] v. to permit or let; to admit or concede; to allocate or allot: 'They allow an hour for lunch'

aloe [al'•o] n. a sweet-smelling succulent plant whose juice is often used as a tonic

alow [uh•lo'] adv. below (nautical): 'They told me to take the men alow, so we went to the ship's hold'

allowed See aloud

alloy, ally

alloy n. a union or mixture of two or more ingredients, usually metals

ally n. a close supporter or helper

ally v. to join together by treaty or marriage; to choose sides: 'Your vote will ally you with either him or me'

all ready, already

all ready adv. prepared or completely set: 'He was all ready to land in the morning'

already adv. previously: 'He was already there'; used as an intensifier: 'Stop already'

all right, all right/alright

all right adj. honest, honorable: 'He's an all right guy'

all right or alright adv. satisfactory; correct; unhurt: 'Despite the crash, they were all right'

all together See altogether

allude, elude, elute

allude *v.* to imply; to refer to something vaguely or obliquely: 'She tends to allude to her many romances, but I'm never sure they existed'

elude *v.* to evade, escape: 'The criminals hope to elude the police'; to shun

elute *v.* to extract a material from another material or to remove by adsorption

allusion, elusion, elution, illusion

allusion *n.* an indirect reference or mention

elusion *n.* a deception; an evasion; a clever escape: 'Their elusion from the enemy's grasp was the subject of a movie'

elution *n.* in chemistry, removal by dissolving

illusion *n.* a false or unrealistic perception or that which produces such a perception, often intentionally: 'She was under the illusion that she would receive a quick promotion'; 'a master of illusion'

alluvion, alluvium, eluvium, illuvium

alluvion *n.* a flood or flow of water against a river bank or ocean shore

alluvium *n.* material such as sand or silt deposited by flowing water

eluvium *n.* material such as rock debris or sand deposited by the wind

illuvium *n.* material leached from one layer of soil into another

all ways *See* always

ally *See* alloy

almighty, all mighty

almighty *adj.* all powerful: 'The almighty dollar took me everywhere in Europe'

all mighty *pron., adj.* each of them powerful: 'They are all mighty men, but they don't always win'

alms, arms

alms *n.* donations, as of food or money, to the poor

arms *n.* (pl.) parts of the body, namely, the upper limbs; instruments of war

arms *v.* 3d person, sing., present tense of arm, to prepare for war or to equip with weapons

aloe *See* allow

aloud, allowed

aloud *adv.* loudly, in a speaking voice: 'The teacher asked me to read the poem aloud, but I was too nervous to be heard'

allowed *v.* past tense of allow, to permit: 'We were allowed to leave when we finished the test'

alow *See* allow

alright *See* all right

altar, alter

altar *n.* a raised table or stage which serves as the center of worship or ritual in religious services

alter *v.* to modify or adjust without changing the essential nature: 'My tailor will alter the jacket to fit me'

altitude, attitude

altitude *n.* the elevation above a given surface, often sea level; in geometry, a perpendicular line segment or its length

attitude *n.* a feeling or idea about a person or a thing: 'His attitude toward her changed as they got older'; a posture or position; a ballet position

altogether, all together

altogether *adv.* completely, entirely, wholly: 'altogether satisfied with the results'; as a total: 'Altogether I will have spent $3,000 on the vacation'; with slight exceptions: 'Altogether, the marriage seems happy'

all together *pron., adv.* everything at the same time or place: 'They went all together in one car to the party'

alumna, alumnae, alumni, alumnus

alumna *n.* a woman who has attended a particular school

alumnae *n.* (pl.) two or more female graduates

alumni *n.* (pl.) two or more male graduates

alumnus *n.* a male former student

always, all ways

always *adv.* constantly, perpetually, ever: 'I'll always love you'

all ways *n.* every possible means: 'I will explore all ways to help you'

amend, amends, emend

amend *[uh•mend']* *v.* to correct; to improve behavior; to revise or alter formally: 'He voted to amend the existing bill'

amends *n.* a fine or a reparation; compensation for loss or injury

emend *[i•mend']* *v.* to make textual corrections

amiable, amicable

amiable *[ay'•mee•uble]* *adj.* pleasant, friendly; agreeable

amicable *[am'•ik•uble]* *adj.* peaceable; characterized by goodwill: 'The two parties were so amiable that they quickly reached an amicable agreement'

amour, armer, armoire, armor

amour *[uh•moor']* *n.* an illicit love affair

armer *n.* one who prepares an explosive for detonation; one who arms or provides with weapons

armoire *[arm•wahr']* *n.* a tall wardrobe or cupboard

armor *n.* defensive clothing protection: 'He wore his aloofness as his armor against society'; combat groups in an army

amputation, imputation

amputation *n.* a cutting off, often referring to limbs: 'The gangrene on his toe required its amputation'

imputation *n.* an indirect accusation; an insinuation: 'He resented the imputation of sexist behavior'

analysis, analyses

analysis *n.* the act of breaking a whole into parts for better understanding; an examination of a whole and its parts; a field of mathematics; a method of treatment by psychoanalysts analyses *n.* (pl.) more than one of the above

analyst, annalist

analyst *n.* a person who studies or carefully details problems; a psychiatrist or psychoanalyst: 'My analyst is a Freudian; she decided my problem is sex'

annalist *n.* a writer of historical records

anchorite, ankerite

anchorite *n.* a religious recluse; a hermit

ankerite *n.* a mineral containing iron

androgenous, androgynous

androgenous *adj.* producing male offspring; tending to promote male traits

androgynous *adj.* having both female and male characteristics; neither specifically masculine nor feminine; suitable for both sexes

anecdotal, antidotal

anecdotal *adj.* relating to an interesting or amusing account of a real or fictious incident

antidotal *adj.* relating to an antidote, something that counteracts the effects of poison

angel, angle

angel *[ayn'•jel] n.* a heavenly or spiritual being; a kind person

angle *[ang'•ul] n.* a mathematical term; a corner; an approach or method, often illicit or improper: 'She played every angle to get the promotion'; a viewpoint

angle *v.* to cast for fish; to seek a favor in a subtle fashion; to shape an event in a particular way: 'He can angle the story so as to cast suspicion on the suspect'

annalist *See* analyst

annals, annuals, annuls

annals *n.* (pl.) chronicles or periodicals dealing with academic or historical subjects

annuals *n.* (pl.) plants living but one season; publications published yearly annuls *v.* 3d person, sing., present tense of annul, to declare void; to abolish or to erase

annunciation, enunciation

annunciation *n.* a public statement; an announcement

enunciation *n.* clear pronunciation or articulation

ant, aunt

ant *n.* an insect

aunt *n.* a sister of one's mother or father

ante, anti, auntie/aunty

ante *n.* a stake in a poker game; a business share: 'We need money; it's time to up the ante'

anti *n.* a person opposed to some proposal or action

auntie *or* aunty *n.* a familiar form of aunt

antecedence, antecedents

antecedence *n.* priority; that which came before; precedence

antecedents *n.* (pl.) ancestors; words that are referred to by pronouns later in a sentence

antenna, antennas, antennae

antenna *n.* a rod to receive audio or TV signals; an insect's sensors

antennas/antennae *n.* (pl.) more than one audio or TV antenna or set of insect feelers

anthesis, antithesis

anthesis *n.* the period or action of a flower opening to full bloom

antithesis *n.* the direct opposite: 'She is the antithesis of her mother'

anti *See* ante

antic, antique

antic *[an'•tik] n.* a prank, a caper

antic *adj.* bizarre; comical; playful

antique *[an•teek'] n.* a relic of ancient or older times; art or furniture that, by law, must be at least 100 years old

antidotal *See* anecdotal

anus, heinous

anus *[ay'•nis] n.* the excretory organ of the alimentary canal

heinous *[hay'•nis] adj.* abominable; grossly wicked: 'The Texas chain-saw massacre was a heinous crime'

anymore, any more

anymore *adv.* at the present; any longer: 'If you do that anymore, I'll leave'

any more *adj.* an additional amount, usually negative: 'I can't eat any more pizza'

anyone, any one

anyone *pron.* anybody; any person; people generally: 'Anyone can win the lottery'

any one *pron.* any of several: 'There are so many candidates, and any one could do a good job'

anything, any thing

anything *pron.* any occurrence, object, or matter: 'anything goes'

any thing *n.* any of several things: 'You can choose any thing in the window'

anytime, any time

anytime *adv.* at any time: 'I can get a job anytime'

any time *n.* one of several times: 'Any time you choose to come would be fine'

anyway, any way, anyways

anyway *adv.* in any case; anyhow; at any rate; nevertheless: 'He objected, but she went anyway'

any way *n.* any method or manner: 'Any way we choose will involve danger'

anyways *adv.* a nonstandard form of anyway

aoul *See* owl

apatite, appetite

apatite *n.* a mineral

appetite *n.* the desire to eat; a craving or urge

aperitif, aperitive

aperitif *n.* a predinner alcoholic drink

aperitive *n.* a laxative

aphagia, aphasia

aphagia *n.* the inability to swallow

aphasia *n.* the inability to understand words or speak, a condition resulting from a brain injury

apiary, aviary

apiary *n.* a place where beehives are kept

aviary *n.* an enclosure for birds

apologia, apologue, apology

apologia *[ap•i•low'•jee•uh] n.* a defense of one's views or actions

apologue *[ap'•i•log] n.* an allegory; a fable with a moral

apology *n.* an expression of regret for wrongdoing

apostil/apostille, apostle

apostil *or* apostille *n.* a marginal note

apostle *n.* one sent to preach the gospel

apparat, apparatus

apparat *n.* the political bureaucracy of the former Russian Communist party

apparatus *n.* a set of instruments or tools

appetite *See* apatite

apposition, opposition

apposition *n.* bringing together; juxtaposition; in grammar, consecutive terms that refer to the same concept and have the same relationship to the rest of the sentence: 'Ronald Reagan, our fortieth president, often fell asleep at meetings'

opposition *n.* a person or group that is against something or someone; the act of being against: 'The environmental activists expressed their opposition to the nuclear plant'

appraise, apprise, apprize

appraise *v.* to assess the quality or value of something

apprise *v.* to inform: 'The school will apprise her of its decision to admit her' apprize *v.* to value or appreciate: 'One should apprize education for its own sake, not just as a means of making money'

appressed, oppressed

appressed *adj.* pressed close to or lying flat against

oppressed *adj.* ruled harshly

arbiter, orbiter

arbiter *n.* a judge

orbiter *n.* one that orbits or revolves around

arc, arch, ark

arc *n.* a segment of a curve; an electrical current

arch *n.* a curved structure over an open space, as in a doorway

arch *adj.* main, principal: 'The murderer is an arch villain'; saucy, impudent, haughty

ark *n.* Noah's boat or a similar ship; a cabinet that holds sacred Torahs in synagogues

area, aria

area *[air'•ee•uh] n.* the measure of a surface in square units: 'The room has an area of 100 square feet'; an extent of space or surface

aria *[are'•ee•uh] n.* an operatic solo

areola, areole, aureole

areola *n.* a part of an eye; a dark-colored ring, as around a breast nipple

areole *n.* a small pit or cavity

aureole *n.* a halo; a ring of light around the sun

See also oriel

ark *See* arc

armer, armoire, armor *See* amour

arms *See* alms

arraign, arrange

arraign *[uh•rain'] v.* to call before a court of law to answer a charge arrange *v.* to organize; to work out details; to negotiate or harmonize: 'The generals from both sides will arrange a ceasefire'; to adjust or put in order; to orchestrate (in music)

arrant *See* errand

array, arrêt

array *n.* an orderly foundation; a large number of people or things; a statistical or mathematical sequence

array *v.* to put in a desired order: 'to array the soldiers for inspection'; to put on fine clothes: 'They will array themselves in evening gowns'

arrêt *[uh•ray']* *n.* a court decree

arrhythmic, eurhythmic

arrhythmic *adj.* lacking regular rhythm: 'There was a pressing need to operate on his arrhythmic heart'

eurhythmic *adj.* pertaining to the choreography of harmonious bodily movements to improvised music or rhythmical speaking

arrogate *See* abrogate

arsine, arson

arsine *[are•seen']* *n.* a poisonous gas

arson *[are'•sun]* *n.* an illegal burning of property

artist, artiste

artist *n.* one skilled in a fine art

artiste *[are•teest']* *n.* a public performer; a musical or theatrical performer

artistic, autistic

artistic *adj.* pertaining to artists or the arts; showing artistry: 'Harrods displays food in quite an artistic way'

autistic *adj.* pertaining to a form of mental illness marked by a withdrawal from society and reality and absorption in daydreams and hallucinations

ascend, ascent *See* accent

ascetic *See* acetic

ascian, ashen

> ascian *[ash'•ee•in] n.* one having no shadow; an inhabitant of a torrid zone
>
> ashen *[ash'•in] adj.* very pale: 'When he heard of her death, his face became ashen'; pertaining to the ash tree

ashore, assure

> ashore *adv.* on or toward land
>
> assure *v.* to guarantee: 'I assure you that this order will be delivered on time'; to secure; to spur one's confidence; to stabilize

ask *See* acts

ass, asse

> ass *n.* a donkey; a stubborn person or a fool; buttocks (slang)
>
> asse *n.* a fox indigenous to Southern Africa

assay, essay

> assay *[uh•say'] n.* a test of ore or metals to determine composition; an examination of characteristics
>
> assay *v.* to test or evaluate
>
> essay *[ess'•ay] n.* an analytic or interpretive written composition; an attempt to do something
>
> essay *v.* to try or to attempt

assent *See* accent

assessable *See* accessible

assiduous *See* acidulous

assistance, assistants

> assistance *n.* aid; the help given
>
> assistants *n.* (pl.) helpers or auxiliaries

assure *See* ashore

asterid, asteroid

> asterid *n.* a starfish
>
> asteroid *n.* a minor planet

astray, estray

> astray *adv.* away from the correct path: 'The minister called on all who had gone astray to return to the church'; in error

estray *n.* a domestic animal that strayed

ate *See* ait

attach, attaché, attack

attach *v.* to bind or join together

attaché *[at•a•shay']* *n.* a specialist attached to an embassy

attack *v.* to strike out at; to criticize; to undertake vigorously: 'attack a problem'

attendance, attendants

attendance *n.* the number of people attending: 'The attendance at this fair broke all records'

attendants *n.* (pl.) helpers

attic *See* addict

attitude *See* altitude

auction *See* action

auditor, auditory

auditor *n.* one who listens; one who examines and verifies accounts

auditory *adj.* relating to the sense of hearing

Augean *See* Aegean

auger, augur

auger *n.* a tool used for boring holes in wood

augur *v.* to predict, to foreshadow

aught, ought

aught *n.* zero, zilch

ought *n.* moral obligation, duty

ought *aux. v.* to express one's obligation: 'You ought to pay your bill on time'; to express likelihood or probability: 'It ought to be nice out tomorrow'

aul *See* owl

aunt *See* ant

auntie/aunty *See* ante

aural, oral

aural *adj.* pertaining to the ear or sound

oral *adj.* pertaining to the mouth or speech

oral *n.* a school exam taken or administered orally

aureole *See* areola

auricle, oracle

>auricle *[or'•i•kel] n.* a part of the outer ear; an atrium of the
>heart

>oracle *[or'•ah•kel] n.* one who prophesies; a person or
>shrine through whom a deity speaks or reveals divine
>wisdom; a revelation; a person of great wisdom

autarchy, autarky

>autarchy *n.* autocratic rule

>autarky *n.* a national policy of establishing an independent
>and self-sufficient economy

auteur, hauteur

>auteur *n.* a film director who dominates the movie's style

>hauteur *n.* a haughty manner; arrogance

autistic *See* artistic

automation, automaton

>automation *[awt•ah•may'•shun] n.* the use of automatic or
>mechanical machinery to do work formerly done by
>humans

>automaton *[au•tom'•a•ton] n.* a robot; a person dogmatic or
>mechanical in thinking and action

averse *See* adverse

aversion, eversion

>aversion *n.* dislike, distaste, or antipathy

>eversion *n.* the act of turning inside out or the condition of
>being turned outward

avert *See* advert

aviary *See* apiary

avocation, evocation

>avocation *n.* an activity, such as a hobby, in addition to one's
>regular work

>evocation *n.* the act of summoning; the state of calling to
>mind

avoid, ovoid

>avoid *v.* to escape, evade, or shun

ovoid *n.* an egg-shaped object

avulsion, evulsion

avulsion *n.* a forcible separation; a sudden cutting off

evulsion *n.* an extraction

aw, awe, oar, o'er, or, ore

aw *interj.* exclamation of sympathy, dislike, protest, or disgust

awe *n.* respect combined with wonder or fear; fearful
reverence

oar *n.* a paddle for rowing a boat

o'er *adv.* over (poetic): 'O'er the land of the free / and the
home of the brave'

or *conj.* other, introduces alternatives: 'Either she or I will
speak for the family'; expresses approximation: 'It will
take two or three days'

ore *n.* a mineral from which metal can be extracted

away, aweigh

away *adv.* from a place: 'During the coffee break, he goes
away from his desk'; at once: 'Do it right away'

away *adj.* absent: 'I will be away on vacation for two weeks';
at some distance: 'He lives far away'; in baseball, an out:
'The bases were loaded, with two away'

aweigh *adj.* hanging just above the bottom of the sea:
'anchors aweigh'

aweful, awful, offal

aweful *adj.* inspiring adoration, worship, dread, or awe

awful *adj.* terrible, unpleasant, or dreadful

offal *n.* waste or by-products of a process; garbage; the
entrails of an animal

awhile, a while

awhile *adv.* for a short time: 'Rest awhile before you go'

a while *n.* an indefinite period of time: 'I haven't seen him
for a while'

See also while

awl *See* all

ax/axe *See* acts

axes, axis

    axes *n.* (pl.) tools for heavy cutting or chopping; more than one axis

    axis *n.* a mathematical straight line

    See also access

axiom, axion

    axiom *n.* a self-evident truth; a rule of law; a principle; a maxim

    axion *n.* a hypothetical particle of matter

axle, axel, axial, axil, axile, exile

    axle *n.* a shaft around which wheels revolve

    axel *n.* a jump in figure skating

    axial *[ak'•see•il] adj.* pertaining to an axis in mathematics

    axil *n.* the angle between a stem or upper face of a leaf and the supporting stem or branch which forms the axis

    axile *[aks'•ile] adj.* situated in or pertaining to the axis of a plant

    exile *[egg'•zile] n.* a person who is forced to leave his or her country; one who is expelled

axseed *See* accede

aye/ay, eye, I

    aye *or* ay *n.* an affirmative vote; yes; OK

    eye *n.* the organ of sight

    eye *v.* to look at: 'You can eye the photo on page 92'

    I *pron.* the self

    See also eyed

B

baal, Baal

baal *n.* a false god

Baal *n.* the sun god of several ancient Middle East peoples

babbitt, Babbitt

babbitt *n.* a kind of metal

Babbitt *n.* a smug, mediocre, conventional American
businessman, uninterested in cultural values; from the
name of the title character, George F. Babbitt, in a novel
by Sinclair Lewis.

babble, babel, Babel

babble *n.* chatter: 'There was so much babble around us that
we could not hear the speaker'

babel *[bay'•bil] n.* a racket, noise, din

Babel *[bay'•bil] n.* the city where the biblical tower was built

bach, bache, batch

bach *[batch] v.* to live as a bachelor

bache *[batch] n.* a valley containing a small stream

batch *n.* a group; a lot; a quantity

batch *v.* to combine; to mix

backdoor, back door

backdoor *adj.* secret, devious: 'We don't know the details
because it was a backdoor deal'

back door *n.* a door in the back of a room or building:
'She came in the front door but went out the back
door'

back-out, back out

> back-out *n.* the reversal of steps when a space launch countdown is to be aborted
>
> back out *v.* to withdraw

backstairs, back stairs

> backstairs *adj.* secret: 'She had a backstairs affair with her best friend's husband'
>
> back stairs *n.* stairs in the back of a building, sometimes those used by servants

backup, back up

> backup *n.* one who reinforces or protects another; an overflow due to an obstruction: 'The overturned truck caused a nine-mile traffic backup'
>
> back up *v.* to support: 'I will back up the team all the way'; to move backward: 'She had to back up the truck to make room for the ambulance to get through'

bad, bade

> bad *adj.* the opposite of good; wrong; naughty; evil; rotten; or downcast
>
> bade *[bad] v.* the past tense of bid: 'He bade his army goodbye when the fighting ceased'

bagfuls, bags full

> bagfuls *n.* (pl.) one bag filled more than one time: 'I used this bag to collect three bagfuls of leaves'
>
> bags full *n.* (pl.) individual bags: 'I ordered five bags full of cement'

bahr *See* bar

bai *See* bay

bail, bale

> bail *n.* security given to insure one's court appearance
>
> bail *v.* to scoop or empty water, usually from a boat
>
> bale *n.* a large tightly wrapped package

bailee, bailey

> bailee *n.* one who holds goods for another and returns them: 'The bailee is holding their property until the court resolves their conflicts'

bailey *n.* a castle wall

bailer, bailor

bailer *n.* a person who attaches handles to buckets and pails; a cricket ball bowled so that it hits one or both bails; a melon-shell, a type of mollusk; one who bails

bailor *n.* one who hands over money or goods

bailout, bail out

bailout *n.* an emergency rescue, usually financial

bail out *v.* to pay someone's bail; to provide emergency relief; to leave an aircraft in an emergency

bait, bate, bet/beth

bait *n.* a lure; a decoy; an enticement

bait *v.* to lure; to put food into a trap or on a fishing line; to harass or heckle: 'They like to bait the marchers with obscenities and epithets'

bate *n.* an alkaline solution used to remove lime in tanning leathers

bate *v.* to decrease force; to abate

bet *or* beth *n.* *[rhymes w.* fate*]* the second letter of the Hebrew alphabet

baize, bays, beys

baize *n.* a thick fabric

bays *n.* (pl.) bodies of water; animal sounds

bays *v.* 3d person, sing., present tense of bay, to howl: 'The coyote bays at the moon'

beys *n.* (pl.) titles of respect

bald, balled, bawled

bald *adj.* without hair

balled *adj.* made into the shape of a ball

bawled *adj.* past tense of bawl, to cry: 'The baby bawled all night'

bale *See* bail

balky, bulky

balky *[baw'•key] adj.* uncooperative; contrary; ornery

bulky *[bul•key] adj.* unwieldy; difficult to handle: 'The balky mule rebelled against the bulky load'

ball, bawl

ball *n.* a formal party with dancing; a round object

bawl *n.* a loud outcry

ballad, ballade

ballad *[bal'•id] n.* a romantic song, often telling a story

ballade *[bu•labd'] n.* a verse form or a piano composition

balled *See* bald

ballet, ballot

ballet *[bal•lay'] n.* a stylized form of classical dance

ballot *[ba'•lot] n.* a paper on which a voter indicates his or her choice

balm, barm, bomb, bombe

balm *n.* a soothing, healing, or fragrant lotion

barm *n.* the yeast formed during alcohol fermentation

bomb *n.* an explosive weapon; a theatrical flop; a mass of lava

bomb *v.* to drop an explosive weapon from the air; to fail: 'I won't bomb in my attempt to become a comic'

bombe *[bomb] n.* a confection or frozen dessert

balmy, barmy

balmy *adj.* mild: 'The weather in May is usually balmy'; having a pleasant smell

barmy *adj.* crazy: 'That barmy man walks around talking to himself'; foamy

band, banned

band *n.* a musical group; a tribe; a ring; a circle

band *v.* to gird; to belt; to combine

banned *v.* past tense of ban, to forbid

banded, bandied

banded *v.* past tense of band, to gird

bandied *v.* past tense of bandy, to toss back and forth: 'She bandied words with him'

bands, banns, bans

bands *n.* more than one band

bands *v.* 3d person, sing., present tense of band

banns *n.* a notice of intended marriage: 'The minister announced the banns for Harold and Mildred'

bans *n.* (pl.) prohibitions: 'The city bans on spitting and littering are strictly enforced'

bang, bhang

bang *v.* to hit noisily

bang *n.* a thrill; pleasure; enjoyment; a blow or a wallop; a loud noise

bhang *n.* hemp; hashish

banquet, banquette

banquet *[bang'•kwit] n.* a sumptuous meal

banquette *[bang•ket'] n.* a raised walk; a bench

baptist, Baptist, batiste

baptist *n.* a person who baptizes

Baptist *n.* a member of a Protestant denomination

batiste *[ba•teest'] n.* a sheer fabric

bar, barre, bahr

bar *n.* a rod or a stick; a barrier; an obstacle; a place where alcoholic drinks are served; a court of law; the legal profession

bar *prep.* except, excluding: 'Every student, bar freshmen, must complete the assignment'

barre *[bar] n.* a wooden railing used for ballet practice

bahr *n.* a body of water, such as a river, lake, or sea

barbet, barbette

barbet *[bar'•bit] n.* a curly-haired dog; a tropical bird

barbette *[bar•bet'] n.* a part of a warship

barcode, bar code

barcode *v.* to imprint lines and numbers to be read by a computer

bar code *n.* markings read by a laser and computer

bard, barred

bard *n.* a poet; armor to cover a horse's head; an ornamental cloth; a bacon slice used to cover roasting meat

barred *v.* past tense of bar

bare, bear

bare *adj.* naked: 'His bare skin shone in the water'; empty: 'The cupboard was bare'

bare *v.* to uncover: 'He loves to bare his body in the water'

bear *n.* a large furry animal

bear *v.* to carry; to suffer: 'How long can you bear the pain?'

bareback, bare back

bareback *adj.* without a saddle: 'She was a bareback rider'

bare back *n.* a back which is not covered: 'Her bare back was quite suntanned'

barefoot, bare foot

barefoot *adv.* wearing no shoes or socks: 'He walked barefoot'

bare foot *n.* a foot that is not covered: 'He got a splinter in his bare foot'

barely, barley

barely *adv.* scarcely: 'We had barely enough money to pay for dinner'

barley *n.* a grain, often used in cereals and whiskey

barer, bearer

barer *adj.* comparative of bare

bearer *n.* a porter; a person or thing that sustains

bearer *adj.* unregistered; free or negotiable: 'His briefcase containing bearer bonds was stolen'

bargainer, bargainor

bargainer *n.* one who offers terms for an agreement or contract

bargainor *n.* a legal term for the seller in a sale

baric, barrack

baric *[bar'•ic] adj.* pertaining to atmospheric pressure

barrack *[bar'•uk] n.* a building to house soldiers

baring, bearing

baring *v.* present participle of bare; exposing or uncovering

bearing *n.* conduct or deportment: 'His bearing exuded confidence'

bearing *v.* present participle of bear; carrying or enduring

bark, barque

bark *n.* the outer part of a tree; a guttural sound like that made by a dog

bark *v.* to snarl or command: 'The sergeant loved to bark his orders'

barque *[bark] n.* a sailing ship

barley *See* barely

barm *See* balm

barmy *See* balmy

barney, barny

barney *n.* a noisy row; a good time; a small vehicle used in a mine

barny *adj.* characteristic of a barn in smell, size, etc.

baron, barren, barrens

baron *n.* a member of the nobility

barren *adj.* unproductive; infertile; bare

barrens *n.* a bleak, poorly forested area; a wasteland

barrack *See* baric

barre *See* bar

barré, barret, barrette, beret

barré *[bah•ray'] n.* a textile pattern of colored stripes

barret *[bar'•it] n.* a small cap

barrette *[buh•ret'] n.* a hair clasp

beret *[buh•ray'] n.* a small cap, originally from France

barrelfuls, barrels full

barrelfuls *n.* (pl.) a barrel filled more than once: 'I brought two barrelfuls of water into the house with this barrel'

barrels full *n.* (pl.) more than one filled barrel: 'Here are three barrels full of beer'

barrenness, baroness

barrenness *n.* the quality of being incapable of growing crops or of producing offspring

baroness *n.* a titled woman

basal, basil

basal *[bay'•zal] adj.* fundamental or elementary: 'They use basal readers in elementary school'

basil *[ba'•zul or bay'•zul] n.* an herb

base, bass

base *n.* a foundation; a bottom; a basis

base *v.* to ground; to serve as a basis

base *adj.* lowborn, common, vile: 'That base allegation is a lie'

bass *[base] n.* a deep tone; a male singer of the lowest vocal range

bass *[rhymes w. pass] n.* a fish; a palm tree fiber

based, baste

based *v.* past tense of base; founded on or in that location: 'Our group is based in Paris'

baste *[based] v.* to moisten meat; to sew loosely; to scold, strike, or abuse

bases, basis, basses

bases *[bay'•siz] n.* (pl.) foundations; the lowest parts; the main constituents; military installations; the four infield corners of a baseball field

basis *[bay'•siss] n.* support; the fundamental principle: 'The basis of education is an inquiring mind'

basses *[bay'•siz] n.* (pl.) singers in a low register

bask, basque

bask *v.* to relax; to luxuriate; to enjoy favor or warmth

basque *n.* a tight-fitting bodice

bat, batt

bat *n.* a flying rodent; a club or cudgel; a hag; a blow

bat *v.* to hit; to gallivant; to blink: 'She likes to bat her eyes seductively when she's at a party' batt *n.* matted cotton

batch *See* bach

bate *See* bait

bath, bathe

bath *n.* a washing of the body in a tub, or the water-filled tub itself; a bathroom; a bathtub

bathe *v.* to take a bath; to make something wet or steep it in liquids; to swim; to be filled with or immersed in: 'The end rooms bathe in sunlight'

bathetic, pathetic

bathetic *adj.* trite, cliched, hackneyed; maudlin: 'The average television drama is bathetic, rarely showing true feeling or originality'

pathetic *adj.* pitiful: 'The pathetic performances were appropriate to that bathetic show'

bathos, pathos

bathos *n.* false or pretentious sympathy; trite or common

pathos *n.* a quality that moves one to sorrow or pity

batiste *See* baptist

baton, batten

baton *[ba•ton']* *n.* a short stick or club passed in a race; a sticklike article used to conduct an orchestra; a smooth staff used by a drum major

batten *[bat'•in]* *n.* a wooden strip used to cover a joint between boards; a strip of wood used to close a tarpaulin over a hatch

batt *See* bat

batterie, battery

batterie *n.* a ballet movement

battery *n.* a military grouping; a source of electricity; a physical beating: 'She was charged with assault and battery'

bauble, bubble

bauble *n.* a worthless trinket

bubble *n.* a globule of air enclosed in liquid

bubble *v.* to seethe; to boil: 'Water will bubble at 212 degrees
    Fahrenheit'

bawl *See* ball

bawled *See* bald

bay, bai, bey

    bay *n.* an inlet of a sea

    bay *v.* to howl: 'I heard the dog bay at the moon'

    bai *[by] n.* a yellow mist

    bey *[bay] n.* a title of respect in several Middle Eastern
        countries

Bayreuth, Beirut

    Bayreuth *[by'•roit] n.* a Bavarian city

    Beirut *[bay•root'] n.* the Lebanese capital

bays *See* baize

bazaar/bazar, bizarre

    bazaar *or* bazar *n.* an oriental market; a charity sale or fair; a
        store where miscellaneous merchandise is sold

    bizarre *adj.* unconventional; odd or eccentric

bazooka, bouzouki

    bazooka *[bu•zoo'•kuh] n.* an antitank weapon

    bouzouki *[buh•zoo'•key] n.* a stringed musical instrument

be, bee

    be *v.* to exist

    bee *n.* an insect; the letter *B*; a competition: 'He won the
        spelling bee'

beach, beech

    beach *n.* the sandy edge where land meets water

    beech *n.* a type of tree

beachy, bitchy

    beachy *adj.* like a beach

    bitchy *adj.* pertaining to a nasty or promiscuous person

beadle/bedel, beetle, betel

    beadle or bedel *n.* a church officer; a town crier

    beetle *n.* an insect

    beetle *v.* to overhang; to scurry

betel *[bee'•tel]* *n.* a leaf that is chewed as a stimulant or narcotic

bean, been, bin

bean *[been]* *n.* a vegetable

been *[bin]* *v.* past tense of be: 'I've been there before'

bin *n.* a compartment or box

bearing *See* baring

beat, beet

beat *v.* to strike a person or thing repeatedly; to pulsate: 'His heart will beat faster after exercise'; to win or to surpass: 'I beat him in the race'; to circumvent: 'I left the office early to beat the rush hour'

beat *n.* a measure of rhythm in music; a patrol area: 'The police officer walked her beat'

beat *adj.* exhausted: 'By the end of the party, she was beat'

beet *n.* a root vegetable

beatify, beautify

beatify *[bee•at'•i•fie]* *n.* to proclaim one to be blessed in a Christian rite

beautify *[byoo'•ti•fie]* *v.* to make beautiful or to adorn

beat-up, beat up

beat-up *adj.* in very poor condition: 'I bought a beat-up jalopy for 500 dollars'

beat up *v.* to hit with fists or a weapon

beau, beaus/beaux, bow

beau *[rhymes w. go]* *n.* a dandy; a boyfriend

beaus *or* beaux *[rhymes w. goes]* *n.* (pl.) more than one beau

bow *n.* *[rhymes w. go]* anything curved; a decorative knot; a weapon used for shooting arrows; a stick used in playing a violin

bow *[rhymes w. cow]* *n.* the forward part of a ship

bow *[rhymes w. cow]* *v.* to bend the head or body in respect; to submit

See also bode; bough

bedel *See* beadle

bee *See* be

beech *See* beach

been *See* bean

beer, bier

beer *n.* a drink

bier *n.* a coffin and its stand

beet *See* beat

beetle *See* beadle

beget, bigot

beget *v.* to procreate; to cause: 'His actions will beget more hostility'

bigot *n.* a person with intolerant prejudices and opinions

begin, béguin, beguine, Beguine

begin *v.* to start

béguin *[bay'•gin] n.* a flirtation; an infatuation

beguine *[bu•geen'] n.* a dance

Beguine *n.* a member of a lay sisterhood

begum, begun

begum *[bee'•gim] n.* a Muslim princess; an Indian woman of wealth or rank

begun *v.* past tense of begin, to start: 'Have you begun the work yet?'

Beirut *See* Bayreuth

Belgian, Belgium

Belgian *n.* a native or inhabitant of Belgium

Belgium *n.* a country in Europe

bell, belle

bell *n.* a hollow object with a clapper that rings when moved

belle *n.* a beauty: 'She was the belle of the ball'

bellboy, bell buoy

bellboy *n.* a person who carries luggage, usually in a hotel

bell buoy *n.* a floating device that warns ships of danger

bellow, bellows, below, billow

bellow *[bell'•oh] n.* a loud roar

bellows *n.* a device for blowing air on fires or through a
musical organ

below *[bi•loh']* *adv.* under, beneath: 'The subway runs below
the ground'

billow *[bill'•oh]* *n.* a wave of water, sound, or fabric

berg, burg, burgh

berg *n.* an iceberg

burg *n.* a fortified or walled town

burgh *n.* a town in Scotland

berried, buried

berried *adj.* having berries; bearing eggs, used in reference
to a lobster

buried *adj.* that which is covered or not visible

berry, burry, bury

berry *n.* a fruit

burry *[burr'•ee]* *adj.* prickly, like a burr; covered with burrs

bury *[berry]* *v.* to conceal; to cover with earth: 'We bury our
dead quickly'

berth, birth

berth *n.* a place to sleep; a place at a wharf; a position of
employment

birth *n.* a coming into life

beseech, besiege

beseech *v.* to beg, implore, or plead

besiege *v.* to surround an enemy; to beleaguer

beside, besides

beside *prep.* at or by the side of: 'She placed the book on the
table beside the bed'

besides *prep.* in addition to: 'Besides being fat, he is also
short'

betel *See* beadle

bet/beth *See* bait

better, bettor

better *v.* to improve: 'Get a job and better your life'

better *adj.* higher in quality; more worthy, useful or desirable than an alternative: 'There is a better way to make a mousetrap'

bettor *n.* a gambler, a person who bets

better-off, better off

better-off *adj.* indicates relative wealth: 'The better-off families live in this gentrified neighborhood'

better off *adv.* having an advantage: 'I am better off since I got this job'

bey *See* bay

beys *See* baize

bhang *See* bang

biannual, biennial

biannual *adj.* twice a year

biennial *adj.* every two years

bib, bibb, Bibb

bib *n.* a napkin tied under the chin; a part of a pair of overalls

bibb *n.* a part of a ship's mast

Bibb *n.* a type of lettuce

bible, Bible

bible *n.* an authoritative book: 'His compilation is considered to be the bible of baseball'

Bible *n.* the Old Testament and/or the New Testament

bid, bide

bid *v.* to make an offer; to command; to invite; to attend

bide *v.* to stay; to wait: 'Bide your time until the baby is born'

bidden, bitten

bidden *v.* past participle of bid, to command: 'You were bidden to clean up this yard, and you didn't do it'; to greet: 'They were always bidden a warm hello when they arrived'

bitten *v.* past participle of bite: 'He was bitten by a dog'

bier *See* beer

big-city, big city

big-city *adj.* stylish or sophisticated: 'She was not used to the big-city ways'

big city *n.* a city that is large in area or population: 'Los Angeles is a big city'

bighorn, big horn

bighorn *n.* a kind of sheep

big horn *n.* a horn that is large

bight, bite, byte

bight *n.* a loop; a curve; a bend; a bay: 'the Bight of Benin'

bite *n.* a morsel; a snack; a share

bite *v.* to cut into with teeth; to corrode; to sting

byte *n.* a unit of computer memory

bigmouth, big mouth

bigmouth *n.* one who gossips or boasts: 'Will that bigmouth please shut up!'

big mouth *n.* a mouth that is large: 'He has a big mouth'

bigot *See* beget

billed, build

billed *v.* past tense of bill, to charge: 'They billed me too much'

build *n.* physique: 'After working out for months in the gym, he developed a nice build'

build *v.* to construct; to make; to increase

billion, bouillon, bullion

billion *n.* a thousand million, in the United States; a million million in Great Britain

bouillon *[bool'•yon] n.* a clear soup

bullion *[bull'•yin] n.* uncoined gold or silver; a heavy twisted cord fringe

billow *See* bellow

bin *See* bean

biped, bipod

biped *n.* a two-footed animal: 'A bird is a biped'

bipod *n.* a two-legged stand: 'She placed the camera on a bipod'

bird, burred
>bird *n.* a winged, feathered, egg-laying, two-legged creature
>burred *adj.* having a rough edge or sound

birn, burn
>birn *n.* a pear-shaped socket used in clarinet-type instruments to fit the mouthpiece
>burn *n.* an injury caused by fire, acid, or intense heat; a firing of a space rocket
>burn *v.* to set on fire; to scorch or scald; to shine or glow; to feel hot

birr, buhr, burr/bur
>birr *n.* a whirring sound
>buhr *n.* a type of rock, namely a buhrstone
>burr *or* bur *n.* a rough, guttural, or whirring sound; a prickly seed case; a trilling pronunciation of the letter *R:* 'The Scot spoke with a thick burr'

birth *See* berth
bit, bitt
>bit *n.* the tiniest amount; a morsel, smidgeon, or fragment; a tool
>bit *v.* past tense of bite: 'The child bit into the doughnut'
>bitt *n.* the part of a ship to which mooring lines are attached
>*See also* bid

bitchy *See* beachy
bite *See* bight
bitten *See* bidden
bivalence, bivalents
>bivalence *n.* the ability of an atom to combine with two other atoms
>bivalents *n.* (pl.) double chromosomes

bizarre *See* bazaar
black-bag, black bag
>black-bag *adj.* pertaining to illegal entry, usually by a government agency (slang): 'Since they were unable to get a search warrant, they conducted a black-bag operation'
>black bag *n.* a bag which is black

blackbird, black bird
> blackbird *n.* a bird, an English thrush
> black bird *n.* a bird that is black

black-letter, black letter
> black-letter *adj.* disastrous: 'The day the factory closed was a
>   black-letter day'
> black letter *n.* a heavy typeface

blackout, black out
> blackout *n.* a loss of consciousness; an elimination of all light;
>   the censorship of news
> black out *v.* to censor; to faint: 'Passengers can black out from
>   lack of oxygen'

blackstrap, black strap
> blackstrap *n.* molasses
> black strap *n.* a strap that is black

blacktail, black tail
> blacktail *n.* a deer
> black tail *n.* a tail that is black

blacktop, black top
> blacktop *n.* asphalt
> black top *n.* a top that is black

blanch, blench
> blanch *v.* to whiten; to scald by cooking
> blench *v.* to flinch

bland, blend, blende
> bland *adj.* very mild or gentle; insipid or dull
> blend *v.* to combine or intermingle: 'Red and yellow blend
>   into orange'
> blende *n.* a mineral

blanket, blanquette
> blanket *[blan' • kit] n.* a covering
> blanquette *[blang • ket'] n.* a stew

blasé, blaze
> blasé *[blah • zay'] adj.* satiated; uninterested; sophisticated or
>   world weary: 'He's so blasé that even those spectacular
>   fireworks bored him'

blaze *n.* a sudden fire; a bright display or outcropping: 'a blaze of color amidst the greenery'

bleat, bleed

bleat *v.* to make a plaintive cry; to say something sadly or plaintively

bleed *v.* to lose blood or other fluids; to draw blood; to extort money: 'You'll bleed me dry with your insistent demands for money'; in printing, to run material to the edge of a page

blew, blue

blew *v.* past tense of blow: 'He blew out his birthday candles'

blue *adj.* pertaining to the color blue; a melancholy or depressed mood: 'Losing the race made her blue'; obscene or profane: 'blue movies'

blight, blite

blight *n.* a plant disease

blight *v.* to cause a blight; to ruin or destroy: 'The recession will blight his hopes for college'

blite *n.* a weedy plant

bloc, block

bloc *n.* a group united for joint action: 'The Soviet bloc came apart at the seams'

block *n.* an obstacle, delay, or obstruction; a device used with a cord: 'The captain ordered the cargo hoisted with the block and tackle'

block *v.* to prevent; to cut off a view; to lay out a design; to delay a football opponent

blond, blonde

blond *n.* a yellow-haired male

blonde *n.* a yellow-haired female

blowback, blow back

blowback *n.* a backward draft of air; the recoil of a firearm bolt or the escape of gases as a weapon is fired

blow back *v.* to return something by a strong gust of air

blowdown, blow down

blowdown *n.* a sudden rupture in a nuclear plant

blow down *v.* to expel breath downward

blowhard, blow hard

blowhard *n.* a braggart

blow hard *v.* to forcibly expel breath

blowoff, blow off

blowoff *n.* expelled vapor or water

blow off *v.* to gripe; to remove something by a strong gust of breath or wind; to stand up: 'He'd better not blow off our date'

blowout, blow out

blowout *n.* an explosion; a rowdy party

blow out *v.* to extinguish with breath or air

blowup, blow up

blowup *n.* an explosion; a bad fight; a photo enlargement

blow up *v.* to explode; to enlarge a photo; to fill a balloon with air or gas

blue *See* blew

bluebird, blue bird

bluebird *n.* a North American bird

blue bird *n.* a bird that is blue

blue-chip, blue chip

blue-chip *adj.* high-priced; especially safe for investment: 'Widows and orphans should own only blue-chip stocks'

blue chip *n.* a poker disk colored blue; the stock of a major corporation: 'That Wall-Street broker deals only in blue chips'

blue-collar, blue collar

blue-collar *adj.* pertaining to manual labor: 'The union is composed mainly of blue-collar workers'

blue collar *n.* a collar that is blue, as on a shirt or blouse

bluefish, blue fish

bluefish *n.* a species of fish

blue fish *n.* a fish whose color is blue

blue-pencil, blue pencil

blue-pencil *v.* to edit; to change a manuscript

blue pencil *n.* a pencil that has blue lead or is colored blue

bluepoint, blue point

> bluepoint *n.* a type of oyster
>
> blue point *n.* a breed of Siamese cat

blue-ribbon, blue ribbon

> blue-ribbon *adj.* preeminent: 'A blue-ribbon panel was chosen to consider the case'
>
> blue ribbon *n.* a ribbon that is blue: 'She wore a blue ribbon in her hair'; a first prize, an award for excellence

blue-sky, blue sky

> blue-sky *adj.* having little value: 'It's a blue-sky stock; don't buy it.'
>
> blue sky *adj.* + *n.* a sky that is blue

bluestocking, blue stocking

> bluestocking *n.* a pedantic or literary woman
>
> blue stocking *n.* a stocking that is blue

boar, Boer, boor, bore

> boar *n.* a male pig
>
> Boer *n.* a South African of Dutch descent
>
> boor *n.* a rude or crude person
>
> bore *n.* a person or thing that is uninteresting or tiresome; a high-crested wave; the interior diameter of a firearm; a hole made by boring

board, bored

> board *n.* prepaid meals: 'room and board'; a flat slab of wood; an organized corporate or governmental body: 'The board of directors elected a new CEO'
>
> board *v.* to embark; to put up; to billet
>
> bored *v.* past tense of bore: 'The woodpecker bored three holes in that branch'

boarder, border, bordure

> boarder *n.* a person who pays for regular meals in someone's home
>
> border *n.* an edge or frontier

border *v.* to be close to: 'Illinois borders Indiana'; 'Your remarks border on defamation of character'

bordure *n.* part of a coat of arms

boast, boost

boast *v.* to try to impress other people with one's real or alleged accomplishments; to be proud of something one possesses: 'The town boasts a great swimming pool'

boost *v.* to raise; to promote; to enhance: 'His scholarship will boost him up the economic ladder'; 'The holiday party should boost morale'

boost *n.* an increase; an upward push: 'He gave her a boost over the fence'

boating, boding

boating *n.* the sport or act of using a boat

boding *n.* an ominous prediction or feeling about the future: 'I have a boding that the stock market is going to crash again'

bobbin, bobbing

bobbin *n.* a cylinder, such as a spool, that holds thread or wire

bobbing *v.* present participle of bob, to move up and down: 'He is bobbing for apples'

boccie/bocce, botchy

boccie *or* bocce *[botchy] n.* an outdoor bowling game

botchy *adj.* poorly done; spotty

bode, bowed

bode *v.* to provide an omen; to predict or feel the future: 'That doesn't bode well for the future'

bowed *[bode] v.* past tense of bow, to play a string instrument: 'The violinist bowed for more than an hour without interruption'

bowed *[bode] adj.* curved or bent into the shape of a bow

bowed *[rhymes w. loud] v.* past tense of bow, to incline one's head

bodies, body's

bodies *n.* (pl.) more than one body

body's *n.* possessed by a body: 'Her body's temperature is normal'

boding *See* boating

Boer *See* boar

bogey, boggy, bogy

bogey *[boh'•gee] n.* an unidentified flying object; in golf, one stroke over par on a hole

boggy *[bah'•gee] adj.* waterlogged

bogy *[boh'•gee] n.* a goblin or evil spirit

boggle, bogle

boggle *[bahg'•il] v.* to bungle; to botch; to hesitate; to astound: 'Your ideas boggle my mind'

bogle *[boh'•gil] n.* a hobgoblin

bold, bowled

bold *adj.* brave, courageous; sassy

bowled *v.* past tense of bowl: 'I bowled a perfect game today'

bolder, boulder/bowlder

bolder *adj.* the comparative of bold: 'Lila is bolder than Tom'

boulder *or* bowlder *n.* a large rock

bole, boll, bowl

bole *n.* a tree trunk; soft clay

boll *n.* a seed capsule

bowl *n.* a concave vessel; a stadium

bowl *v.* to play a game which involves rolling a ball at ten pins

bomb *See* balm

bombard, bombarde

bombard *v.* to attack with heavy fire or to drop bombs

bombarde *n.* a reed stop on a musical organ

bomb bay, bombe, bombé

bomb bay *n.* a compartment on a military aircraft

bombe *[bomb] n.* a round frozen mold filled with ice cream or custard

bombé *[bomb•bay']* *adj.* rounded or curving outward
See also balm

bona fide, bona fides

bona fide *[bone'•uh•fied]* *adj.* genuine or in good faith: 'She
said that it was a bona fide antique'

bona fides *[bon•uh•feed'•ase]* *n.* (pl.) authentic credentials:
'She presented her bona fides to the selection
committee'

bondman, bondsman

bondman *n.* a serf or slave

bondsman *n.* a person who provides bail

bonny, bony

bonny *[bon'•ee]* *adj.* beautiful, comely, good-looking

bony *[boh'•nee]* *adj.* lean, scrawny

booboisie *See* bourgeois

bookie, booky

bookie *n.* someone whose profession is to take and place
bets

booky *adj.* one who is studious

boor *See* boar

boos, booze

boos *n.* (pl.) vocal sounds of disapproval: 'When he was
introduced, boos rang throughout the stadium'

booze *n.* whiskey or liquor

boost *See* boast

bootee/boutie, booty

bootee *or* boutie *n.* a child's knitted shoe; a woman's half-
boot

booty *n.* plunder or spoils of war

bora, borer

bora *n.* an initiation rite of Australian aborigine boys; a
violent wind in the Adriatic

borer *n.* one who bores; any of various animals that bore; a
hagfish

border, bordure *See* boarder

bore *See* boar

bored *See* board

born, borne, bourn/bourne

born *adj.* to have emerged into life: 'Her baby was born on Thursday'

borne *v.* past participle of bear: 'She has borne four daughters'; 'He has borne that load for three miles'

bourn *or* bourne *n.* a rivulet

borough, borrow, burro, burrow

borough *[buh'•row] n.* a town; a subdivision of a town

borrow *[bar'•row] v.* to receive a loan

burro *[buh'•row] n.* a donkey

burrow *[buh'•row] n.* a lair or den

burrow *[buh'•row] v.* to cuddle; to dig

Börse *See* bourse

botchy *See* bocce/boccie

bough, bow

bough *[rhymes w.* now] n. a large tree branch

bow *[rhymes w.* now] v. to bend one's knee; to submit: 'They all were seen to bow as the queen passed by'

See also beau; bode

boulder/bowlder *See* bolder

bourgeois, bourgeoise, bourgeoisie, booboisie

bourgeois *[boor•jwa'] n.* a male of the middle class

bourgeoise *[boor•'jwaz'] n.* a female of the middle class

bourgeoisie *[boor•jwa•zee'] n.* the middle class; in Marxist jargon, the capitalist class

booboisie *[boob•wa•zee'] n.* the class composed of fools and oafs

bourn/bourne *See* born

bourse, Bourse, Börse, burse

bourse *n.* a stock exchange

Bourse *n.* the French stock exchange

Börse *n.* the German stock exchange

burse *n.* a purse; a lined case used in a church ritual

boutie *See* bootee

bouzouki *See* bazooka

bow *See* beau; bough

bowed *See* bode

bowels, bowls

> bowels *[bow'•ils; bow rhymes w. cow] n.* the intestines; the inner part of anything: 'Miners go into the bowels of the earth'
>
> bowls *[bohlz] n.* (pl.) more than one bowl

bowl *See* bole

bowlder *See* bolder

bowled *See* bold

box-office, box office

> box-office *adj.* popular, pertaining to performers or performances of plays, films, opera, etc.: 'She is a box-office smash'
>
> box office *n.* the place where theater tickets are sold

boy, buoy

> boy *n.* a male child
>
> buoy *[boo'•ee] n.* a device to warn ships of danger
>
> buoy *[boo'•ee] v.* to support, to bolster

brae, bray, brey

> brae *n.* a hillside
>
> bray *v.* to utter a harsh sound
>
> brey *n.* a barnacle
>
> brey *v.* to soften and make pliable using the hands

braid, brayed, breyed

> braid *v.* to weave or intertwine
>
> brayed *v.* past tense of bray, to make a harsh sound
>
> breyed *v.* past tense of brey, to soften

brail, braille

> brail *n.* a line used in sailing
>
> braille *n.* raised-dot characters that can be read by a blind person

braise, braize/braise, braze

braise *v.* to slowly cook in fat in a closed pot

braize/braise *n.* a fish

braze *v.* to make something with brass; to fuse metals

brake, break

brake *n.* a device for slowing or stopping motion by applying friction

break *n.* the place where a rupture, separation, or interruption occurs; good fortune: 'This job is a lucky break'

break *v.* to crack or fracture: 'Did the fall break your arm?'; to separate into parts: 'Please don't break the window'; to violate: 'break the law'; to end or disrupt: 'break a strike'; 'break the connection'

braker, breaker

braker *n.* a person who rolls dough to make baked goods; a wooden brace used to help in launching a boat; one who slows a vehicle

breaker *n.* one who breaks; a machine to break hemp, etc.; a circuit breaker; a wave; a small water cask

brands, brans

brands *n.* (pl.) a specific make of a product: 'GM produces several car brands'; marks made by a hot iron or poker: 'cattle brands'

brans *n.* (pl.) different quantities or types of coarse grains: 'We have wheat and rye brans'

brasserie, brassier, brassiere, brazier/brasier

brasserie *[brass'•uh•ree] n.* a food-and-drink bar

brassier *[brass'•ee•yer] adj.* more impudent; more like brass

brassiere *[bri•zeer'] n.* a woman's undergarment, a bra

brazier *or* brasier *[bray'•zher] n.* a cooking utensil holding live coals; one who works with brass

brassie, brassy

brassie *n.* a golf club

brassy *adj.* bold; resembling brass

brava, bravo

brava *n.* verbal applause for a woman

bravo *n.* verbal applause for a man; a cutthroat, a hitman

bray *See* brae

brayed *See* braid

braze *See* braise

breach, breech

breach *n.* a rupture, gap or violation: 'The inspectors
discovered a breach of the treaty'; 'breach of contract'

breach *v.* of a whale, to leap out of the water and fall with a
loud splash

breech *n.* the buttocks; the back of a weapon

breech *v.* to clothe with trousers

bread, bred

bread *n.* food made from flour

bread *v.* to cover food with bread: 'bread the veal chop'

bred *v.* past tense of breed, to cultivate or propagate: 'They
bred horses for years'

See also brede

bread-and-butter, bread and butter

bread-and-butter *adj.* mundane; staple sustaining: 'Shoes are
the bread-and-butter products of the store'

bread and butter *n.* bread spread with butter: 'I had a piece
of bread and butter'; livelihood: 'Peddling is his bread
and butter'

breadth, breath, breathe

breadth *n.* the distance from side to side; width; scope: 'The
breadth of his knowledge of history was astonishing'

breath *n.* inhaled and exhaled air

breathe *[rhymes w. seethe] v.* to inhale and exhale air; to
whisper: 'Don't breathe a word of it to him'

break *See* brake

breakdown, break down

breakdown *n.* a mechanical failure or human collapse: 'He
had a nervous breakdown'

break down *v.* to stop working: 'This machine will break
   down easily'; to damage or to destroy: 'Break down the
   door'; to simplify: 'Break down the theory so that we can
   understand it'

breaker *See* braker

break-even, break even

break-even *n.* the point at which income and expenditures
   meet without profit or loss: 'Ten million dollars is our
   break-even'

break even *v.* to balance wins and losses: 'You win five and
   lose five, so you break even'

break-in, break in

break-in *n.* a forcible entry

break in *v.* to enter by force; to overcome the stiffness of a
   new item; to accustom someone to a new activity: 'Will
   you break in your replacement before you leave?'

breakout, break out

breakout *n.* an action that frees one from constraint: 'A prison
   breakout occurred at 3 P.M. today'

break out *v.* to get a skin eruption; to produce or to emerge
   suddenly: 'I will break out the card table right after
   dinner'

breakup, break up

breakup *n.* the disintegration of a relationship: 'After the last
   argument, the breakup of their marriage was inevitable'

break up *v.* to disrupt continuity; to end a relationship; to
   abandon oneself to laughter: 'Lily Tomlin always makes
   me break up'

breathe *See* breadth

bred *See* bread

brede, breed

brede *n.* braid or embroidery

breed *n.* a genetic strain or new type: 'They developed a new
   breed of cow which gives twice the amount of milk'

breed *v.* to reproduce and raise by selective mating

See also bread

breech *See* breach

brees, breeze, Bries

    brees *n.* (pl.) stocks, broths, or gravies; an eyebrow

    breeze *n.* a gentle wind; an easy job (slang)

    breeze *v.* to move fast without expending much effort

    Bries *n.* (pl.) Brie cheeses

Breton *See* Britain

brewed, brood

    brewed *v.* past tense of brew, to make tea or beer: 'They
        brewed beer by boiling and fermenting the malt'; to
        simmer: 'The insult brewed until it became a fight'

    brood *v.* to hatch by sitting on eggs; to mope: 'She will brood
        over an insult for days'

    brood *n.* offspring: 'The goose and her brood swam in the
        lake'

brews, bruise

    brews *v.* 3d person, sing., present tense of brew, to make tea
        or beer, to simmer

    bruise *v.* to inflict a bruise; to crush

brey *See* brae

breyed *See* braid

bridal, bridle

    bridal *adj.* pertaining to marriage: 'The bridal gown was all
        white lace'

    bridle *v.* to restrain; to show resentment: 'That sexist remark
        makes me bridle'

brilliance, brilliants

    brilliance *n.* intense brightness; great talent or intellect

    brilliants *n.* (pl.) diamonds; typefaces of a small size

brisk, brisque

    brisk *adj.* lively; quick; invigorating: 'The brisk Northeast wind
        put roses in their cheeks'; abrupt or curt

    brisque *n.* an ace or ten in certain card games

Britain, Breton, Briton, Brittany

    Britain *n.* short for Great Britain

Breton *n.* a native or inhabitant of Brittany

Briton *n.* a native or inhabitant of Great Britain

Brittany *n.* a region of France

broach, brooch

broach *v.* to make known for the first time: 'broach the
subject carefully'; to pierce: 'We'll broach a beer barrel'

broach *n.* a tapered tool; part of a lock

brooch *[broach] n.* a piece of jewelry

brood *See* brewed

broom, brougham, brume

broom *n.* an implement used for sweeping

brougham *[broo'•im] n.* a carriage

brume *n.* a mist or fog

brownie, browny

brownie *n.* a flat chocolate cake

browny *adj.* tending toward brown, somewhat brown or
browned

brows, browse

brows *n.* (pl.) eyebrows; the forehead; the upper part of the
face; steep hills

browse *v.* to look around casually as in a store; to graze
upon; to leaf through

bruise *See* brews

bruit, brut, brute

bruit *[brute] v.* to spread news or a rumor; to declare

brut *[brute] adj.* very dry, specifically champagne

brute *n.* a savage animal; a man with beastlike qualities

brume *See* broom

brunet, brunette

brunet *n.* a dark-haired male

brunette *n.* a dark-haired female

brushback, brush back

brushback *n.* a baseball pitch thrown close to the batter

brush back *v.* to push toward the back

brush-off, brush off

brush-off *n.* an abrupt dismissal: 'She gave him a quick brush-off'

brush off *v.* to remove particles like dust with a brush; to dismiss abruptly

brushup, brush up

brushup *n.* a renewal of skills; a refreshment of memory

brush up *v.* to eliminate imperfections; to refresh memory or skills

brut, brute *See* bruit

buccal, buckle

buccal *[buckle] adj.* oral; pertaining to or involving the cheeks

buckle *n.* a clasp

buckle *v.* to fasten with a buckle; to cause to bend or warp; to collapse

bucketfuls, buckets full

bucketfuls *n.* (pl.) one bucket filled a number of times: 'I drew three bucketfuls of water from the well with this bucket'

buckets full *n.* (pl.) buckets filled separately: 'Here are five buckets full of earth'

buffa, buffe, buffer, buffi, buffo, bufo

buffa *[boo'•fuh] n.* a woman who sings comic opera

buffe *[boo'•feh] n.* (pl.) women who sing comic opera

buffer *n.* something that cushions a blow

buffi *[boo'•fee] n.* (pl.) men who sing comic opera

buffo *[boo'•foh] n.* a man who sings comic opera

bufo *[boo'•foh] n.* a toad

buhr *See* birr

build *See* billed

buildup, build up, built-up

buildup *n.* an accumulation: 'The armaments buildup will cost a fortune'; publicity: 'The starlet received a massive buildup'

build up *v.* to develop: 'They plan to build up downtown
Philadelphia'
built-up *adj.* covered with buildings; layered, reinforced: 'His
built-up shoes made him appear much taller'
bulbil, bulbul
bulbil *[bil'•bil] n.* a small bulb, a leaf, or a bud
bulbul *[bull'•bil] n.* a bird
Bulgar, bulgur
Bulgar *n.* A native or inhabitant of Bulgaria
bulgur *[bul'•ger] n.* cracked wheat
bulky *See* balky
bull's-eye, bull's eye
bull's-eye *n.* the center of a target
bull's eye *n.* the eye of a bull
bunco/bunko, buncombe/bunkum
bunco *or* bunko *n.* a swindle
buncombe *or* bunkum *n.* insincere or untrue talk; nonsense
or flimflam
buoy *See* boy
burg, burgh *See* berg
burger, burgher
burger *n.* a meat patty
burgher *n.* a solid citizen; a middle-class inhabitant of a town
buried *See* berried
burley, burly
burley *n.* a tobacco
burly *adj.* bulky; beefy; lusty; having burls or lumps
burnout, burn out
burnout *n.* mental or physical exhaustion; engine trouble
burn out *v.* to excavate with heat; to lose strength; to
completely destroy a motor
burr/bur *See* birr
burro, burrow *See* borough
burry, bury *See* berry
burse *See* bourse

bury *See* berry

bus, buss

bus *n.* a vehicle

buss *n.* a kiss

business, busyness

business *n.* work or activity: 'What business are you in?'; a
company; the volume of trade: 'Business was good this
month'; concern: 'It's none of your business'

busyness *n.* the state of being busy

but, butt, butte

but *adv.* only, merely: 'When she first met him, he was but
recently divorced'

but *conj.* only, except: 'Everybody but she understood the
lesson'

butt *n.* an end; a stub; a target, a laughing stock or a fool; a
flatfish; a cigarette; backside (slang)

butt *v.* to hit the head against something; to lock horns; to
adjoin

butte *[byoot] n.* a small steep mountain with a flat surface

butt-in, butt in

butt-in *n.* a busybody, a meddler

butt in *v.* to intrude or to meddle

button-down, button down

button-down *n.* a type of shirt collar

button-down *adj.* conventional: 'All their top executives were
button-down types;

button down *v.* to make final: 'It took great skill to button
down the deal'

buy, by, bye, 'bye

buy *v.* to purchase; to bribe; to redeem; to believe: 'I buy
your argument'

buy *n.* a purchase; a bargain

by *prep.* near

bye *n.* of minor importance; skipping a turn in a tournament:
'The top team gets a bye in the first playoff round'

'bye *n.* goodbye

buyer, byre

buyer *n.* one who purchases

byre *n.* a cow stable; a hut

buy-in, buy in

buy-in *n.* the accumulation of stock in a company or of goods for future use

buy in *v.* to purchase an interest in a company; to agree to deal at an auction

buy-off, buy off

buy-off *n.* the purchase of all rights to a product or service

buy off *v.* to pay or bribe for an illegal service

by, bye, 'bye *See* buy

byte *See* bight

C

cabal, cabala/cabbala, cable

cabal *[kuh•bal']* *n.* a secret political plot or a group of secret
plotters: 'This government is really run by a despotic
cabal'

cabala *or* cabbala *[kuh•bal'•ah]* *n.* a system of mysticism in
Judaism [also kabala/kabbala(h)]

cable *n.* a strong wire or metal rope; a unit of nautical length;
a long-distance telegraphic message

cacao *See* coco

cache, cash, cachet

cache *[cash]* *n.* a hiding place; items that are carefully hidden:
'They thought he had a cache of cash'; a section of a
computer's central processor

cache *v.* to conceal; to stash

cash *n.* money: 'Did he pay in cash?'

cash *v.* to pay or receive money: 'Did you cash my check?'

cachet *[cash•ay']* *n.* a seal of authenticity of high quality,
status, or stature: 'Eating in that restaurant gave him a
certain cachet'

cachou, cashew

cachou *[cuh•shoo']* *n.* a pastille to sweeten the breath

cashew *[ca'•shoo]* *n.* an edible nut from the tropical tree

caddie, caddy, catty

caddie *n.* one who carries clubs for a golfer

caddy *n.* a tea container; a small box to store things

catty *adj.* spiteful, malicious: 'She's very catty, gossiping about all her friends'

caduceus, caducous

caduceus *[ka•doo'•shus] n.* the rod of Hermes with two snakes intertwined, symbol of the medical profession

caducous *[ka•doo'•kus] adj.* falling early, as of flowers or leaves

café, coffee

café *n.* a small, informal restaurant, often with an outdoor section; a night club

coffee *n.* a beverage; the bean or plant of the coffee tree

cala, calla

cala *[kuh•lah'] n.* a picnic ham

calla *[kal'•uh] n.* a plant, particularly the calla lily

calculous, calculus

calculous *adj.* characterized by the presence of stones or gravel in the gall bladder, kidney, etc.

calculus *n.* a stone in the gall bladder; a system of mathematics

calendar, calender, colander

calendar *n.* a table or chart showing divisions of the year, i.e., days, weeks, and months; a schedule of activities

calender *v.* to press through a machine with rollers to smooth cloth or paper

colander *n.* a perforated bowl used to rinse or drain foods

calibrate, celebrate, celibate, cerebrate

calibrate *v.* to note or correct the gradations on a measuring instrument like a gauge; to measure the caliber of a gun

celebrate *v.* to engage in festivities to mark a birthday, wedding, or other happy occasion; to officiate at a religious ceremony: 'celebrate Mass'

celibate *n.* an unmarried person; one who abstains from sexual relations

cerebrate *v.* to think

calk, caulk, cawk

>calk *n.* a metal plate on a shoe, boot, or horseshoe that prevents slipping
>
>caulk *v.* to make watertight with a putty
>
>cawk *v.* to mate, said of hawks

call, caul, cawl

>call *v.* to say out loud: 'call my name'; to convene: 'call a meeting'; 'call a strike'; to order or command: 'call up the troops'; to phone; to name: 'We'll call the child Daphne'; to halt: 'We'll call this game due to rain'; to predict: 'call that shot'; to request payment: 'call a loan'
>
>caul *n.* a part of the membrane around a fetus
>
>cawl *n.* a wooden basket

callous, callus

>callous *adj.* insensitive; cold in manner: 'The doctor was so callous I could not confide in him'
>
>callus *n.* a thick, hard skin layer

calm, cam

>calm *n.* quiet, or a lull: 'the calm before the storm'
>
>calm *v.* to relieve; to bring an end to distress: 'We tried to calm him after the accident'
>
>cam *n.* the part of a wheel or shaft that affects the motion of other parts of a machine

calvary, Calvary *See* cavalry

campaign, champagne

>campaign *n.* activities leading to a specific goal: 'a military campaign'
>
>champagne *n.* a white, effervescent wine

can, cann

>can *n.* a container; jail (slang); buttocks (slang)
>
>can *v.* to be able to; to have the right or permission to; to dismiss (slang)
>
>cann *n.* a drinking mug

canapé, canopy

>canapé *n.* a small piece of bread or toast covered with tasty food

canopy *n.* a rooflike covering or shelter

canasta, canaster, canister

canasta *[ki•nass'•tuh] n.* a rummylike card game

canaster *[ka'•ni•stir] n.* a kind of tobacco

canister *[kan'•i•stir] n.* a case or box

cancer, canker, chancre

cancer *[kan'•sir] n.* a malignant growth in the body; any
wicked, spreading action or idea: 'Racism is a cancer in
our society'

canker *[kang'•ker] n.* a sore, usually in the mouth; a wood-
destroying disease in forests

chancre *[shan'•ker] n.* an ulcer caused by venereal disease

candid, candida, candied

candid *adj.* frank, honest

candid *n.* in photography, an unposed shot

candida *[can'•dee•duh] n.* a yeastlike infection

candied *adj.* cooked or preserved in sugar

candor, condor

candor *n.* honest speech: 'You rarely find a politician who
speaks with candor'

condor *n.* a large bird, a kind of vulture

cane, Cain, kain

cane *n.* a stick used to help one walk; the stem of certain
grasses like bamboo or sugar cane; a weasel

Cain *n.* a murderer, based on Adam and Eve's son who killed
his brother: 'Murderers all bear the mark of Cain'; to act
boisterously: 'raise Cain'

kain *n.* a sarong

cann *See* can

cannon, canon, cañon/canyon

cannon *n.* a weapon used to fire heavy projectiles

canon *n.* a clerk; a broad set of principles; a set of writings
embodying authoritative precepts

cañon *or* canyon *n.* a deep gorge

cannonry, canonry

cannonry *n.* artillery

canonry *n.* the office of a cleric attached to a cathedral

canopy *See* canapé

cant, can't

cant *n.* argot; jargon; hypocritical speech; an angular or slanted surface; a sudden movement causing a tilting or overturning

can't *v.* can not: 'I can't stand his cant about women's roles'

canter, cantor

canter *n.* a horse's gait between a trot and a gallop

cantor *n.* a church choir leader; a singer of Hebrew religious music

canvas, canvass

canvas *n.* a fabric used in sails and by artists; a boxing ring

canvass *v.* to look out carefully; to solicit orders or votes: 'We tried to canvass the entire district before the election'

caper, capper

caper *n.* joyful play; an illegal act like a robbery: 'The bank caper netted $1 million'; the bud of a caper plant, pickled and used as a seasoning in cooking

capper *n.* someone who puts caps on bottles; something that matches or tops an item or event: 'The capper was his second home run'

capital, Capitol, capitol

capital *n.* a seat of a national government; money invested in a business: 'To handle the business downturn, the owner invested more capital'; wealth: 'Our nation's capital is our children'

capital *adj.* most important; first rate; having to do with wealth; punishable by death: 'Murder is a capital offense'

Capitol *n.* the building in which the United States Congress meets

capitol *n.* a building in which a state legislature meets

carat/karat, caret, carrot

carat *or* karat *n.* a unit of weight for precious stones: 'Her engagement ring has a six-carat diamond'; a measure of gold content: 'Her wedding band was 18 karat'

caret *n.* an editing mark which indicates the place for an
insert

carrot *n.* a vegetable; an inducement, often accompanied by a
threat: 'the carrot or the stick'

card, cart

card *n.* a small piece of cardboard used for notes, as in index
cards; part of a deck of playing cards; the program for
boxing matches or horse races: 'The boxing card features
two ex-champions'; a funny person; a wire cleaning
brush

cart *n.* a horse-drawn vehicle

cart *v.* to carry

caries, carries

caries *[care'•eez] n.* tooth decay

carries *v.* 3d person, sing., present tense of carry: 'He carries
the world on his shoulders'

carnal, charnel

carnal *adj.* relating to physical desires or sexual pleasure,
desires of the flesh

charnel *n.* a place where dead bodies are kept

carol, carole/carol, carrel

carol *n.* a joyous song, sung especially at Christmas

carole/carol *n.* a round dance

carrel *n.* a small cubicle used for individual study in a library

carotene, keratin

carotene *n.* a source of vitamin A found in carrots and other
yellow vegetables

keratin *n.* a protein that aids in the building or strengthening
of hair and nails

carousal, carousel

carousal *[kuh•rowz'•il] n.* drinking or fun making to excess;
a binge

carousel *[kar•uh•sell'] n.* a merry-go-round: 'During their
carousal, they loved to go riding on a carousel'

carrot *See* caret

cart *See* card

carting, karting

    carting *v.* present participle of cart, to carry in a cart, a two-wheeled, horse-drawn vehicle

    karting *n.* the sport of racing with karts, lightweight vehicles

carton, cartoon

    carton *n.* a cardboard box

    cartoon *n.* a comic strip; a political drawing on current events; a TV show featuring drawings giving the illusion of movement: 'Saturday morning TV is dominated by cartoons'

cash *See* cache

cashew *See* cachou

cast, caste

    cast *v.* to select actors for a play; to throw dice or a fishing line: 'Be careful of the fish hook when you cast your line'; to throw something off: 'the skin cast by a reptile'; to vote: 'cast a ballot'; to look at: 'Cast your eyes on this dirty room'; to state: 'He cast aspersions on my character'; to shape a material by putting it in a mold: 'She cast the sculpture in a plaster mold first'

    caste *n.* a hereditary, exclusive group based on rigid distinctions of birth or occupation

caster, castor

    caster *n.* a sprinkler for salt or pepper; a wheel placed under furniture; one who casts, as in sculpture

    castor *n.* an oil used as a medicine or in perfume

casual, causal

    casual *adj.* occasional; happening by chance; not intimate: 'He's just a casual acquaintance'

    causal *adj.* relating to cause and effect: 'There is a causal relationship between poverty and crime'

casualty, causality

    casualty *n.* a person who is killed or injured

    causality *n.* the relationship between cause and effect

cat, CAT, khat

cat *n.* a small feline pet; the large animals of the same family, such as tigers; a malicious, gossiping woman; a jazz devotee; any male (slang)

CAT *n.* acronym for computerized axial tomography, a brain scanner: 'Before operating, they decided to do a CAT scan'

khat *[rhymes w. got] n.* a plant whose leaves are chewed for their stimulant effect

cataclasm, cataclysm, catechism

cataclasm *n.* a breakdown or a disruption: 'The civil strife is creating a cataclasm in all areas of the city'

cataclysm *n.* a major disaster or war

catechism *n.* basic Christian beliefs or other types of instruction in a question-and-answer format

catch, ketch

catch *v.* to capture; to grasp and hold: 'The outfielder should catch the deep drive'; to find: 'I'll catch him stealing again'; to watch: 'We'll catch the TV show tonight'; to intercept or overtake: 'I have to catch the 5:16 to the city'; to contract: 'Careful, don't catch the cold from her'

ketch *n.* a small sailboat

catch up, catchup, catsup *See* ketchup

catholic, Catholic

catholic *adj.* comprehensive, universal: 'He has a catholic view of history'

Catholic *n.* members of the Roman Catholic Church, or of the Anglican, Episcopal, or Eastern Orthodox Churches

catty *See* caddie

caudal, caudle

caudal *adj.* relating to a tail

caudle *n.* a drink

caul *See* call

caulk *See* calk

caulker, corker

caulker *n.* a person who makes things watertight; a tool used for this purpose

corker *n.* an amazing person (slang); a person who corks bottles

causal *See* casual

causality *See* casualty

cause, caws

cause *n.* someone or something that leads to an effect or result; a principle or movement: 'He is devoted to the feminist cause'

cause *v.* to bring about, or to produce

caws *n.* (pl.) sounds made by crows

cavalry, calvary, Calvary

cavalry *n.* soldiers or troops on horses or in armored vehicles

calvary *n.* a painful ordeal

Calvary *n.* the hill where Jesus was crucified

cave-in, cave in

cave-in *n.* a collapse of earth or of a building; the act of surrendering: 'Management's cave-in was cause for celebration'

cave in *v.* to give in, to surrender: 'They hoped the dictator would cave in to their demands for more democracy'

cawk *See* calk

cawl *See* call

cease, seas, sees, seize

cease *[rhymes w. lease] v.* to stop; to bring to an end: 'Cease this complaining'

seas *n.* (pl.) more than one sea or body of water

sees *v.* 3d person, sing., present tense of see: 'The cat sees in the dark'

seize *v.* to grab forcibly, to take hold of: 'Iraq tried to seize Kuwait'

cedar, ceder, cedor, cedre, Seder, seeder

cedar *n.* a pine tree

ceder *n.* a person who gives in or surrenders

cedor *n.* a person who assigns a claim to another

cedre *n.* a color

Seder *[say'•dur] n.* the Jewish ritual meal observing the holiday of Passover

seeder *n.* a planting tool; one who places chemicals in clouds to cause rain

cede, seed

cede *v.* to relinquish, to transfer, or to yield: 'The demonstration forced the old rulers to cede power'

seed *n.* a small grain containing an embryo; offspring; the origin of an idea or movement: 'The seed of the revolt lay in the peasants' misery'; ancestry; sperm; one's ranking in a sports tournament

seed *v.* to plant; to remove fruit seeds; to place chemicals in clouds to cause rain; to rank and match contestants in sports; to spread one's ideas

ceil, ciel, seal, seel

ceil *v.* to put in a lining or ceiling

ciel *[rhymes w. seal] n.* a blue color

seal *n.* a symbol, die, or disk that is a guarantee of authenticity; a sea mammal; something that fastens tightly

seal *v.* to close: 'seal this letter'; to firm up: 'seal a deal'; to set permanently: 'His speech will seal his fate'

seel *v.* to close a falcon's eyes

ceiling, sealing

ceiling *n.* the inside top of a room; the uppermost limit: 'The contract places a ceiling on cost'

sealing *v.* fastening tightly: 'She is sealing the envelopes for mailing'

sealing *n.* the hunting of seals

celebrate *See* calibrate

celesta/celeste, cellist

celesta *or* celeste *[sell•es'•tuh] n.* a musical instrument similar to a piano which uses steel plates instead of strings cellist *[chell' • ist]* *n.* one who plays the cello, an instrument similar to a large violin

celibate *See* calibrate

cell, sell

cell *n.* the smallest living part of an organism; a small, bare, single room as in a prison or religious institution; a small group of people organized to work together: 'He belonged to a cell in the I.R.A.'; a space or cavity in a honeycomb or plant; a unit that converts chemical into electrical energy: 'A battery cell'; a computer unit of storage

sell *v.* to provide goods or services in exchange for money, to promote the sale of an item or personality; to convince

cellar, seller

cellar *n.* the basement of a house, a storage place; a stock of wines

seller *n.* a person who sells: 'The seller and the buyer came to terms after much haggling'

cemetery, symmetry

cemetery *n.* a burial place

symmetry *n.* a correspondence of opposite sides in shape, position, or size

cense, cents, scents, sense

cense *v.* to perfume, mainly with incense

cents *n.* (pl.) pennies, the plural of cent

scents *n.* (pl.) odors

sense *n.* the ability to appreciate or enjoy: 'a sense of humor'; the ability to know or understand: 'a good sense of direction'; a point of view or opinion: 'Get the sense of the voters'

sense *v.* to become aware through the five senses; to believe or understand: 'I sense that you are uncomfortable'

censer, censor, censure, sensor

censer *n.* an incense burner

censor *n.* a person who deletes or suppresses ideas or
materials

censure *[sen'•shur] n.* blame or disapproval; an official
rebuke: 'The senator received a vote of censure for his
financial dealings'

sensor *n.* a device that detects automatically

census, senses

census *n.* a count of population

senses *n.* (pl.) the faculties of sight, touch, smell, hearing, and
taste; good judgment: 'I hope she'll come to her senses
and leave him'

senses *v.* 3d person, sing., present tense of sense, to become
aware of; to understand

cent, scent, sent

cent *n.* a coin, a penny

scent *n.* a smell

sent *v.* past participle of send

centaur, center, scenter

centaur *n.* a Greek mythological creature with the head and
torso of a man and the body and legs of a horse

center *n.* the middle: 'The center of the city'; a football player
who puts the ball in play; a site of heavy activity: 'a
shopping center'; a moderate political party, group, or
view: 'He held that all politicians must move to the
center once elected'; the focus of interest: 'Everywhere
he went, he became the center of attention'

scenter *n.* one who scents or smells

cents *See* cense

cêpe/cep, seep

cêpe or cep *[rhymes w.* pep*] n.* a mushroom

seep *v.* to leak, to ooze

See also cyp

cercal, circle

cercal *adj.* relating to a tail

circle *n.* a curve on which all points are the same distance from the center; a group of people with common concerns or interests: 'my circle of friends'; 'the artists' circle'

circle *v.* to surround, to form a circle; to move in circles: 'Let's watch the birds circle the tree'

cere, sear, seer, sere

cere *n.* a part of a bird's beak

cere *v.* to wrap in a special waxed cloth

sear *n.* a part of a gun

sear *v.* to burn or scorch

seer *[see'•er] n.* an observer; a person who sees

seer *[rhymes w. sear] n.* a prophet: 'Edison was a seer who foresaw the potential of electricity'

sere *adj.* withered

cereal, serial

cereal *n.* an edible grain; prepared breakfast food

serial *n.* a television, radio, or newspaper story appearing in a number of installments

serial *adj.* happening or arranged in order: 'The murders were the work of a serial killer'

cerebrate *See* calibrate

cereus, serious

cereus *[seer'•i•us] n.* a cactus plant

serious *adj.* solemn; earnest; important; deeply thoughtful; done with much effort: 'He made a serious study of highway accidents'

cerise, sears, seers, series

cerise *[su•rees'] n.* a light reddish color

sears *v.* 3d person, sing., present tense of sear, to burn

seers *n.* (pl.) prophets

series *n.* an orderly arrangement of similar things; a group of games played as a unit: 'the World Series'; a number of books or articles on the same topic; a radio or TV program with the same cast and story continuity

cerous, cirrous, cirrus, scirrhus/scirrus, scirrhous, serous

cerous *[seer'•is] adj.* relating to cerium, a metallic element

cirrous *[si'•ris] adj.* resembling a cirrus cloud

cirrus *[si'•ris] n.* a high, thin cloud; a plant's tendril

scirrhus *or* scirrus *[ski'•ris] n.* a cancerous tumor

scirrhous *adj.* having a hard cancer

serous *[si'•ris] adj.* pertaining to serum

cessation, cession, session

cessation *n.* a halt or stoppage: 'After the treaty there was a cessation of hostilities'

cession *n.* a yielding or giving up of rights or property

session *n.* a single meeting

cetaceous, sebaceous, setaceous

cetaceous *adj.* pertaining to aquatic mammals such as whales

sebaceous *adj.* fatty or secreting fat

setaceous *adj.* having bristles

cete, seat

cete *n.* a whale; a group of badgers

seat *n.* a place where one sits; the buttocks or the clothing covering same: 'the seat of his pants'; the base for an activity; 'the seat of operations'; a governmental center: 'the county seat'

chagrin, shagreen

chagrin *[shi•grin'] n.* embarrassment: 'To everyone's chagrin, she wore a very low-cut gown to church'

shagreen *[shi•green'] n.* untanned leather

chair, chare

chair *n.* a seat; an authoritative office or officeholder; the electric chair (slang); a chairperson

chare *n.* a chore, or an odd job

chalet, chalice, challie/challis

chalet *[sha•lay'] n.* a typical Swiss house

chalice *[chal'•iss] n.* a goblet or cup

challie *or* challis *[shal'•ee] n.* a lightweight fabric

champagne *See* campaign

chance, chants

chance *n.* luck; fate; occurring without a known reason; a
    gamble: 'Take a chance and try this ride!'; or an
    opportunity: 'Here's your chance to improve your status'
chance *adj.* accidental or unplanned: 'a chance encounter'
chants *n.* (pl.) rhythmical, religious songs or shouts

chancre *See* cancer

chank *See* cinque

chantey, shanty

chantey *n.* a song of the sea
shanty *n.* a hutlike structure, a shack

chard, charred

chard *n.* a beet
charred *v.* past tense of char, to scorch or burn; to work as a
    charwoman; to convert to charcoal

charnel *See* carnal

chary, cheery, cherry

chary *[char'•ee] adj.* cautious, stingy, slow to grant: 'He's
    chary of giving praise or money'
cheery *adj.* showing joy or good spirits
cherry *n.* a small red round fruit with a pit; the tree that
    produces it or its wood; a red color

chased, chaste

chased *v.* past tense of chase, to run after or to cause to leave:
    'They chased away the stray cat'
chaste *adj.* pure in thought; virginal; austere in design

chatelain, chatelaine

chatelain *[shat'•il•ane] n.* a governor of a fort or castle
chatelaine *[shat'•il•ane] n.* the mistress of a chateau; an
    ornamental chain worn by a woman

cheap, cheep

cheap *adj.* of little cost; of inferior quality: 'cheap fabric';
    stingy: 'He's so cheap that a fancy dinner with him
    consists of hamburgers'; vulgar: 'That was a cheap joke'
cheep *n.* a birdlike sound, a peep

cheaper, cheeper

cheaper *adj.* costing less; of poorer quality; of less value

cheeper *n.* a bird that peeps or chirps

checkup, check up

checkup *n.* an examination: 'I went for my annual medical checkup yesterday'

check up *v.* to review for accuracy: 'The supervisor will usually check up on my reports'

cheek, chic, chick, sheik/sheikh

cheek *n.* the side of the face; a part of the buttocks (slang); arrogance: 'He's got a lot of cheek to say that'

chic *[sheek] adj.* very elegant, stylish

chick *n.* a baby chicken; a girl or woman (slang)

sheik *or* sheikh *[shake] n.* an Arab leader

cheery *See* chary

chef, chief

chef *[shef] n.* a cook, usually one in charge of a kitchen

chief *n.* a head or leader of a group

chief *adj.* the highest in rank: 'The chief justice of the U.S. Supreme Court is appointed by the president'

cherry *See* chary

chert, shirt

chert *n.* a rock resembling flint

shirt *n.* an article of clothing worn on the upper part of the body

chews, choose

chews *v.* 3d person, sing., present tense of chew, to grind food with one's teeth; to think about: 'She always chews things over in her mind before letting you know'

choose *v.* to select, to pick; to want: 'I choose to remain at home'

chickery, chicory

chickery *n.* a poultry farm hatchery

chicory *n.* a plant used as a substitute for coffee, or to enhance the flavor or cut the bitterness of coffee

chili, chilly
>chili *n.* a hot pepper
>
>chilly *adj.* cold

chlor, chlore
>chlor *n.* a yellowish-green hue
>
>chlore *v.* to apply a weak solution of bleach

choir, quire
>choir *n.* a chorus, an organized group of singers, often in church
>
>quire *n.* a set of 24 sheets of paper

choler, cholera, collar, color, culler
>choler *[collar] n.* anger, rage
>
>cholera *[co'•luh•ruh] n.* a disease affecting the gastrointestinal system
>
>collar *n.* a part of clothing around the neck; a restraint used on animals; an arrest (slang)
>
>color *n.* light waves of the spectrum reflected on the eye, i.e., red, green, blue, yellow; one's complexion; distinctive speech or writing; a dye; background commentary, often done by a sportscaster
>
>color *v.* to give color to: 'I told the child to color the paper with crayons'; to modify or distort; to blush
>
>culler *n.* a person who selects or picks

choose *See* chews

choral, chorale, coral, corral
>choral *[kor'•uhl] adj.* pertaining to music for a choir
>
>chorale *[kuh•ral'] n.* a hymn or psalm that is sung; a chorus
>
>coral *[kor'•uhl] n.* marine skeletons formed in reefs; a pinkish-red color
>
>corral *[kuh•ral'] n.* an animal holding pen
>
>corral *v.* to round up animals, or to capture

chord, cord, cored
>chord *n.* musical notes played together for harmony; a line in mathematics that connects two points on a curve

cord *n.* a material used to tie things; part of the spine; a
measure of cut wood; electric, insulated wire: 'an
extension cord'

cored *v.* past tense of core, to remove the center of a fruit:
'He cored the apples before cooking them'

chorea, correa

chorea *n.* a nervous disorder

correa *n.* a plant or flowering shrub

choreography, chorography

choreography *n.* the art of composing and arranging dances;
written dance notation; the art of dancing

chorography *n.* the art of mapmaking

chou, shoe, shoo

chou *[rhymes w. shoe] n.* a cabbage; a cabbage-shaped
ornament

shoe *n.* an outer garment for the foot; a tire casing or tread; a
part of a car brake

shoe *v.* to provide shoes: 'shoe the horse'

shoo *interj.* an exclamation meaning 'go away!'

chow, ciao

chow *n.* a dog breed; food (slang)

ciao *[chow] interj.* a greeting, hello and good-bye

christen, Christian

christen *[kris'•sen] v.* to baptize; name a baby or name a
major object in a ceremony: 'christen this boat'; to use
something for the first time

Christian *[kris'•chin] n.* a believer in the teachings of Jesus
Christ

chronic, chronical, chronicle

chronic *adj.* continuing, persistent, of long standing: 'They are
chronic smokers'; frequent recurrence; always present:
'chronic disease'

chronical *adj.* pertaining to a long-standing disease

chronicle *n.* a listing of events in a set order

chute, shoot

   chute *n.* a parachute; a steep slide or trough

   shoot *v.* to propel with force: 'shoot a weapon'; to wound or
        kill; to film; to make a move in sports: 'shoot the ball'; to
        hunt; to move quickly: 'Race cars shoot off at a
        tremendous speed'

   shoot *n.* a young plant growth

   shoot *interj.* used to express annoyance or surprise

ciao *See* chow

ciel *See* ceil

cingle, single

   cingle *n.* a belt or a girdle

   single *n.* a person who is unmarried; a room for one person;
        in baseball, a one-base hit; in cricket, one run

   single *v.* to choose; to prefer: 'The teacher will always single
        out my children for praise'; to hit a single in baseball

cingular, singular

   cingular *adj.* relating to those bodily features that tend to
        circle a part of the body, such as a muscle; ring-shaped;
        banded

   singular *adj.* peculiar; unique; extraordinary; unusual

   singular *n.* in grammar, the singular form

cinque, sank/chank

   cinque *[sank] n.* the number five in dice or playing cards

   sank/chank *n.* a mollusk in the tropics

   sank *v.* past tense of sink: 'He sank the shot with seconds to
        spare'

circle *See* cercal

cirrous, cirrus *See* cerous

cis, siss

   cis *[siss] adj.* having certain groups of atoms on the same side
        of the molecule

   siss *v.* to hiss

cist, cyst, schist, sissed

   cist *n.* an ancient burial site; an ancient Roman receptacle for
        utensils

cyst *n.* a harmless growth or sac developing in the body or on the skin

schist *[shist] n.* a mineral-laden rock

sissed *v.* past tense of siss, to hiss

cite, cyte, sight, site

cite *v.* to refer to material as an example or authority: 'She'll try to cite the Bible to support her argument'; to summon one to a hearing; to give a commendation

cyte *n.* a maturing germ cell

sight *n.* the power of vision; an eyesore; something worth seeing: 'That's a sight to behold'; a device on top of a weapon used to improve aim; something ludicrous looking: 'You're a sight!'

site *n.* a location for a building, facility, or special event: 'the site of the concert'

clack, claque

clack *n.* a sharp sound made by hitting together two solid objects like wood

claque *n.* a group of fawning admirers: 'Sinatra's claque was known as the rat pack'; a crowd hired to applaud a performer

clamber, clammer, clamor

clamber *v.* to climb with effort; to climb on both hands and feet

clammer *n.* someone who digs up clams

clamor *n.* a loud noise or uproar; voiced anger or strong approval

clan, Klan

clan *n.* a clique; a social group; a family: 'The whole clan is coming for Thanksgiving dinner'

Klan *n.* as in Ku Klux Klan, a racist, white supremacist organization

clatch, klatch/klatsch

clatch *n.* a lump of mud

klatch *or* klatsch *n.* a gathering of people for informal conversation: 'The candidate spoke at our klatch'

clause, claws

> clause *n.* a section of a legal document; a grammatical part of a sentence with a subject and predicate
>
> claws *n.* (pl.) sharp nails of animals which they use to grasp, clutch, or pull; mechanical devices that hold or pull

cleek, click, clique

> cleek *n.* a big hook
>
> click *n.* a light sharp sound or the movement that produces that sound
>
> clique *[cleek] n.* a close, usually snobbish group of people who exclude outsiders

clench, clinch

> clench *v.* to hold tightly; to close: 'Clench your fist'
>
> clinch *v.* to make final; to firm up an arrangement: 'clinch a deal'

clew, clou, clue

> clew *n.* a part of a sail; a ball of yarn
>
> clew *v.* to roll something, like yarn, into a ball
>
> clou *[clue] n.* the chief attraction or point of interest
>
> clue *n.* piece of evidence used in solving a problem or puzzle: 'Detectives always search for a clue at a crime site'
>
> clue *v.* to offer a clue, or to provide useful information: 'Clue us in on the new personnel change'

climb, clime, cline

> climb *v.* to go up: 'climb the ladder of success'
>
> clime *n.* the climate
>
> cline *n.* a gradual change in organisms of similar species often due to environmental or geographical changes

clinic, clink

> clinic *n.* a low-cost medical center; doctors who share facilities; an instructional program on a specific topic: 'a math clinic'; 'a sports clinic'
>
> clink *v.* to make or cause a light ringing sound: 'They like to clink their champagne glasses in celebration'

clique *See* cleek

cloaca, cloak, clock

cloaca *[kloh•a'•kuh] n.* an internal cavity in birds, fish, and some mammals

cloak *n.* a loose outer garment, a cape; a disguise: 'She used flattery as a cloak over her true feelings'

clock *n.* a device that measures time

cloche, closh

cloche *[klohsh] n.* a woman's bell-shaped hat; a bell-shaped cover for food or plants

closh *[klahsh] n.* a post used to hang blubber to dry on whaling ships

clomp, klomp

clomp *n.* a clump

klomp *n.* a wooden shoe worn in the Low Countries of Europe

clone, clown

clone *n.* an exact copy of someone or something: 'I bought a computer that's an IBM clone'

clown *n.* a circus performer; someone who jokes a lot

close, clothes, cloths, cloze

close *[kloze] n.* the end of a time period: 'the close of day'; the end of an activity: 'the close of the meeting'

close *[kloze] v.* to shut: 'Please close the door'; to bring or come to an end; to fill up: 'close the gap'; to join or bind together: 'close the tear with tape'; to complete an arrangement: 'close the deal'

close *[klohss] adj.* near, either physically or in one's relationship: 'They live close to us'; 'my close cousins'; almost even in competition: 'The teams were close until the last few minutes'; similar: 'That's a close copy of my bracelet'; crowded

clothes *[kloze] n.* (pl.) garments

cloths *[klawths] n.* (pl.) materials made by weaving: 'The clothes were made of silk and wool cloths'; attire worn by the clergy; wash cloths; boat sails cloze *adj.* pertaining to a test of reading comprehension which requires the testee to fill in the deleted words in a written text

close-up, close up

close-up *[klohss'•up] n.* a camera shot made at very close range

close up *[klohz•up'] v.* to draw near: 'The sergeant barked, "Close up the ranks!" '

closure, cloture

closure *[kloh'•zher] n.* anything that shuts or closes

cloture *[kloh'•cher] n.* a vote of Congress to end a filibuster

clou *See* clew

clough, clow

clough *[clow] n.* a ravine

clow *n.* a sluice or floodgate

clown *See* clone

clue *See* clew

clyster, klister

clyster *[klis'•ter] n.* an enema

klister *n.* a soft ski wax

coak, coke, colk

coak *n.* a dowel; a strengthening pin

coke *n.* a solid fuel; cocaine (slang)

colk *n.* a duck

coal, cole

coal *n.* a mineral used as fuel; carbon

cole *n.* various plants in the mustard family, such as kale

coaled, cold

coaled *adj.* charred; burned

coaled *v.* past tense of coal, to take on coal: 'The boat coaled when it hit port'

cold *n.* an inflammation of the nasal mucous membranes leading to flulike symptoms; chilly weather or a lack of warmth

cold *adj.* of low temperature: 'a cold drink'; chilled: 'I feel
   cold'; sexually frigid; unconscious: 'knocked cold';
   certain: 'I have this down cold'; unprepared: 'I went into
   the meeting cold but managed to succeed'; unfeeling,
   indifferent: 'After he stood her up, she was very cold to
   him'

coaler, cola, colla, koala, kola

coaler *n.* a ship or freight car that transports coal
cola *n.* a carbonated soft drink with sugar and caffeine; (pl.)
   colon, part of the large intestine
colla *n.* (pl.) collum, the neck or necklike bones
koala *[koh•ah'•la] n.* a bearlike animal found in Australia
kola *n.* a type of tree found in Africa; the bitter, caffeine-
   containing nut from that tree

coat, cot, cote

coat *n.* an outer garment; animal's hair or fur; any covering or
   layer: 'This needs another coat of paint'
cot *n.* a narrow, light bed; a small house or shelter
cote *n.* a shelter for animals or birds

cob, kob

cob *n.* a corncob; a horse; a male swan; a beating, especially
   on the buttocks
kob *n* a South African antelope

cobble, coble

cobble *n.* a stone often used for paving; a ball of waste iron
   or steel; a red-throated bird
coble *n.* a fishing boat

cockscomb/cock's comb, coxcomb

cockscomb *or* cock's comb *n.* the fleshy red excrescence on
   the head of a rooster; a garden plant; a cap worn by
   clowns
coxcomb *n.* a fop; a conceited dandy

cocky, kaki, khaki

cocky *adj.* too sure of oneself, vain
kaki *n.* a Japanese persimmon

khaki *n.* a type of cloth; a garment, often part of a military
uniform, made of this material; a light yellow-brown or
tan color

cacao, coco, cocoa, koko

cacao *[keh•kay'•o] n.* a South American tree; the dried seeds
of this tree which are used in making cocoa, chocolate,
and cocoa butter

coco *n.* the coconut palm or nut; taro; a tree cut for timber in
Argentina

cocoa *[ko'•ko] n.* a chocolate drink prepared from cacao
beans

koko *n.* a plant, such as the taro, cultivated for its edible nuts;
a honey-eating bird of New Zealand

coda, code, coed

coda *n.* an independent passage added to the end of a
musical score; a concluding or summarizing part that is
somehow separate from the whole

code *n.* a set of rules; symbols, such as those used in radio
transmissions: 'Morse code'; words used in secret
messages

coed *[co•ed'] n.* a female student

coed *adj.* having male and female students

coddle, cuddle, cuttle

coddle *v.* to treasure; to pamper or be overprotective: 'If she
continues to coddle him, she'll make him into a big
baby'; to cook slowly in water, such as eggs

cuddle *n.* a hug or a close affectionate embrace

cuttle *n.* a fish

coffee *See* café

coffer, cougher

coffer *n.* a treasury; a strong box; a hidden panel that holds
valuables

cougher *n.* one who coughs

Cohen *See* cone

coign, coin, quoin

coign *n.* a corner or advantageous position for viewing

coin *n.* money, a flat piece of metal stamped and authorized as legal tender

coin *v.* to make coins; to invent: 'coin a phrase'

quoin *[kwoyn] n.* a wedge or outside angle of building

coke *See* coak

cola *See* coaler

colander *See* calendar

cold *See* coaled

colds, colts, cults

colds *n.* (pl.) nasal inflammations or similar ailments: 'She kept on catching colds all winter long'

colts *n.* (pl.) young male horses

cults *n.* (pl.) religious sects, often considered unorthodox, which show extravagant devotion to particular leaders, rituals, or principles: 'Some young people join several different cults'

cole *See* coal

coliseum, Colosseum

coliseum *n.* a large stadium

Colosseum *n.* the ancient ampitheatre in Rome

colk *See* coak

colla *See* coaler

collage, college

collage *[ku•lazh'] n.* a piece of art made of bits of paper, string, wood, etc., attached to a surface; a group of shifting, unrelated scenes in a film

college *n.* an institution of higher learning: 'After graduating from high school, he went to college'; a specially empowered organization: 'the electoral college'

collar *See* choler

collard, collared, colored

collard *n.* a vegetable leaf similar to kale

collared *adj.* wearing a collar

collared *v.* past tense of collar, to put on a collar or to arrest (slang)

colored *adj.* having color

colored *v.* past tense of color; to give pigment or hue to

colonel *See* kernel

color *See* choler

Colosseum *See* coliseum

colts *See* colds

coma, comma, karma

coma *[coh'•ma] n.* an unconscious condition caused by accident or disease: 'After the accident, he was in a coma for weeks'; a tuft of hair; the surroundings of a comet

comma *n.* a mark of punctuation that looks like (,) and indicates a pause in the sentence

See also comer

karma *n.* the Hindu belief that actions determine a person's destiny in his or her next life

comeback, come back

comeback *n.* a recovery from behind: 'After losing his crown, Muhammad Ali made a spectacular comeback and recaptured it'; a witty reply

come back *v.* to return: 'If you leave me now, don't come back'

comedian, comedienne

comedian *[ku•meed'•ee•in] n.* a male comic

comedienne *[ku•meed•ee•en'] n.* a female comic

comer, cummer

comer *n.* a person who is likely to do well: 'That rookie is a real comer'

cummer *n.* a godmother

See also coma

comet, commit

comet *[kah'•mit] n.* a starlike object that moves around the sun and when near it develops a tail commit *[kuh•mit']* *v.* to do: 'commit murder'; to consign: 'commit a person to prison'; to obligate or pledge oneself: 'I'll commit myself to the Civil Rights movement'; to refer bills to a committee in a legislative body

comics, comix

comics *n.* (pl.) comedians; comic strips or books that feature cartoon characters

comix *n.* (pl.) comic strips produced by an underground press (slang)

comity, committee

comity *[kahm'•it•ee]* *n.* diplomatic or legal courtesy; civility; social harmony

committee *[kuh•mit'•ee]* *n.* a group of people assembled to investigate, report, or decide on something; a person or group legally responsible for another person or estate

comma *See* coma

command, commend

command *n.* top officers or officials: 'The U.S. command issued strict orders to the soldiers'

command *v.* to have a dominant or strategic location: 'That hill should command the entire valley'; to merit or demand special behavior: 'A leader should command respect'; to give orders

commend *v.* to praise, to speak favorably of: 'She should commend his initiative in solving the problem'

common, commune

common *n.* a public community area or space

common *adj.* shared; familiar; widespread: 'It's common knowledge that this company is weak'; ordinary; ill-bred

commune *[kah'•myun]* *n.* a place where people share resources and responsibilities

commune *[kuh•myun']* *v.* to be in close harmony with: 'She likes to commune with nature'

complacence, complaisance

complacence *n.* the state of being satisfied with oneself or having a false sense of security: 'Their complacence was astonishing in light of the impending cutbacks'

complaisance *[kum•play'•sense] n.* a willingness to please others: 'Her complaisance was often misinterpreted as weakness'

complement, compliment

complement *n.* the number or amount which fulfills a goal or makes something complete: 'The three recruits bring us up to our full complement'; a grammatical expression for a word or words that completes a predicate; something that goes well with something else or that completes it: 'The baked potatoes make an excellent complement to the roast beef'

compliment *n.* an expression of approval or praise

composed, composite, compost, compote

composed *v.* past tense of compose, to put together; to make up: 'It is composed of wood and metal'; to resolve a dispute; to create: 'Beethoven composed his Ninth Symphony while deaf'; to become calm: 'The pause in the argument gave her time to become composed'

composite *n.* something made up of separate elements or pieces; the combination of characteristics of several individuals in a group to make up one

compost *[kahm•post'] n.* a mixture, especially of vegetable materials, decomposing to make fertilizer

compote *n.* a dessert composed of several cooked fruits

comptroller, controller

comptroller *n.* a government official who oversees finances

controller *n.* a person in a business or organization who oversees finances; one who controls an operation

con, conn

con *n.* a convict (slang)

con *v.* to trick or swindle

con *adv.* on the negative side: 'We'll vote pro or con'

conn *n.* one who steers a ship

concave, conclave

concave *adj.* curved like the inside of a bowl

conclave *n.* a private meeting or session: 'The cardinals held a conclave to elect a new pope'

concede, conceit

concede *v.* to give up; to agree: 'I concede the point; you're right'

conceit *n.* excessive pride or self-admiration

conch, conk

conch *n.[kongk]* an edible mollusk notable for its spiral-shaped shell

conk *n.* the head; a blow on the head (slang)

conk *v.* to strike the head (slang); to faint; to slow down or break down: 'I hope my car doesn't conk out on the highway'

concord, conquered

concord *n.* an agreement or harmony: 'At the beginning the two groups lived in concord'; a type of grape often used to make jelly or juice

conquered *v.* past tense of conquer, to overcome, subdue, or be victorious

condemn, condom, contemn

condemn *v.* to criticize strongly; to put in a sorry condition: 'Their lack of education will condemn them to poverty'; to pronounce guilty and sentence a person: 'The judge will condemn the action and condemn him to seven years in prison'; to judge unfit for use: 'I hope they don't condemn this building'

condom *n.* a protective sheath used in sexual activity, a contraceptive device

contemn *n.* to despise, to look down on, to treat with contempt

condor *See* candor

cone, Cohen, koan

> cone *n.* a geometric solid with a circular base tapering to a point opposite the base, for example, a pine cone, an ice cream cone
>
> Cohen *n.* a member of the Jewish priestly class; a member of one of the three divisions of Orthodox Jewry
>
> koan *[koh'•ahn] n.* a paradox posed to a student of Zen Buddhism to help bring about enlightenment

confectionary, confectionery

> confectionary *n.* a place or store for confections
>
> confectionery *n.* (pl.) sweet things such as candy, cake, or ice cream: 'The confectionary sells mainly confectionery'

confer, conifer

> confer *v.* to bestow an award; to consult
>
> conifer *n.* an evergreen

confidant, confident

> confidant *[kon•fi•dahnt'] n.* a close friend with whom secrets are shared
>
> confident *[kon'•fi•dent] adj.* sure of oneself or of something: 'I am confident that my confidant will not spill the beans to you'

conk *See* conch

conn *See* con

consign, cosign, cosine

> consign *v.* to transfer; to give to another's care or control: 'We will consign the goods to you for sale'
>
> cosign *v.* to sign a loan agreement with others
>
> cosine *n.* a mathematical term used in trigonometry

consul *See* council

consulter, consultor

> consulter *n.* a person who consults
>
> consultor *n.* one selected for specialized knowledge, especially one selected by the Roman Catholic Church to advise a bishop or congregation

contest, context

> contest *[kahn'•test] n.* a competition: 'The prize in this
> contest is $100,000'; a struggle; a dispute
>
> contest *[kun•test'] v.* to compete; to try to win; to argue; to
> challenge: 'I contest the election because of fraud'
>
> context *n.* words that surround a word or phrase and help
> clarify its meaning; the conditions or environments that
> surround an event: 'The context of the vote was the
> growing resentment of high tax levels'

controller *See* comptroller

convey, convoy

> convey *v.* to move; to carry; to communicate: 'Please convey
> my greetings to him'; in law, to transfer title
>
> convoy *n.* a protected group of vehicles, such as ships,
> moving together
>
> convoy *v.* to escort; to protect

coo, coup

> coo *n.* the sound made by a pigeon or dove, a cooing sound
>
> coup *[coo] n.* a sudden act, as in overthrowing a government:
> 'coup d'état'; winning something by surprise
>
> *See also* coop

coolly, coulee

> coolly *adj.* acting calmly, in a cool manner, or deliberately
>
> coulee *n.* a ravine; a steep valley with a stream; a stream of
> lava

coop, co-op, coupé

> coop *n.* a small enclosure for housing birds or animals
>
> coop *v.* to confine to a small area; to malinger on a job
> (slang): 'The cops coop under the bridge for hours at a
> time'
>
> co-op *[koh•op'] n.* a cooperative, something owned and
> operated by its users: 'I just bought a two-bedroom co-op
> apartment for a song'
>
> coupé *[koo•pay'] n.* a two-door car; a ballet step
>
> *See also* coo

cops, coppice/copse

cops *n.* (pl.) the police

coppice *or* copse *n.* a thicket or grove; a wood with small
trees

coquet, coquette

coquet *v.* to flirt

coquet *adj.* flirtatious

coquette *n.* a woman who flirts insincerely

coral *See* choral

cord *See* chord

core, corps

core *n.* the center, as of an apple; the center or mainstay of
any organization or system: 'This computer is the core of
our management system'; in electricity, the iron part of a
transformer or coil

core *v.* to remove the core of an apple or other fruit

corps *[core] n.* a large or specialized military unit; a group of
people with common tasks or goals: 'the press corps'

cored *See* chord

corespondent, correspondent

corespondent *[koh'•ri•spon•dent] n.* the other person in a
divorce suit, that is, the one who committed adultery
with the person who is being sued

correspondent *[kah•ri•spon'•dent] n.* one who writes, either
for a publication or as a letter writer: 'He was the Paris
correspondent for this paper for many years'

corker *See* caulker

corner, coroner

corner *n.* the point where two streets or lines meet; a difficult
or desperate position: 'backed into a corner'; a
geographical section: 'a corner of the state'; a monopoly:
'a corner on the market'

corner *v.* to put an opponent into a hopeless position; to get
complete control over something; to turn a corner: 'That
sports car corners well'

coroner *n.* an official who conducts inquiries into the causes of certain deaths

cornet, coronet

cornet *n.* a musical instrument similar to a trumpet

coronet *n.* a tiny crown or a jewelled band

corporal, corporeal

corporal *n.* the rank below sergeant in the army

corporeal *n.* something real or bodily, as opposed to spiritual

corps *See* core

corpse, corpus

corpse *n.* a dead body; any lifeless or helpless object or function: 'Communism is now a corpse'

corpus *n.* a collection of one's writings; a complete body of knowledge; a body of work

corral *See* choral

correa *See* chorea

correspondent *See* corespondent

cos, cose, coze

cos *n.* a kind of lettuce; cousin (slang)

cose *v.* to make oneself cozy

coze *n.* a cozy, friendly chat

cosign *See* consign

cosine *See* consign

costard, custard

costard *n.* an English cooking apple

custard *n.* a dessert made of eggs, milk, and sugar

costume, custom

costume *n.* a prevailing style of dressing; special clothing worn in a play or masquerade

custom *n.* the usual way of doing things: 'It is the custom, or expectation, to wear the appropriate costume to this affair'

custom *adj.* made or done to order: 'I bought a custom-made suit'

cot, cote *See* coat

couac *See* quack

cougher *See* coffer

could, cud

> could *v.* past tense of can; to be able to: 'Years ago, you could walk the streets safely at night'; would like to: 'I could go to this movie'
>
> cud *n.* food that cows return to their mouths from their stomachs to be rechewed

coulee *See* coolly

council, counsel, consul

> council *n.* a body of people who are authorized to advise and make decisions: 'The city council's counsel told them that the new law was unconstitutional'
>
> counsel *n.* a lawyer; the advice given, as by a council or as a result of consultation
>
> counsel *v.* to advise
>
> consul *n.* a representative of a foreign government

councilor, counselor

> councilor *n.* a member of a council or official body
>
> counselor *n.* one who gives advice, sometimes even to councilors

coup *See* coo

coupé *See* coop

coupled, couplet

> coupled *v.* joined together, as in marriage
>
> couplet *n.* a poetic unit of two lines, often with a similar rhythm or rhyme scheme

courier, currier

> courier *n.* a special messenger
>
> currier *n.* someone who tries to win favor by flattery; one who works with leather

courtesy, curtsy

> courtesy *n.* polite behavior: 'Courtesy suggests that you write thank-you notes for gifts'

curtsy *n.* a bending of the knees as a formal bow, usually made by women

cousin, cozen

cousin *n.* your aunt's or uncle's child

cozen *v.* to cheat, to deceive, or to delude

covert, covet

covert *n.* a shelter or hiding place; a disguise; a thicket; a cloth

covert *adj.* secret: 'Congress criticized the CIA for its covert actions in many countries'; covered or protected

covet *v.* to want very much something belonging to another; to enviously and wrongfully desire someone else's property

cover-up, cover up

cover-up *n.* an attempt to conceal dishonest or illegal acts: 'The attempted cover-up of the Iran-contra scandal will taint the administration for years'

cover up *v.* to cover entirely or to wrap: 'You can cover up your body with a longer garment'

coward, cowered

coward *n.* someone who is without courage

cowered *v.* past tense of cower, to crouch as a sign of fear

coze *See* cos

coy, koi

coy *adj.* bashful, demure, playfully coquettish; hesitant to reveal one's ideas or plans: 'He's being very coy about the new promotion'

koi *n.* a carp

craft, kraft

craft *n.* skill in making things by hand; guile; an occupation using hand skills: 'The craft of carpentry'

kraft *n.* a tough paper, usually brown

crap, crape, creep, crêpe

crap *n.* a losing throw of the dice

crape *n.* a black mourning fabric, often worn as a band on the sleeve; an ornamental Chinese plant

creep *n.* someone whom you don't like (slang); the act of creeping; a slow metallic flow

creep *v.* to move slowly or near the ground

crêpe *[rhymes w. tape] n.* a crinkled fabric or paper; a small thin pancake

crass, cross, crosse

crass *adj.* insensitive, tasteless: 'After a few drinks, his remarks turn crass'

cross *n.* two lines intersecting at right angles; a wooden or metal structure built that way; a crucifix; a mark for an error (X); a hybrid in biology

cross *v.* to go from one side to another: 'cross the street'; to cancel: 'Cross out that word, and insert this one'; to betray (slang): 'Don't cross her'; to make the sign of the cross; to encounter casually: 'We hope to cross paths again some day'

cross *adj.* irritated, annoyed; intersecting

crosse *n.* the stick used in the game of lacrosse

crater, creator, creature

crater *n.* a large cavity in the ground caused by a heavy impact; the mouth of a volcano; a hole caused by an explosion

crater *v.* to form or produce a crater

creator *n.* someone who creates or produces something: 'He's the creator of that great ad campaign'

creature *n.* a person or other animal; an indefinite being: 'That monster is a creature of your imagination'; a subservient person or instrument: 'That politician is a creature of the arms producers'

crawl, kraal

crawl *v.* to move on one's hands and knees along the ground; to move slowly; to act in a servile manner: 'He'll crawl before his bosses'; to swim a certain stroke; to feel or be covered by crawling objects

CREWED, CRUDE

kraal *[crawl] n.* a fenced enclosure for people or animals

creak, creek

creak *n.* an unpleasant squeaking sound

creek *n.* a small stream

cream, crème

cream *n.* the fatty part of milk; a lotion; the best part: 'That
play was the cream of this season's crop'

crème *[rhymes w.* hem] *n.* a sweet liqueur, as in crème de
cacao or crème de menthe; the very best, as in crème de
la crème

crease, criss

crease *n.* a wrinkle or sharp fold in clothes or paper: 'Press
my pants to hold a neat crease'

crease *v.* to make sharp folds or wrinkles

criss *n.* a stand with a curved top on which crist tiles are
produced

creatine, cretin

creatine *[kree'•uh•teen] n.* an amino acid that assists
muscular movements

cretin *[kree'•tin] n.* a person with a very low intelligence due
to a hormone deficiency; an insensitive person

creator, creature *See* crater

creed, credo

creed *n.* a set of religious or other basic beliefs: 'Their creed
called for complete harmony with nature'; religion: 'race,
color, or creed'

credo *n.* a synonym for creed; a special named set of beliefs:
'One such credo is the Apostles' Creed'; the music to
which creeds are set for church choirs

creep, crêpe *See* crap

crevasse, crevice

crevasse *[kri•vas'] n.* a major crack in large ice formations or
in the earth's surface

crevice *[kre'•viss] n.* a small crack in places like walls or rocks

crewed, crude

crewed *v.* past tense of crew, to serve on a boat

crude *adj.* rough; not finished; vulgar, lacking refinement; blunt

crude *n.* unrefined petroleum

crewel, cruel

crewed *n.* a thin piece of yarn used in embroidery

cruel *adj.* causing intense suffering or damage: 'Making us work outdoors in that heat is cruel and inhuman punishment'

crews, cruise, crus, cruse

crews *n.* (pl.) workers on a cruise or boat trip; groups working together or under a common master; a crowd

cruise *v.* to travel in a leisurely manner; to take a boat trip

crus *n.* part of the lower leg

cruse *n.* a small vessel designed to hold a liquid such as oil or water

cricked, cricket

cricked *v.* past tense of crick, to hurt one's neck or head by twisting

cricket *n.* the game played with bats, balls, and wickets; an insect that makes loud chirping counds; sportsmanship or fair behavior: 'Telling a lie is not cricket'

crisis, crises

crisis *[kry'•sis] n.* a critical phase; an unstable time requiring decisiveness: 'The Middle East crisis was finally resolved by negotiations'; the turning point in an illness

crises *[kry'•sees] n.* (pl.) more than one crisis

criss *See* crease

critic, critique

critic *[kri'•tik] n.* someone who faults others; someone who evaluates creative works: 'That critic reviews the worst plays in town'

critique *[kri•teek'] n.* a criticism of a creative work

croaked, crocked

croaked *v.* past tense of croak, to make a throaty sound; to die (slang) crocked *adj.* drunk (slang): 'He always got crocked on payday'

crochet, crotched, crotchet

crochet *n.* a type of knitting using a single needle

crotched *adj.* angled by the separation of two parts like legs, branches, etc.

crotchet *n.* a musical note; a hook; an odd kind of trick; an eccentric opinion or preference

croquet, croquette

croquet *[kro•kay']* *n.* a game played on a lawn with mallets, balls, and wickets

croquette *[kro•ket']* *n.* a food made from chopped fish or meat that has been formed in a mound and deep-fried

cross, crosse *See* crass

crossed, crust

crossed *v.* past tense of cross: 'She always obeyed the traffic lights when she crossed the street'

crust *n.* the harder outer layer of bread or of the earth; a pastry shell; any hard covering; a scab; insolence or gall (slang): 'She has a lot of crust to order him around'

crossover, cross over

crossover *n.* a vote for a party you don't belong to or generally vote for; a biological switch of genetic material

cross over *v.* to pass from one side to another

crotch, crouch, crutch

crotch *n.* the bodily area where one's legs fork; any angle formed by the parting of two legs, branches, or members

crouch *v.* to bend the legs down low

crutch *n.* an underarm support; any prop or special support, often emotional

crowed, crowd

crowed *[rhymes w.* load*]* *v.* past tense of crow, to make a sound like a rooster; to make a triumphant sound: 'They crowed over their unexpected victory' crowd *[rhymes w.* loud] *n.* a lot of people; a group of people with something in common: 'Only certain people belong to my crowd'

crowd *v.* to put a lot of people together in an inadequate space; to watch someone too closely or get too close physically: 'Don't crowd me; I'll do it right away'

crows, croze

crows *n.* (pl.) black or gray songbirds

crows *v.* 3d person, sing., present tense of crow, to make a sound like a rooster

croze *n.* a tool used in making barrels

crude *See* crewed

cruel *See* crewel

cruise, crus, cruse *See* crews

crust *See* crossed

crutch *See* crotch

cubical, cubicle

cubical *adj.* shaped like a cube

cubicle *n.* a small partitioned private space: 'My bedroom was just a cubicle'

cud *See* could

cuddle *See* coddle

cue, queue

cue *n.* a signal for someone to do something, particularly in acting; a hint; a stimulus in psychology used to test a person's response; a long stick used in billiards

queue *n.* a line of people or vehicles waiting, as at a movie; a braid of hair worn down the back; stored computer data awaiting processing

culler *See* choler

cults *See* colds

cummer *See* comer

cupfuls, cups full

cupfuls *n.* (pl.) the same cup filled three times: I drank three cupfuls of water from my favorite glass

cups full *n.* (pl.) three filled cups: Please line up three
separate cups full of water side by side

cupola, cupula, cupule

cupola *[kyoo'•puh•luh] n.* a domed structure or roof

cupula *[kyoo'•pyula] n.* a part shaped like a cup

cupule *[kyoo'•pyool] n.* a concave bodily structure, usually in
trees

cups, cusps

cups *n.* (pl.) small drinking containers

cups *v.* 3d person, sing., present tense of cup, to create a
cuplike shape: 'He cups his hands to drink from the
stream'

cusps *n.* (pl.) the meeting points of two curved lines; an
ornamental design of the meeting point of two arcs;
pointed ends; in astrology, a point of transition between
signs

cure, curé, curie

cure *n.* a remedy for an ailment: 'Aspirin is a cure for a
headache'; a solution to a general problem: 'Tax cuts are
no cure for deficits'; a method of preserving foods

curé *[kyu•ray'] n.* a parish priest

curie *n.* a unit of radiation

cure-all, cure all

cure-all *n.* a universal remedy or panacea for all ailments or
difficulties: 'Tough laws are not a cure-all for crime'

cure all *v.* 'The doctor will cure all his patients'

currant, current

currant *n.* a berry much like a raisin

current *n.* a flow of water, air, or electricity: 'The electrical
current in this building is inadequate to its needs'

current *adj.* modern, happening now; in general use or
circulation: 'These are the current fashions'

currier *See* courier

curtsy *See* courtesy

cusps *See* cups

custard *See* costard

custom *See* costume

cutoff, cut off

> cutoff *n.* a short route; something that stops a mechanism: 'a cutoff switch'
>
> cut off *v.* to end contact with or financial help to someone

cuttle *See* coddle

cyclar, cycler

> cyclar *adj.* relating to or moving in cycles; cyclic
>
> cycler *n.* one who rides on a cycle

cygnet, signet

> cygnet *n.* a young swan
>
> signet *n.* a person's seal, often used in place of a signature; a ring with a seal on it

cymbal, symbol

> cymbal *n.* a loud brass percussive instrument
>
> symbol *n.* a sign or object that represents something else or has a special meaning in culture, psychoanalysis, art, or mathematics: 'That building is a symbol of all that's wrong with modern architecture'

cyp, sip

> cyp *n.* princewood, an American tropical tree or its wood
>
> sip *n.* the act of sipping; a small quantity of liquid taken
>
> sip *v.* to drink in small quantities in order to taste

cypress, cypris

> cypress *n.* a tree; an olive-green color; a gauzelike fabric
>
> cypris *n.* a crustacean

cyst *See* cist

cyte *See* cite

D

daily, dally

daily *adj.* happening every day: 'It's a daily newspaper'

dally *v.* to waste time; to play with someone's emotions: 'Don't dally with me; let's set the wedding date'

dairy, diary

dairy *n.* a business dealing with milk products

diary *n.* a personal written record; an appointment book

dam, dame, damn

dam *n.* any barrier, such as one that stops the flow of water: 'The beavers built a dam made of twigs and mud'; a female parent of animals

dame *n.* a woman (slang); a titled woman, equivalent to a knight

damn *n.* a curse; a bit: 'This car isn't worth a damn'

days, daze

days *n.* (pl.) day, the time of light between sunrise and sunset; more than one 24-hour period from midnight to midnight; a period of time

daze *n.* a state of shock, stun, or bewilderment: 'After the accident, he wandered around in a daze'

dead, deed

dead *n.* the time of greater darkness: 'Dead of night'; those no longer alive: 'The dead littered the field of battle'

deed *n.* a specific action, such as a good or bad deed; a special accomplishment; a legal document

deadbeat, dead beat

deadbeat *n.* one who reneges on his or her debts; a moocher; a loafer

dead beat *adj.* exhausted: 'By Friday, I'm just dead beat'

dean, dene

dean *n.* a school or church official; the senior or honored member of a profession: 'Bernstein was the dean of American composers'

dene *n.* a sandy tract of land

debauch, debouch

debauch *[di•baw'•tch] v.* to seduce

debouch *[di•bow'•tch] v.* to come into open country, a military term; to emerge

decade, decayed

decade *[deck'•aid] n.* a period of ten years

decayed *[di•kaid'] v.* past tense of decay, to rot or fall apart from age or disease: 'The trees decayed because of pollution'; to produce radioactive disintegration

decadent, decedent

decadent *[deck'•i•dent] n.* a person who has low moral standards

decedent *[di•seed'•ent] n.* a dead person

deceased, diseased

deceased *[di•sees'•t] n.* a dead person

deceased *adj.* dead

diseased *[di•seez'•d] adj.* sick or unhealthy, relating to both people and society: 'This is a diseased society with drugs, crime, etc.'

decent, descend, descent, dissent

decent *[dee'•sint] adj.* respectable, honest, modest, proper, or kind

descend *[di•send'] v.* to move to a lower place; to stoop; to sink

descent *[di•sent'] n.* lineage or ancestry: 'Her descent was from a line of actresses'; a downward movement of people or objects: 'The airplane's descent was rapid'

dissent *[di•sent']* *n.* the act of disagreement; a minority
    judicial opinion

dissent *v.* to disagree strongly: 'Her new book will dissent
    from the view that Poe was a great poet'

decree, degree

decree *n.* a legal or religious order: 'His divorce decree was
    issued last week'

degree *n.* the certification of completion of a higher level
    school; the extent or amount of something: 'The degree of
    crime has risen sharply'; a unit of measurement, usually
    associated with temperature or a mathematical angle

deed *See* dead

deep freeze, deep-freeze

deep freeze *n.* cold storage: 'They put the food into a deep
    freeze'

deep-freeze *v.* to postpone: 'The group will deep-freeze the
    plan'; to store in a frozen condition

deep six, deep-six

deep six *n.* a place for trash or burial

deep-six *v.* to throw overboard; to discard

defer, differ

defer *[di•fur']* *v.* to submit or comply: 'I defer to your
    superior judgment in this matter'; to delay: 'We must
    defer a vote on that issue until fall'

differ *[diff'•er]* *v.* to be unlike; to disagree; to quarrel

deference, difference

deference *n.* respect, submission, yielding: 'In deference to
    your views, I will withdraw my objection'

difference *n.* disparity, being unlike: 'I won't vote because
    there's little difference between the candidates'; a
    quarrel; 'We had a difference about the trip'

deferential, differential

deferential *adj.* marked by courteous yielding or respect

differential *n.* the amount of difference; the relationship
    between two mechanical forces; a function in
    mathematics

differential *adj.* showing a difference

definite, definitive, difinitive

definite *adj.* having distinct limits; precise; positive: 'You can't stay out after midnight, and that's definite'

definitive *adj.* precisely defined or conclusive: 'That's the definitive work on Lincoln'

difinitive *n.* a special postage stamp used as part of a series

defuse, diffuse

defuse *[dee•fyooz']* *v.* to remove an explosive device, hence, to calm things in a dangerous situation: 'The police defused the gang confrontation'

diffuse *[di•fyooz']* *v.* to spread, to scatter; to disseminate: 'Pragmatic philosophy was diffused throughout education years ago'

diffuse *adj.* widespread; rambling: 'His speeches are always diffuse'

degree *See* decree

deli, Delhi

deli *[del'•ee]* *n.* a delicatessen

Delhi *[del'•ee]* *n.* the capital of India

delude, dilate, dilute

delude *[di•lood']* *v.* to deceive someone or one's self: 'The owners were either deluded about the true state of the company, or were trying to delude the public'

dilate *[die•late']* *v.* to expand; to widen: 'Bright light will dilate the pupils of your eyes'; to write or speak at length: 'His planned speech will dilate on the issue of abortion'

dilute *[die•loot']* *v.* to water down or to weaken: 'Don't dilute my drink'

demeaner, demeanor

demeaner *n.* one who degrades, debases, or demeans

demeanor *n.* behavior, particularly toward others

demesne, domain

demesne *[di•main']* *n.* a district; the possession of land; an estate worked by oneself domain *[do•main']* *n.* an area over which one has control: 'For two centuries England had domain over the high seas'; owned land

demote, denote

demote *v.* to reduce someone's job status to a lower level: 'Due to budget reductions, the city must demote 50 supervisors to case workers'

denote *v.* to make something clear or precise; to symbolize: 'The six-sided signs on the highway denote "stop"'

demur, demure

demur *[di•mur']* *v.* to take exception: 'I demur from your views that Shakespeare didn't write his plays'

demure *[di•myoor']* *adj.* modest, shy, or coy

dene *See* dean

dengue, dung

dengue *n.* a dangerous tropical disease

dung *n.* animal manure

dense, dents

dense *adj.* crowded or thick: 'The room was so dense with smoke, we had to go outside'; thickheaded; complex: 'That's a very dense discussion of deconstruction'

dents *n.* (pl.) depressions or hollows caused by blows: 'The car was full of dents'

dental, dentelle, dentil

dental *[den'•til]* *adj.* pertaining to teeth: 'My dental plan doesn't cover root canal'

dentelle *[den•tell']* *n.* lace or lacework

dentil *[den'•til]* *n.* an architectural term for small blocks forming a molded projection on a building

dependance/dependence, dependents

dependance *or* dependence *n.* the condition of being in a dependent, controlled, or subordinate role: 'His dependence on drugs made him unemployable'

dependents *n.* (pl.) those who rely on others for support: 'She claimed four dependents on her tax return'

depose, depots

depose *[di•pose']* v. to dismiss; to give evidence

depots *[deh'•pose]* n. (pl.) railway or bus stations; warehouses

depositary, depository

depositary *n.* a person to whom you give something in trust

depository *n.* a safe place for keeping valuables

deposition, disposition

deposition *n.* testimony given under oath: 'He gave his lawyers a deposition about the accident'

disposition *n.* one's temperament: 'She has a pleasant disposition'

deprecate, depreciate

deprecate *[dep'•ri•kate]* v. to disapprove or to speak critically: 'He tends to deprecate his colleague's ideas about how meetings should be run'

depreciate *[di•pree'•shee•ate]* v. to reduce the value of something, such as money; to lose value; to deduct equipment costs for tax purposes; to disapprove

descend, descent *See* decent

desert, dessert

desert *[dez'•ert]* n. a dry, barren region: 'the Sahara Desert'

desert *[di•zert']* v. to abandon or to forsake: 'I'll bet that no-good husband will desert her in a year'; to run away or to leave one's military post without permission

dessert *[di•zert']* n. the last course of a meal, usually a sweet dish

desperate, disparate

desperate *adj.* extreme need or hopelessness: 'The homeless are in a desperate plight'; ultimate: 'The doctors made a desperate attempt to save the victim'

disparate *adj.* quite different or distinct: 'Their views were so disparate that there was little likelihood of agreement'

deter, detour, detur

deter *[di•tur']* v. to prevent or to persuade one not to do something: 'The fear of not being believed can deter many women from pressing sexual harassment charges' detour *[dee'•toor]* n. a temporary roundabout deviation from a direct route

detur *[dee'•ter]* n. a prize awarded to a student for meritorious work

deuce, douce, duce

deuce *n.* the number two in the game of cards or dice; a tie score in a tennis game; devil (an exclamation of annoyance): 'They gave me the deuce of a time about my clothing'

douce *adj.* sweet; sedate

duce *[doo'•chay]* n. a chief, a commander; the leader
See also douse

deviser, devisor, divisor

deviser *n.* someone who plans, organizes, or schemes

devisor *n.* one who transmits property through a will

divisor *n.* the number by which another number is divided in mathematics

dew, do, doux, due

dew *n.* condensed moisture forming drops; something refreshing or pure

do *v.* to act; effect; accomplish; work; to cheat: 'That scam can do poor people out of their last savings'; to visit or travel: 'We'll do Paris next year'; to serve time; 'He'll do eight years in prison'; to get along: 'We can do without fancy furniture'

doux *adj.* of champagne, very sweet

due *n.* fair treatment; credit for accomplishments: 'Give her her due'; that which is owed

due *adj.* owing: 'The bill is due on the tenth'; appropriate, something to which a person is entitled; scheduled: 'My plane is due to arrive at noon'

due *adv.* precisely: 'We'll have to head due North'
See also do

dewar, doer, dour

dewar *[dyu'•er]* n. a glass container for holding liquid

doer *[do'•er] n.* one who does, who accomplishes things
vigorously and effectively

dour *[dow'•er] adj.* gloomy, harsh, unyielding

diagnosis, diagnoses

diagnosis *n.* an evaluation of a physical condition; any analysis
of a problem

diagnoses *n.* plural of diagnosis

diagram, diaphragm

diagram *n.* a plan, a drawing, or a sketch

diaphragm *n.* a muscular membrane in the human body; a
contraceptive device

dialectal, dialectical

dialectal *adj.* pertaining to a dialect or to regional speech

dialectical *adj.* a philosophical term for a method of arriving
at the truth

diary *See* dairy

dictate, diktat

dictate *[dik•tate'] n.* a command or guiding principle: 'They
issued a dictate governing public assembly'

dictate *[dik'•tate] v.* to issue orders; to read or speak aloud to
be recorded by another: 'She will dictate several letters
to her secretary'

diktat *[dik•tot'] n.* a unilaterally imposed harsh decree on a
defeated government or political party

die, dye

die *n.* a stamp for impressing coins; a device used to cut or
form metals; the singular of dice

die *v.* to cease to live; to suffer greatly; to wither or languish;
to desire greatly: 'I'd die for chocolate'; to form with a
mechanical die

dye *n.* a pigment used to give color to cloth, hair, etc.

differ *See* defer

difference *See* deference

differential *See* deferential

diffuse *See* defuse

difinitive *See* definite
dilate, dilute *See* delude
dinar, diner, dinner

    dinar *[di•nahr']* *n.* a monetary unit in Yugoslavia
    diner *n.* an inexpensive restaurant: 'They ate dinner at the
        diner because it served large, cheap portions'
    dinner *n.* a meal eaten late in the day

dine, dyne

    dine *v.* to eat or entertain at dinner; to eat any meal
    dyne *n.* unit of energy

ding, dinge, dinghy, dingy

    ding *v.* to hit; to make a ringing sound
    dinge *n.* the state of being dull or shabby
    dinghy *[ding'•gee]* *n.* a small boat
    dingy *[din'•jee]* *adj.* shabby, worn, dark, or dull: 'They lived
        in a dingy apartment'

diplomat, diplomate

    diplomat *n.* person who represents a national government;
        someone with great tact
    diplomate *n.* a person who holds a diploma

dire, dyer

    dire *adj.* having serious or terrible consequences; desperate:
        'They are in dire need of medical treatment'
    dyer *n.* one who colors material with dye

disapprove, disprove

    disapprove *v.* to censure, to condemn; to refuse to approve: 'I
        disapprove of his leadership style; he's too autocratic'
    disprove *v.* to prove false: 'She can disprove the prevailing
        theory about acid rain'

disbursal, dispersal

    disbursal *n.* the act of paying out
    dispersal *n.* the act of dispersing, scattering, or separating

disburse, disperse

    disburse *v.* to pay out: 'The city will disburse $500,000 for
        neighborhood cleanups'

disperse *v.* to scatter: 'After the concert, the audience will disperse quickly'

discomfit, discomfort

discomfit *v.* to frustrate or thwart, to foil; to embarrass: 'You discomfit him with your laughter'

discomfort *n.* an annoyance: physical pain or distress; something that makes one feel uncomfortable: 'The persistent cold caused him discomfort'

discreet, discrete

discreet *adj.* to show tact or reserve; to lack ostentation; to be unobtrusive; to keep secrets: 'You can tell me your problem; I'll be discreet'

discrete *adj.* consisting of unconnected or distinct parts: 'This organization has seven discrete units'

discus, discuss, discous

discus *[diss'•kis] n.* a heavy disk thrown in athletic events

discuss *[dis•kuss'] v.* to debate; to consider a matter by talking about it: 'Let's discuss this issue calmly'

discous *[diss'•kiss] adj.* resembling a disk

diseased *See* deceased

disillusion, dissolution

disillusion *n.* the state of being free from false or unrealistic ideas or illusions; disenchantment

dissolution *n.* the breakup of a group, authority, or close relationship: 'The dissolution of the partnership was acrimonious'

disinter, dysentery

disinter *[diss•n•tur'] v.* to remove a body from a grave; to revive an unused custom or idea: 'They love to disinter old plays'

dysentery *[diss'•n•ter•ee] n.* a serious disease of the lower intestine, causing dehydration and extreme diarrhea

disparate *See* desperate

dispersal *See* disbursal

disperse *See* disburse

disposition *See* deposition

disprove *See* disapprove

dissent *See* decent

dissidence, dissidents

>dissidence *n.* disagreement, particularly opposition to authority: 'Their dissidence resulted in imprisonment'

>dissidents *n.* (pl.) people who disagree or oppose authority

dissolution *See* disillusion

diva, dive

>diva *n.* an opera singer, usually quite temperamental

>dive *n.* a rapid descent: 'The airplane made a sudden dive'; a cheap bar or nightclub (slang)

divers, diverse

>divers *[die'•verz] n.*(pl.) people who dive

>divers *[die'•verz] adj.* various or sundry: 'Her bag was filled with divers cosmetics.'

>diverse *[die•verss'] adj.* unlike, distinct, or multiform: 'New York City comprises people with diverse interests and backgrounds'

divisor *See* deviser

divorce, divorcé, divorcée

>divorce *n.* the end of a marriage; the dissolution or separation of two items or ideas that were linked

>divorcé *n.* a divorced man

>divorcée *n.* a divorced woman

do, doe, dough

>do *n.* a tone in the musical scale

>doe *n.* a female deer or rabbit

>dough *n.* a mixture of flour and water; money (slang)

>*See also* dew

doer *See* dewar

does, doze

>does *n.* (pl.) several female deer or rabbits

>does *v.* 3d person, sing, present tense of do, to act, to produce, or to solve: 'She does the crossword puzzle in ten minutes'

doze *v.* to sleep lightly: 'I usually doze off at my desk in the afternoon'

doggy, dogie

doggy *[daw'•gee] n.* a small dog

dogie *[doh'•gee] n.* a stray calf

dol, dole, doll, dull

dol *n.* a measure of the degree of pain

dole *n.* unemployment compensation; charitable payments or distributions: 'He's been on the dole for one year'

dole *v.* to provide charity; to give out sparingly: 'They'll dole out the food once a week'

doll *n.* a toy figure resembling a person

doll *v.* to dress up: 'She'll doll up for the party'

dull *adj.* boring: 'That was a dull play'; not clear; stupid

dollar, dolor, duller

dollar *[doll'•er] n.* paper currency equal to 100 cents

dolor *[doh'•ler] n.* a state of extreme sorrow or pain

duller *[dull'•er] adj.* slower to understand; more boring

domain *See* demesne

done, dun

done *adj.* finished; cooked adequately: 'The roasted chicken is done'; performed: 'The job is done'

dun *n.* a brownish gray color; an urgent request

dun *v.* to ask repeatedly for payment of a debt: 'Collection agencies dun debtors in unpleasant ways'; to darken; to cure fish

dun *adj.* dark or gloomy

dotty, doty, doughty, dowdy

dotty *[dot'•ee] adj.* slightly mad or eccentric

doty *[doh'•dee] adj.* decayed or discolored (of timber)

doughty *[dow'•tee (dow rhymes w. cow)] adj.* brave: 'The doughty boxer kept going even after several knockdowns'

dowdy *[dow'•dee] adj.* dressed poorly, or in old-fashioned styles

double time, double-time

> double time *n.* to pay at twice the regular rate for overtime work; a fast marching count used in the army or sports: 'The sergeant barked, "Double time, march!"'
>
> double-time *v.* to move at the fast count

douce *See* deuce

dough *See* do

dour *See* dewar

douse, dowse

> douse *v.* to make wet: 'She doused his hair with water from the pipe'; to extinguish: 'Douse the light'
>
> dowse *v.* to search for water or minerals with a special stick: 'In dry spells, they dowse frequently'

doux *See* dew

doze *See* does

dragon, dragoon

> dragon *n.* a mythological scaly monster with wings; a fierce person: 'She was a dragon about protecting her children'
>
> dragoon *n.* a soldier
>
> dragoon *v.* to pressure someone to do something: 'He will dragoon us to contribute to this charity'

drier, dryer

> drier *adj.* having less moisture
>
> dryer *n.* a machine that eliminates moisture: 'He moved his clean laundry from the washing machine to the dryer'

driven, drive-in drive in

> driven *adj.* compulsive: 'He's driven to be the best pianist'
>
> driven *v.* past participle of drive: 'He was driven to the concert in a Rolls Royce'
>
> drive-in *n.* a store or movie that permits customers to enter while remaining in their cars
>
> drive in *v.* to go in a vehicle: 'He likes to drive in the rain'

droop, drop, drupe

> droop *v.* to bend downward; to hang: 'If you do not water the plant, it will droop'

drop *n.* a small liquid particle: 'A drop of rain won't hurt you'; a small amount: 'Just a drop of syrup, please'; a steep decline: 'a drop in stock prices'

drop *v.* to fall or to let fall; to act exhausted: 'After that workout, I'm ready to drop'; to come down sharply: 'If that giant company fails, stocks could drop 100 points'

drupe *n.* a fruit with a single hard stone

drop-off, drop off

drop-off *n.* a sharp decline: 'A drop-off in student scores'

drop off *v.* to leave something: 'I'll drop off this package tomorrow'; to fall asleep

dropout, drop out

dropout *n.* one who quits school

drop out *v.* to withdraw from participation: 'She'll have to drop out of the tournament because of an injury'

dryer *See* drier

dual, duel

dual *adj.* double; made up of two parts; having two functions: 'She has the dual role of mother and professional'

duel *n.* combat: 'That's a duel unto death'; a struggle for ascendancy

dualist, duelist

dualist *n.* a proponent of dualism, a view that reduces life or ideas to two basic substances or concepts

duelist *n.* one who takes part in a duel

ducat, ducked, duct

ducat *[duh'•kit] n.* a ticket; an old European gold coin

ducked *v.* past tense of duck; to lower quickly; to evade or dodge: 'He ducked the draft'

duct *n.* a tube or passage that carries liquid, gas, or air; a bodily tube that conveys fluids

duce *See* deuce

due *See* dew

dull *See* dol

duller *See* dollar

dully, duly

> dully *adv.* in a dull manner, not intense or acute: 'His broken
> wrist throbbed dully'
>
> duly *adv.* in a proper manner: 'This was the duly elected
> council'

dun *See* done

dung *See* dengue

dye *See* die

dyeing, dying

> dyeing *v.* coloring fabrics
>
> dying *v.* present participle of die; to be near death; to want
> very much to do something: 'I'm dying to see that movie'

dyer *See* dire

dyne *See* dine

dysentery *See* disinter

E

earn, erne, urn

> earn *v.* to receive payment for one's labor: 'He can earn $500 a week on that job'
>
> erne *n.* a European eagle
>
> urn *n.* a vase used as a receptacle for cremated ashes; a large coffee or tea maker

earthly, earthy

> earthly *adj.* worldly: 'An earthly existence is all too brief'; conceivable or possible: 'There is no earthly reason for him to say that'
>
> earthy *adj.* of the earth; coarse and unrefined: 'He uses very earthy language'

eave, eve

> eave *n.* the edge of a sloping roof
>
> eve *n.* the night before a holiday or an event

eccentric *See* acentric

eclipse, ellipse, ellipsis, ellipses

> eclipse *n.* the obscuring of one heavenly body by another; a state of decline or disgrace
>
> ellipse *n.* a mathematical curve
>
> ellipsis *n.* the grammatical term for the omission of words that are conceptually understood but grammatically necessary; the linguistic term for the omission of sounds, or slurring in speech; the symbol indicating the omission of words from a sentence, that looks like (. . .)

ellipses *n.* the plural of ellipsis

economic, economical

economic *adj.* refers to the management of income, production, distribution, and consumption: 'The economic plan of the former Soviet Union requires an influx of billions of dollars from the West'

economical *adj.* thrifty, efficient: 'She is very economical with the family's meager income'

ecru *See* accrue

edible *See* addable

edict *See* addict

edition *See* addition

e'er *See* air

eerie/eery *See* aerie

effect *See* affect

effective *See* affective

effluent *See* affluent

efflux *See* afflux

egoism, egotism

egoism *n.* the view in ethics that self-interest motivates all action and propels society

egotism *n.* self-importance, conceit, or self-centeredness

egression *See* aggression

egret *See* aigrette

eight *See* ait

either, ether

either *[ee'•ther (th as in the)] adj.* one of two: 'I will take either the blue one or the red one'

either *adv.* also, as well: 'If you don't see him, I won't either'

ether *[ee'•ther (th as in throw)] n.* a chemical: 'The doctor gave the patient ether to put him to sleep'

el, ell

el *n.* an elevated railroad; the letter *L*

ell *n.* an elbow in a pipe; a right angled extension to a building ; various units of cloth measurement

elapse, illapse

elapse *v.* to slip or glide away

illapse *n.* an influx

elation, illation

elation *n.* a state of great happiness; the elevation of the mind or spirit

illation *n.* an inference, or that which is inferred

elder, older

elder *n.* a tree; a person with authority: 'He is an elder of the church'

elder *adj.* refers to higher rank, earlier times, or earlier birth

older *adj.* comparative of old: 'He is older than his sister'

eldest, oldest

eldest *adj.* the first born: 'Jacob's eldest son was Reuben'

oldest *adj.* superlative of old; of greater age than all its predecessors or related persons

elegy, eulogy

elegy *[ell'•i•gee] n.* a poem or a musical composition, usually sad and mournful

eulogy *[you'•li•gee] n.* a funeral oration: 'The eulogy for the dead president brought tears to the eyes of all who heard it'

elementary *See* alimentary

elicit, illicit

elicit *[ee•liss'•it] v.* to draw forth, to evoke: 'His letter should elicit a quick reply'

illicit *[ill•liss'•it] adj.* unlawful; not allowed by custom or morality: 'He had an illicit affair with his secretary for over a year'

ell *See* el

ellipse/ellipsis/ellipses *See* eclipse

elude *See* allude

elusion/elution *See* allusion

elusory, illusory

elusory *[i•loose'•ory] adj.* evasive

illusory *[ill•loose'•ory] adj.* deceptive or based on illusion

elute *See* allude
eluvium *See* alluvion
emend *See* amend
emerge, immerge

> emerge *v.* to become visible; to become apparent; to develop as something new: 'After billions of years, life emerged on this planet'
>
> immerge *v.* to plunge: 'The blacksmith immerged the molten steel in the water'

emersed, immersed

> emersed *adj.* standing out above the water, usually referring to leaves on plants
>
> immersed *adj.* engrossed, absorbed: 'He did not hear me as he was immersed in his reading'; placed under water; baptised

emigrant, immigrant

> emigrant *n.* a person who leaves a country in order to settle in another country
>
> immigrant *n.* a person who comes to settle in a country

emigrate, immigrate

> emigrate *v.* to leave one's country
>
> immigrate *v.* to come into a new country in order to settle there

eminent, immanent, imminent

> eminent *adj.* distinguished, prominent, or outstanding: 'The meeting was addressed by three eminent Nobel laureates'
>
> immanent *adj.* inherent; transcendent; present throughout the world: 'It is said that God is immanent'
>
> imminent *adj.* likely to happen soon: 'War is imminent, the president concluded, if the aggression does not stop immediately'

emolient, emolument

> emolient *n.* a substance for soothing or softening the skin
>
> emolument *n.* salary, wages, or gain from employment

empire, umpire

empire, *n.* a group of territories, colonies, or countries under one sovereign: 'The British Empire was at its zenith during the reign of Queen Victoria'

umpire *n.* an arbiter of disputes; a sports official chosen to rule on plays

empties, emptys

empties *v.* 3d person, sing., present tense of empty, to pour out: 'He empties the bottles before cleaning them'

emptys *n.* (pl.) bottles, freight cars, or trucks that are empty: 'They shipped the emptys back to the Coca-Cola plant to be refilled'

enable, unable

enable *v.* to make able, to make possible: 'The four years in medical school should enable her to pass the medical boards'

unable *adj.* not able, lacking the ability: 'He is unable to finish anything he starts'

enervate, innervate

enervate *v.* to debilitate, to deprive of vigor: 'The broiling sun completely enervated him'

innervate *v.* to stimulate a muscle or organ

enunciation *See* annunciation

enroot, en route

enroot *v.* to implant; to fix; to establish

en route *[on•root']* *adv.* along the way: 'They'll stop off here en route to Canada'

ensure, insure

ensure *v.* to guarantee; to make safe; to protect; to make sure: 'This lock will ensure your safety'

insure *v.* to provide insurance; to take out insurance: 'If you ensure your safety, we will insure you at a lower rate'

entomology, etymology

entomology *n.* the study of insects

etymology *n.* the study of word origins

envelop, envelope

envelop *[en•vell'•up] v.* to wrap up; to cover completely; to surround: 'Oceans envelop most continents'; 'This blanket will envelop you with warmth'

envelope *[en'•vi•lope] n.* a wrapper, a covering; a container for a letter

epic, epoch

epic *n.* a long poem or other writing telling of a nation's heroic acts or of an heroic act

epoch *n.* a period of time in history or in geology: 'a peaceful epoch'

equable, equatable, equitable

equable *[ehk'•wi•bil] adj.* unvarying or even tempered: 'While everyone else was shouting, his behavior was equable'

equatable *[ee•kwate'•able] adj.* capable of being made equal

equitable *[eh'•quit•able] adj.* fair, just, right, or reasonable: 'That's an equitable division of the inheritance'

era, error

era *n.* an age or epoch

error *n.* a fault, mistake, or blunder; a sin; a baseball misplay

erasable, irascible

erasable *[i•race'•ible] adj.* able to be effaced, rubbed out, or wiped out: 'That tape is erasable'

irascible *[i•rass'•ible] adj.* quick-tempered; easily angered: 'When he drank, he became irascible'

ere *See* air

erect, eruct

erect *v.* to raise; to construct; to assemble; to found

eruct *v.* to belch

erne *See* earn

erotic, erratic

erotic *adj.* relating to or arousing sexual desires or feelings: 'That's an erotic movie'

erratic *adj.* moving unevenly: 'The erratic movement of the plane made him nervous'; eccentric or odd: 'His erratic ways drove her up the wall'

err *See* air

errand, errant, arrant

    errand *n.* a brief trip to do something specific: 'My errand
        was to pick up a package'

    errant *adj.* wandering, straying, moving aimlessly; mistaken:
        'those errant economists who still defend supply-side
        theories'

    arrant *adj.* thoroughly; outstanding bad: 'That is arrant
        nonsense'

error *See* era

eruption, irruption

    eruption *n.* a bursting forth; an outbreak of volcanic activity; a
        sudden skin rash

    irruption *n.* a sudden invasion: 'No one foresaw the irruption
        of the Iraqis into Kuwait'; a violent bursting into space

esoteric, exoteric

    esoteric *adj.* understood by only a chosen few: 'Her esoteric
        poetry developed a cult following'; confidential; private

    exoteric *adj.* simple; commonplace, meant for public
        understanding (the opposite of esoteric)

essay *See* assey

estray *See* astray

ether *See* either

etymology *See* entomology

eulogy *See* elegy

eunuch, unique

    eunuch *[you'•nick] n.* a castrated male; one lacking power or
        force

    unique *[you'•neek] adj.* having no equal or like; belonging
        solely to

euphemism, euphuism

    euphemism *n.* an agreeable or inoffensive word or phrase
        used in place of another word considered offensive or
        distasteful: 'The administration used a euphemism for its
        unpopular move, calling its war a "police action" '

euphuism *n.* an affected, artificial elegance in speaking or
writing

eurhythmic *See* arrhythmic

eve *See* eave

eversion *See* aversion

evert *See* advert

everyday, every day

everyday *adj.* daily; ordinary: 'Robbery is an everyday event in
the large city'

every day *adj.* each separate day: 'It happens every day';
'Every day in prison seemed to be an eternity'

everyone, every one

everyone *pron.* all the people in a group or in the whole
world: 'Everyone at the party dressed informally'

every one *n.* each one: 'Winning the battle depends on every
one of the airmen being in the right place at the right
time'

everything, every thing

everything *pron.* all the things: 'He does everything for his
aged father'; life in general; extremely important:
'Winning is everything to me'

every thing *n.* each thing: 'Every thing he touched turned to
gold'

evocation *See* avocation

evulsion *See* avulsion

ewe, hew, hue, whew, yew, you, yu

ewe *n.* a female sheep

hew *v.* to chop; to shape with an axe or knife; to conform:
'She'll hew to the party line'

hue *n.* a color or tint; a shout: 'hue and cry'

whew *interj.* dismay, relief, or astonishment

yew *n.* an evergreen tree

you *pron.* the person or persons to whom you are speaking;
the third person, or 'one'; people in general: 'Things that
you can't believe!'

yu *n.* precious jade

ewer, hewer

ewer *n.* a pitcher or jug

hewer *n.* a person who chops or shapes wood with an axe

See also yore

exalt, exult

exalt *v.* to praise: 'Their prayers exalt God'

exult *v.* to be very glad or jubilant, or to rejoice: 'They'll exult over their victory'

exceed *See* accede

except *See* accept

exceptionable, exceptional

exceptionable *adj.* objectionable: 'His remarks about the trial were exceptionable'

exceptional *adj.* above average; not ordinary: 'She received A's in all her subjects; she is an exceptional student'; physically or mentally impaired: 'After receiving severe head injuries, he was sent to a school for exceptional students'

excerpt *See* accept

excess *See* access

exercise, exorcise

exercise *v.* to use or employ: 'He will exercise caution when crossing the ravine'; to engage in regular physical activity; to have an effect on someone or something: 'She might exercise undue influence on him'

exercise *n.* a practice or drill: 'The teacher gave the students a tough exercise in arithmetic'; physical activity: 'He likes his exercise too much'

exorcise *v.* to drive out evil spirits; to purify

exhilarate *See* accelerate

exile *See* axle

exoteric *See* esoteric

expansive, expensive

expansive *adj.* able to expand; to be friendly or expressive: 'He was in an expansive mood and talked for hours' expensive *adj.* high-priced: 'That car is too expensive for our budget'

expos, expose, exposé

expos *n.* (pl.) expositions: 'That city is the host to many expos'

expose *v.* to open one to risk or harm: 'If you expose yourself to the sun you might get a nasty burn'; to reveal harmful acts: 'The D.A. will expose the credit card fraud'; to make known, or to bare

exposé *[ex•po•zay] n.* the act of revealing a scandal to the public: 'That tabloid would love to run an exposé exposing the president's tax evasion'

extant, extent

extant *adj.* still in existence: 'She owns all of Smith's extant paintings'

extent *n.* amount, area, degree: 'The extent of his holdings would astonish you'

exult *See* exalt

eye *See* aye/ay

eyed, I'd, id, ide/id

eyed *v.* past tense of eye, to watch; to look at: 'He eyed the street carefully before going out'

I'd *contr.* I had, I should, or I would: 'If I'd gone to the movies, this would never have happened'

id *[rhymes w.* lid*] n.* a psychological term, defined by Freud, to describe the unconscious; that part of the psyche that is completely driven by instinctual needs and drives

ide/id *[rhymes w.* bide*] n.* a carp-like fish

See also aye/ay

eyelet, islet

eyelet *n.* a grommet; a peephole; a small eye or hole designed to receive a lace

islet *n.* a small island; a mass of human tissue within another type of tissue

F

faces, feces

faces *n.* (pl.) more than one face, the front part of the head

faces *v.* 3d person, sing., present tense of face, to confront or
to deal with: 'He faces heavy opposition in the election';
to turn toward or about: 'Our living room faces the
sun'

feces *n.* excrement

facet, faucet

facet *n.* a polished surface of a cut gem; an aspect or phase of
something: 'Every facet of this system is operating well'

faucet *n.* a device that allows water to flow

faction, fraction

faction *n.* a small, often contentious, political group working
for a common cause inside a larger group: 'The left
faction opposed any settlement'

fraction *n.* a small part; a portion; a mathematical term

factious, factitious, fatuous, fictitious

factious *adj.* quarrelsome; taking part in factions or small
organized groups

factitious *adj.* artificial, lacking authenticity or genuineness:
'He bought a factitious antique at the flea market'

fatuous *adj.* silly, inane: 'He doesn't realize how fatuous his
remarks about politics are'

fictitious *adj.* fictional, invented: 'He gave a wholly fictitious
account of his background'

facts, fax

facts *n.* (pl.) real and true things; 'He never gets his facts straight'

fax *n.* a machine that transmits written messages over telephone lines

fadeaway, fade away

fadeaway *n.* a baseball term for a base runner's slide to avoid a tag; a basketball shot made by a player falling back from the basket

fade away *v.* to disappear after gradually losing intensity: 'Old soldiers never die, they just fade away'

faerie/faery, fairy, ferry

faerie *or* faery *adj.* visionary; enchanted

fairy *n.* an imaginary being in human form with magical powers

ferry *n.* a boat designed to transport passengers or goods across a stretch of water

fain, fane, feign

fain *adv.* ready; eager; happily: 'I would fain die for thee'

fane *n.* a place of worship; a pennant

feign *v.* to pretend, to make believe: 'He'll feign illness before the next test'

faint, feint

faint *v.* to temporarily lose consciousness

faint *adj.* very light: 'Those colors are faint'; weak or timid

feint *n.* a pretended blow or attack; a deceptive move

fair, fare, phare

fair *n.* a gathering of people; a carnival; a bazaar; an agricultural exhibit; an exhibition or sale, often for a charity

fair *adj.* light-skinned or good-looking; pleasant: 'fair weather'; just or impartial: 'He's a fair judge'

fare *n.* the price of passage, food, or drink, as in a 'bill of fare'

phare *n.* a lighthouse

fairer, farer

> fairer *adj.* comparative of fair; pretty; equitable; average;
> sunny; light-skinned; probable; without blemishes
>
> farer *n.* a traveler or a wayfarer

fairy *See* faerie/faery

faker, fakir

> faker *n.* a bluffer; a swindler; an impostor
>
> fakir *[fi•keer']* *n.* a Muslim or Hindu ascetic considered to be
> holy

fallout, fall out

> fallout *n.* particles emanating from a nuclear explosion; the
> negative side effects of any action
>
> fall out *v.* to break with someone as a result of a quarrel; in
> the military, to break ranks

familial, familiar

> familial *adj.* pertaining to one's family: 'familial pride'
>
> familiar *adj.* well-known; friendly; knowledgeable: 'He's
> familiar with Mexican history'; intimate: 'He's too familiar
> with her when he hardly knows her'

fane *See* fain

fare *See* fair

farer *See* fairer

faro, farrow, pharaoh

> faro *n.* a game of cards
>
> farrow *n.* a litter of pigs
>
> pharaoh *n.* a king of ancient Egypt

farther, father, further

> farther *adj.* both farther and further mean beyond a certain
> point, but farther means at a greater distance: 'We can't
> go any farther than this without collapsing'
>
> further *adj.* means more or additional: 'Further action seems
> unnecessary'
>
> further *v.* to support or help someone or something: 'further
> his career'
>
> father *n.* a male parent; a founder: 'George Washington is the
> father of our country'

fat, phat

fat *adj.* overweight; highly productive; rich

phat *n.* matter that can be set easily into type

fatal, fetal

fatal *adj.* deadly; critical: 'a fatal encounter'

fetal *adj.* relating to a fetus: 'Smoking may cause a fetal abnormality'

fate, fête

fate *n.* destiny, or final outcome: 'his sister was hurt in the accident, and the other passengers suffered a similar fate'

fête *[feht] n.* a holiday, a lavish celebration, a festival

fated, feted, fetid

fated *[fate'•id] adj.* destined to end badly, doomed, predetermined: 'He was fated to leave office under a cloud'

feted *[fate'•id] adj.* honored, often via a celebration

fetid *[fet'•id] adj.* smelling bad

father *See* farther

fatuous *See* factious

faucet *See* facet

fauna, fawner

fauna *n.* (pl.) animals, as distinguished from plant life (flora)

fawner *n.* one who fawns, a sycophant or toady

faux, foe

faux *[foe] n.* false or artificial: 'faux fur'

foe *n.* the enemy; a person or group that opposes an action or policy: 'The nominee's foe presented his arguments'

fax *See* facts

fay, fey

fay *n.* a fairy; an elf

fay *v.* to fit well

fey *adj.* mischievous; supernatural; strange: 'His fey manner made her nervous'; doomed; fated; clairvoyant; enchanted

faze, phase

faze *v.* to disturb or to bother: 'His bad jokes don't faze me' phase *n.* an aspect or side; the different appearances of the moon or planets; a stage in development: 'He's in an active phase, and runs about constantly'

feat, feet

feat *n.* a special accomplishment: 'Winning three titles in a row was a feat'

feet *n.* the plural of foot

feces *See* faces

feign *See* fain

feint *See* faint

feral, ferrule, ferule

feral *[feer'•il] adj.* not socialized; gloomy; of animals, wild, undomesticated

ferrule *[fer'•il] n.* a metal ring put at the end of a cane; a tool handle

ferule *[fer'•il] n.* a flat stick used to punish children

ferment, foment

ferment *v.* to excite: 'The idea of freedom can still ferment people's imaginations'; to cause fermentation or an enzymatic breakdown

foment *v.* to provide; to encourage; to instigate: 'He did foment a riot'

ferry *See* faerie/faery

fetal *See* fatal

fête *See* fate

feted *See* fated

fetid *See* fated

feudal, futile

feudal *adj.* pertaining to the landowner structure in the Middle Ages: 'The feudal lords held vast estates'

futile *adj.* not useful; ineffective: 'That's a futile gesture'

few, phew

few *n.* a small number: 'A few of them stayed behind'

phew *interj.* an exclamation of disgust

fey *See* fay

fiancé, fiancée, finance
>fiancé *n.* the male partner of an engaged couple
>fiancée *n.* the female of an engaged couple
>finance *v.* to raise money for a firm or project: 'We'll finance this purchase by issuing new stock'

fiche, fish
>fiche *[feesh] n.* a microfiche, a sheet of microfilm used in recording and filing information
>fish *n.* an animal that lives in water, usually a scaly, finned vertebrate which breathes through gills

fictitious *See* factious

fiend, friend
>fiend *n.* an evil spirit; a person strongly involved in or addicted to something: 'an exercise fiend;' 'a drug fiend'
>friend *n.* a close acquaintance; an ally; a person of whom one is fond

file, phial
>file *n.* a cabinet for keeping pages; a folder or other container to hold papers; an orderly arrangement of papers; a line of persons or things; a tool used to smooth uneven surfaces: 'a nail file'
>phial *[fie'•il] n.* a small glass bottle; a small vessel to hold liquids
>*See also* vial

filé, filet, fillet, filly
>filé *[fi•lay'] n.* a sassafras powder used in New Orleans–style cooking
>filet *[fi•lay'] n.* a lace with a simple pattern on a square mesh background; a special steak: 'filet mignon'
>fillet *[fi•lay'] n. adj.* a thin steak or strip of boneless meat or fish
>fillet *[fill'•it] n.* a lacy headband
>filly *n.* a young female horse

filing, filling

filing *v.* scraping material with a file; arranging papers in a folder or sequence

filling *n.* matter used to fill a space, as a tooth; the food used with bread to make a sandwich

filling *v.* completing: 'filling out a form'; stopping up or closing up: 'filling the pothole'

filling *adj.* satisfying: 'That meal was filling'

Filipina, Filipino, Pilipino

Filipina *n.* a female native of the Philippines.

Filipino *n.* a male native of the Philippines

Pilipino *n.* the official language of the Philippines

fillip, flip

fillip *n.* a snap of the fingers; something that creates interest or excitement: 'The new actress was a fillip for the show'

flip *v.* to turn something quickly; to be happy or off the wall

filter, philter

filter *n.* a device to strain out impurities: 'Many people use a filter to provide clean water'; a device to provide better reception on electrical components or appliances; a filter-tipped cigarette

filter *v.* to remove impurities by putting materials through a filter; to move or circulate gradually: 'News of the promotion will quickly filter through the organization'

philter *n.* a magic potion, a love charm

finance *See* fiancé

find, fined, finned

find *v.* to discover; recover; locate: 'They will mount a search to find the missing baby'; to provide: 'We'll find the money to buy the car somehow'; to decide in court: 'The jury will probably find him guilty'

find *n.* a pleasant discovery: 'That cheap restaurant is a real find'

fined *v.* past tense of fine, to be ordered to pay a penalty for illegal parking or other violations of laws or regulations finned *adj.* having fins, like a fish, airplane, or car

fineness, finesse

fineness *[fine'•ness] n.* the state of being fine or of superior quality

finesse *[fi•ness'] n.* an artful or skillful performance, action, or trick

fir, fur

fir *n.* an evergreen tree

fur *n.* the hairy coating of a mammal

fiscal, physical

fiscal *adj.* relating to government or other financial policies or actions, e.g., raising or lowering taxes: 'The fiscal policy of the government is disastrous to the middle class'

physical *adj.* relating to the body: 'physical fitness'; relating to matter and nature, not the spirit: 'the physical world'

physical *n.* a medical examination

fish *See* fiche

fisher, fissure

fisher *n.* a fisherman; an animal like a weasel

fissure *n.* a deep cleft or crack; a strong disagreement

fists, fits

fists *n.* (pl.) tightly closed hands

fits *n.* (pl.) sudden attacks or emotional outbursts: 'He often throws fits'

fits *v.* 3d person, sing., present tense of fit, to be the right size or right match; to make competent: 'His training fits him for this post'

flack, flak, flake

flack *n.* a press agent; a slap; a repeated striking sound

flak *n.* the fire of antiaircraft guns; censure: 'He caught a lot of flak for his mistake'

flake *n.* a light piece of snow or similar flimsy items; an eccentric person (slang)

flacks, flax

flacks *v.* 3d person, sing., present tense of 'flack', to promote or publicize; to flick; to slap

flax *n.* a plant whose seeds yield oil and whose stem is used in textiles; a yellow-gray color

flagrant, fragrant

flagrant *adj.* notorious, outrageous, glaringly bad: 'His flagrant basketball foul caused his ejection from the game'

fragrant *adj.* sweet-smelling

flair, flare

flair *n.* an aptitude: 'She has a flair for painting'; smartness in style: 'She dresses with flair'

flare *n.* a very bright light; a sudden outburst of anger; an outward curve, as of a skirt

flambé, flambeau

flambé *[flom•bay']* *adj.* dressed or served with flaming liquor, usually a dessert

flambeau *[flam•boh']* *n.* a torch; a large candlestick

flap, flop

flap *n.* a hinged or loose part or piece; a blow with a flat item; a scandal: 'The actor's behavior caused a great flap'; the folded-in ends of a book's jacket

flop *n.* a thud; the act of falling suddenly; a failure: 'The show was a flop'; a place to sleep temporarily, a flophouse

flax *See* flacks

flea, flee

flea *n.* a parasitic insect noted for its jumping powers, often living on dogs or cats

flee *v.* to escape; to abscond; to vanish

fleas, fleece, flees

fleas *n.* (pl.) parasitic insects

fleece *n.* a sheep's wool or any similar soft exterior

fleece *v.* to cheat or rob: 'That investor fleeced me of all my savings'

flees *v.* 3d person, sing., present tense of flee, to escape

flêche, flesh

flêche *n.* a spire

flesh *n.* the soft substance of the body; the body as a whole: 'The spirit is willing but the flesh is weak'; the soft pulp of fruits; the physical nature of humans

flecks, flex, flicks

flecks *n.* (pl.) spots; particles; flakes

flex *n.* insulated electrical wires

flex *v.* to bend or contract a muscle: 'The bodybuilder will always flex his muscles on the beach'

flicks *n.* (pl.) sharp sounds made by hitting something with your fingernails; the movies (slang)

flew, flu, flue

flew *v.* past tense of fly: 'The bird flew over the rainbow'

flu *n.* short for the infection influenza

flue *n.* a passageway, such as a shaft that removes smoke from a stove or fireplace

flip *See* fillip

floc, flock

floc *n.* a minute mass of suspended particles

flock *n.* a group of people or animals often attached to a leader: 'a flock of birds'; 'the pastor's flock'; any group of similar items; small pieces of material used as a stuffing for pillows or mattresses; material used to create velveteen wall hangings

flocs, flocks, flux, phlox

flocs *n.* (pl.) suspended chemical particles

flocks *n.* (pl.) groups of certain animals such as sheep or goats; people with a common purpose or direction

flux *n.* the continuing flow of substances, like solder; a condition of change or confusion: 'After the war things were in a state of flux'

phlox *n.* a type of plant

floe, flow

floe *n.* a mass of glacial ice

flow *v.* to move freely or to circulate: 'Water in that river will
flow rapidly in the spring'; 'Today, ideas flow quickly
from one part of the world to another'; to hang loosely:
'He watched her hair flow in the breeze'

flop *See* flap

florescent, fluorescent

florescent *adj.* flowering or blooming: 'A florescent society is
one that is at its peak of development'

fluorescent *adj.* giving off radiant light as a result of radiation:
'She bought some fluorescent bulbs'

flounder, founder

flounder *n.* a fish

flounder *v.* to struggle; to act clumsily: 'He floundered for a
reply'

founder *n.* a person who starts a group or institution:
'Gannett was the founder of a chain of newspapers'

founder *v.* to sink: 'Ships often founder on those rocks'; to
fail: 'The project will founder for lack of support'

flour, flower

flour *n.* a fine substance, usually food, produced by grinding

flower *n.* the colorful part of a plant, picked for display: 'My
favorite flower is a rose'; the best representative or
portion: 'The flower of England's youth died in WWI'; a
special era: 'When Knighthood was in flower'

flu, flue, *See* flew

flux *See* flocs

foaled, fold

foaled *v.* past tense of foal, to give birth to a horse

fold *v.* to bend an object so that one part lies on top of
another: 'fold the blanket'; to intertwine: 'fold one's legs
or arms'; to mix slowly in cooking: 'fold in the egg
whites'; to give in or fail: 'I fold this hand of cards'

fold *n.* an animal enclosure; a group of people with similar
goals: 'Please come back into the fold'

foe *See* faux

foggy, fogy

foggy *[fah'•gee] adj.* full of mental or physical haze; misty: 'a foggy day in London town'

fogy *[foh'•gee] n.* an old-fashioned, conservative person: 'an old fogy'

foment *See* ferment

fondling, foundling

fondling *v.* present participle of fondle, to caress or stroke: 'The new mother was fondling her baby'

foundling *n.* an abandoned infant

fool, fuel, full

fool *n.* a stupid person or act: 'I was a fool to buy that cheap rug'; a devotee: 'a fool for love'

fool *v.* to trick someone; to jest ; to play

fuel *n.* something that creates energy, such as gasoline

full *adj.* complete; entire; top rank: 'a full professor'; ample: 'That blouse is cut full'

full *adv.* exactly or very: 'She knows full well what I want'

for, fore, four

for *prep.* to give or to be used by: 'This present is for you'; to be employed by: 'I work for this company'; a reason or a cause: 'I do this for the money, not satisfaction'; in favor of something: 'I vote for this motion'; to help or please someone: 'He did this for her'; duration: 'We drove for hours'

for *conj.* since, because

fore *n.* to the head or top: 'Martin Luther King, Jr., came to the fore as a civil rights leader'

fore *adj.* former or forward

fore *adv.* situated in front of

fore *interj.* in golf, a shouted warning

four *n.* the number between three and five, 4

forbear, forebear

forbear *v.* to refrain from; to avoid; to be patient or tolerant: 'You will forbear from responding to her insults' forebear *n.* an ancestor

forego, forgo

forego *v.* to go before

forgo *v.* to do without; to abstain from: 'You can forgo desserts for a couple of weeks'

foreword, forward, froward

foreword *n.* a preface: 'The professor wrote the foreword to my book'

forward *n.* a player in basketball, soccer, and hockey who plays in the front line

forward *adj.* bold: 'a forward person'; at or moving to the front; progressive or advanced: 'She's very forward thinking for a politician'

forward *adv.* to face or move to the front: 'He reached forward to pull the handle'; to look to the future; ahead: 'Move the clock forward in the spring'; to anticipate: 'I look forward to this game'

froward *adj.* contrary, unruly: 'His froward daughter will have a hard time making friends'

formally, formerly

formally *adv.* conventionally, properly: 'We haven't been formally introduced'

formerly *adv.* previously: 'We formerly lived in Chicago'

fort, forte, forty, fought

fort *n.* a stronghold, a fortress; a permanent military post

forte *[fort] n.* what one does best: 'Method acting is her forte'

forte *[for'•tay] adj.* in music, loudly

forty *n.* the number between thirty-nine and forty-one, 40

fought *v.* past tense of fight

forth, fourth

forth *adv.* forward in time, place, or position; out into view; abroad; to make known: 'set forth my position on abortion'

fourth *n.* one quarter; a musical interval

fourth *adj.* the next one after third: 'She is his fourth wife'

forward *See* foreword

foul, fowl

>foul *v.* to make an illegal move in sports; to dirty something; to disable: 'Birds often foul airplane engines'

>fowl *v.* a bird

founder *See* flounder

foundling *See* fondling

four *See* for

fraction *See* faction

fragrant *See* flagrant

fraise, frays, fraze, phrase

>fraise *[frays] n.* stakes used in fortifications; a reamer used to enlarge holes; a symbol in heraldry

>frays *n.* (pl.) fights

>frays *v.* 3d person, sing., present tense of fray, to wear out: 'That cheap suit frays easily'; to become irritable or tense: 'Performing always frays my nerves'

>fraze *n.* a tool

>phrase *n.* a group of words, smaller than a sentence, that conveys meaning; a current expression; a musical or dance sentence or thought

frap, frappé

>frap *v.* to bind tightly

>frappé *[fra•pay'] n.* a thick milk shake or a flavored drink with ice

fraud, fraught

>fraud *n.* deception: 'The owners of that bank engaged in fraud'; a person who practices a deception

>fraught *adv.* associated with: 'This trip is fraught with peril'

freak, phreak

>freak *n.* a monstrosity, something abnormal; an addict (slang): 'a drug freak'; a strong fan: 'a football freak'

>phreak *n.* a phone freak, one who uses a device to avoid paying for phone calls (slang)

free-for-all, free for all

free-for-all *n.* a wild fight with many participants

free for all *adj.* at no cost to anybody: 'Drinks are free for all'

frees, freeze, frieze

frees *v.* 3d person, sing., present tense of free, to release, to let go, to become available: 'The boss frees me for special projects'

freeze *v.* to be very cold, to preserve in cold: 'freeze food'; to be unable to move due to fear; to cease, stop, or hold at a certain level: 'freeze salaries or prices'

frieze *n.* a sculptured or patterned strip on a building

freight, fright

freight *n.* cargo; the means or cost of moving cargo; cost (slang): 'I can't handle the freight for that car'

fright *n.* extreme or sudden terror; a person whose appearance is appalling: 'You're a fright'

friar, fryer

friar *n.* a monk; a brown color; a section of a printed page which has received insufficient ink

fryer *n.* a young chicken; a person who fries; a lamp used in color photography

friend *See* fiend

froward *See* foreword

fuel *See* fool

führer, furor

führer *n.* leader; the title used by Adolf Hitler, dictator of Nazi Germany

furor *n.* a rage; an uproar; excitement; fury

full *See* fool

funeral, funereal

funeral *n.* a ceremony to pay respects to a dead person, usually connected with burial

funereal *[fyoo•nee'•ree•ul] adj.* gloomy, mournful, suitable for a funeral

fungous, fungus

    fungous *adj.* like or caused by a fungus or fungi

    fungus *n.* a plant like a mushroom; mildew; mold; rust

fur *See* fir

further *See* farther

fuse/fuze, fuss, fuzz

    fuse *n.* a device used to protect electrical circuits; a cord used to ignite explosives

    fuse *v.* to join or to combine

    fuss *v.* to worry over minor details; to complain about trivial matters: 'They'll fuss for hours about the minor delay'; to dote: 'New grandparents will fuss over the baby'

    fuze *n.* a device used to detonate an explosive

    fuzz *n.* the police (slang); fluffy material

futile *See* feudal

G

Gaelic, Gallic, garlic

Gaelic *adj.* pertaining to natives of Scotland and Ireland

Gallic *adj.* pertaining to the Gauls or to the French

garlic *n.* an edible plant having a distinctive odor and flavor

gaff, gaffe

gaff *n.* a hook used in fishing; a fraud or hoax; harsh criticism: 'He can't stand the gaff'

gaffe *n.* a clumsy remark, a faux pas, a social blunder: 'He committed a gaffe when he called her by her first name immediately'

gage, gauge

gage *n.* a token of challenge used by medieval knights; a form of security against a loan

gauge *n.* an instrument for measuring; the measurement itself

gait, gate

gait *n.* a way of walking or running: 'The horse moves at a fast gait'

gait *v.* to train an animal to move at a particular pace; to display an animal before show judges

gate *n.* a movable barrier: 'You open the gate to enter the yard'; a town's tower erected for defense or as an entryway; the total number of entries or total price paid by them at a public affair: 'The play's gate dropped 10 percent this week'; an entrance: 'The gate to success'

gallop, galop

gallop *n.* a fast gait; the act of doing something quickly

galop *n.* a dance

galosh, ghoulish, goulash

galosh *[guh•losh']* *n.* a rubber boot worn in the rain: 'You left your galosh in the front hall'

ghoulish *[goo'•lish]* *adj.* relating to death, torture, or to people interested in same: 'Their ghoulish behavior frightened the townspeople'

goulash *[goo'•losh]* *n.* a type of Hungarian stew

gambet, gambit

gambet *n.* a type of bird

gambit *n.* a sacrifice of a pawn in chess to gain an advantage; an opening remark; a move to gain an advantage

gamble, gambol

gamble *v.* to play games of chance for money; to take risks generally: 'They'll gamble on moving in the hopes of finding better jobs'

gambol *v.* to skip with joy; to frolic

gamin, gamine, gammon

gamin *[gam'•in]* *n.* a boy with an impish manner; an urchin, a homeless or neglected boy

gamine *[ga'•meen]* *n.* a bright, mischievous small girl; a tomboy

gammon *[gam'•in]* *n.* a side of bacon

gantlet, gauntlet

gantlet *n.* overlapping railroad tracks

gauntlet *n.* a glove, which men used to throw down to challenge someone; a challenge; a protective work glove; a dangerous path one runs while subject to physical or verbal abuse: 'New fraternity pledges have to run the gauntlet'

gap, gape

gap *n.* an opening; a missing portion in a sequence or period of time: 'There's a three-year gap in your résumé'; an incomplete piece of work: 'There is a big gap in this article'; a big difference: 'The gap between rich and poor is getting wider' gape *v.* to look in amazement at an astonishing sight; to stare with one's mouth open; to yearn or to crave; to cleave; to break open

gaps, gasps

gaps *n.* (pl.) openings or spaces

gasps *v.* 3d person, sing., present tense of gasp, to suddenly draw in one's breath: 'When he has an asthma attack, he gasps for air'

garble, gerbil

garble *v.* to speak or write unintelligibly or in a confused manner; to distort one's meaning intentionally: 'He garbled the facts in my paper'

gerbil *[jer'•bill] n.* a tiny rodent often kept as a pet

gargle, gargoyle, gurgle

gargle *v.* to medicate your throat: 'To cure your cold, gargle every three hours'

gargoyle *n.* a grotesque figure often carved on cathedrals

gurgle *n.* the gentle sound of water flowing

garlic *See* Gallic

garnish, garnishee

garnish *v.* to decorate your food with a fancy touch: 'They always garnish their salads with exotic fruits'

garnishee *v.* to withhold part of one's wages to repay debts

garret, garrot, garrote/garote/garotte/garrotte

garret *[gar'•it] n.* an attic

garrot *[gar'•it] n.* a tourniquet; a name for various kinds of ducks

garrote, garote, garotte, *or* garrotte *[gi•rot'] n.* strangulation

gate *See* gait

gauche, gaucho, gosh, gouache

gauche *[go'•sh] adj.* naive, awkward, unsophisticated, or tactless: 'His gauche remarks offended everyone in the room'

gaucho *[gow'•cho] n.* an Argentinian cowboy

gosh *interj.* expression used as a substitute for God: 'My gosh!'

gouache *[gwahsh]* *n.* a manner of painting with opaque
watercolors, or a pigment used in that manner

gauge *See* gage

gauntlet *See* gantlet

gays, gaze

gays *n.* (pl.) homosexual men

gaze *v.* to look intently

gel, jell

gel *[jel]* *n.* a jellylike mixture; a thick, oily substance

jell *v.* to become jellylike; to become clear or come together:
'With that new information, everything will jell'

geld, gelt

geld *v.* to castrate a horse

gelt *n.* money (slang)

gelid, jellied

gelid *[jel'•id]* *adj.* icy, extremely cold

jellied *adj.* food preserved in aspic jelly

gene, jean

gene *n.* the small cell unit that contains DNA and determines
hereditary traits

jean *n.* a durable twilled cotton cloth; in the plural, trousers:
'She wore a pair of blue jeans'

genie, genii

genie *[jean'•ee]* *n.* a spirit with the power to grant one's
wishes

genii *[jean'•ee•ie]* *n.*(pl.) more than one genius

genius, genus

genius *n.* a person gifted with exceptional creative or
intellectual powers

genus *n.* a scientific category of plants or animals

genteel, gentile, gentle

genteel *[jen•teel']* *adj.* polite; refined; pretending to a higher
status: 'She affected genteel behavior in spite of her poor
background'

gentile *[jen'•tile]* *n.* not Jewish or Mormon

gentle *adj.* kind: 'He's a gentle person'; calm: 'She has a gentle voice and movements'; pleasant: 'The weather was gentle today'

gentlemen, gentle men

gentlemen *n.* a formal salutation: 'Ladies and gentlemen, good evening'

gentle men *n.* men who are kind, not rough or violent

gerbil *See* garble

german, German, germane, germen/germin

german *n.* a brother, sister, or cousin; a dance with frequent partner changes

german *[jer'•min] adj.* having the same parents or grandparents on either father's or mother's side

German *n.* an inhabitant or native of Germany

germane *[jer•mane'] adj.* relevant: 'Those facts are not germane to your argument'

germen *or* germin *[jer'•min] n.* a gonad; a rudiment or a shoot

gest, gist, jest

gest *n.* a great adventure or a story about one

gist *n.* the essence of something said or written: 'The gist of this article is buried in the middle'

jest *n.* a joke: 'His jest was lost on me'

gesture, jester

gesture *n.* a movement, either physical or symbolic, to express an attitude: 'He made a feeble gesture of apology'

jester *n.* a person who tells jokes; a fool

get-together, get together

get-together *n.* a gathering: 'The family will have a get-together on Thanksgiving'

get together *v.* to meet: 'We'll get together tomorrow'

ghastly, ghostly

ghastly *adj.* horrible, frightening; unpleasant: 'Those ghastly people down the block make too much noise'; ill: 'She looked ghastly when we visited' ghostly *adj.* looking like a ghost or an apparition

gherkin, jerkin

gherkin *[ger'•kin] n.* a small special cucumber used for pickling

jerkin *[jer'•kin] n.* a sleeveless jacket

ghoulish *See* galosh

gib, jib

gib *n.* a metal plate

jib *n.* a part of a crane

jib *v.* to refuse to proceed further

gibe, jibe

gibe *[jibe] v.* to taunt or insult

jibe *v.* to move suddenly from side to side, particularly on a ship

gild, gilled, guild

gild *v.* to apply a gold covering; to prettify in order to mislead; to decorate unnecessarily: 'To gild the lily'

gilled *adj.* having extra skin; having gills, especially a fish, through which to obtain oxygen from water

guild *n.* a medieval organization of craftsmen or businessmen

gilt, guilt

gilt *n.* a gold surface; a young female pig

gilt *v.* past tense and past participle of gild

guilt *n.* the responsibility for doing something wrong or criminal; the unhappy feeling caused by wrongdoing or the failure to do what one is supposed to do: 'He will bear the guilt of his action forever'

gist *See* gest

glacier, glazier

glacier *n.* a large mass of ice found in valleys above the snow line

glazier *n.* one who works with glass

glair, glare

glair *n.* a liquid made from or resembling egg white

glare *v.* to shine brightly; to stare angrily: 'They often glare at each other for some time after arguing'

glance, glands, glans

glance *v.* to look briefly or quickly: 'At breakfast he likes to glance at the newspapers'

glands *n.* (pl.) bodily organs that create and secrete chemical substances

glans *n.* the tip of the penis or the clitoris

glaze, gleys

glaze *n.* a slippery ice surface; a glossy food coating; a chemical coating for ceramics

gleys *n.* (pl.) clay layers under soil

gleam, glean

gleam *n.* a dim or small bright light; a light or other object that shows up briefly: 'The gleam in your eyes'

glean *v.* to pick up grain on a farm; to obtain information a little at a time; to learn: 'Much of the information you can glean from that course is of little value'

glom, gloom, glum

glom *v.* to steal or to take (slang)

gloom *n.* darkness or dejection: 'After losing her job she fell into a deep gloom'

glum *adj.* extremely low spirits: 'News of his death made me glum'

gluten, glutton

gluten *[glue'•tin] n.* proteins found in cereal grains

glutton *n.* a heavy eater; someone who can take heavy blows or take on heavy tasks: 'He's a glutton for punishment'

glutenin, glutinin

glutenin *n.* a protein found in grains

glutinin *n.* an antibody

gnatty, natty

gnatty *adj.* having or infested with gnats

natty *adj.* smooth, tidy, neat

gnaw, knorr, naw, nor

gnaw *v.* to chew on or bite repeatedly; to worry someone: 'That doubt will gnaw at me all night' knorr *n.* a ship with a single sail

naw *interj.* a regional expression for no

nor *conj.* used to make negative a subsequent item in a clause or sentence, usually used with neither: 'He is neither rich nor hard working'

gneiss, nice, niece

gneiss *[nice] n.* a type of rock

nice *adj.* pleasant; appealing; considerate; precise: 'That's a nice distinction between informal usage and slang'

niece *n.* your brother's or sister's daughter

gnu, knew, new

gnu *[rhymes w. new] n.* a large African antelope

knew *v.* past tense of know

new *adj.* not known, done, or made before now; someone who has just joined a group: 'We have a new president'; something just obtained: 'I bought a new car'

gofer, gopher

gofer *n.* someone who fetches coffee or does other minor errands

gopher *n.* a rodentlike animal

golf, gulf

golf *n.* a sport

gulf *n.* a waterway or gap

golly, gully

golly *interj.* an exclamation of surprise or dismay

gully *n.* a cut in land caused by water

gored, gourd

gored *v.* past tense of gore, to be wounded by an animal tusk; figuratively, it refers to one who is hurt

gourd *n.* a plant; a bowl or instrument made from the plant's rind

gorilla, guerrilla

gorilla *n.* the largest and most powerful of the apes; a hoodlum

guerrilla *n.* one who engages in irregular warfare

gosh, gouache *See* gauche

goulash *See* galosh

goy, guy

goy *n.* a person who is not Jewish, a Gentile, often used with a negative connotation

guy *n.* a fellow, a man; a rope or rod used to hold something in position

guy *v.* to tease or make fun of; to hold something in position by use of a rope or rod

grade, grayed

grade *n.* a level; a class or stage: 'What grade are you in?'; a mark indicating degree of accomplishment

grayed *v.* past tense of gray, to make or become gray

graffito, graffiti, graphite

graffito *[gra•fee'•toh] n.* a wall drawing or defacement

graffiti *[gra•fee'•tee] n.* the plural of graffito: 'The subways are finally free of graffiti'

graphite *[graf'•fite] n.* a form of carbon

graft, graphed

graft *n.* a healthy part of a plant, tree, or human tissue that is transplanted to produce a new variety or renew other tissue growth; money given illegally

graphed *v.* past tense of graph, to draw lines showing a relationship among data

graser, grazer

graser *n.* a device having a similar function to a laser, using gamma rays to produce a beam of energy

grazer *n.* one that grazes

grate, great

grate *n.* a fireplace or metal cover

grate *v.* to rasp; to jar; to have an unpleasant effect on one's nerves; to reduce to small pieces; to grind one's teeth

great *n.* one who is exceptional, remarkable, or notable

grater, greater

grater *n.* a device used to abrade foods or reduce them to small particles greater *adj.* the comparative of great

gray, greige, grès

gray *n.* the shade between black and white

greige *[gray or grazh] n.* cotton, silk, or other materials,
before dyeing; a color, gray-beige

grès *[gray] n.* ceramic stoneware

grayed *See* grade

grease, grece, grise

grease *[rhymes w. peace] n.* a lubricant for machinery or cars;
animal fat

grease *v.* to apply grease; to bribe (slang): 'You can't get a
quick visa unless you grease someone's palm'

grece *[rhymes w. peace] n.* a flight of stairs

grise *[rhymes w. peas] n.* a high-priced gray fur

great *See* grate

greige *See* gray

grew, grue

grew *v.* past tense of grow, to increase in size: 'The baby
grew six inches in two months'; to develop: 'He grew to
understand why we did this'; to change state: 'The sun
grew very hot'

grew *n.* a greyhound

grue *v.* to cry out in horror; to shiver violently

grill, grille

grill *n.* a metal device for broiling food; the food cooked in
that manner

grille *n.* a protective covering for a door or window

grim, grime, grimme

grim *adj.* fierce, cruel, repellent; stern or unyielding

grime *n.* dirt

grimme *n.* a small antelope

grip, gripe, grippe

grip *n.* a strong grasp; a good grasp of a subject; strong
control: 'She took a firm grip on the company when she
took over'; a suitcase

gripe *n.* a complaint: 'He always has a gripe about his boss' grippe *n.* the flu

griper, gripper

griper *n.* someone who gripes or complains constantly

gripper *n.* something or someone that holds something firmly

grise *See* grease

grisly, gristly, grizzly

grisly *[griz' • lee] adj.* horrible: 'He committed a series of
grisly murders'

gristly *[griss' • lee] adj.* containing gristle; meat that's very
tough

grizzly *[griz' • lee] n.* a type of bear

grizzly *adj.* gray haired

groan, groin, grown

groan *v.* to utter a deep moan; to let out a sound of
disappointment, sorrow, or pain

groin *n.* the juncture of the abdomen and the thighs; a
seawall

grown *v.* past participle of grow, to get bigger; older; more
mature: 'He has grown a lot in the past year in size and
wisdom'

grocer, grosser

grocer *n.* a storekeeper who sells food

grosser *n.* something that earns an amount of money (slang):
'*Gone With the Wind* is the all-time big grosser of motion
pictures'

grosser *adj.* comparative of gross, unrefined; fat; disgusting
(slang): 'I can't stand him; he is grosser than any of your
friends'

groove, grove

groove *n.* a cut in a surface, record, or disc; a rut; a great
experience

grove *n.* a group of trees

grope, group

grope *v.* to feel your way physically or mentally in the dark, either for an object or an answer; to fondle sexually (slang)

group *n.* a number of people who are together for a common purpose; a musical combo; a collection of things with similar characteristics; an army unit with two battalions

gross, grouse

gross *n.* 12 dozen; total income or sales

gross *adj.* the total before deductions or discounts: 'gross sales'; vulgar; fat; disgusting (slang)

grouse *v.* to complain or gripe: 'Soldiers always grouse about army food'

grouse *n.* a pheasant or pheasants

grosser *See* grocer

grown *See* groan

grue *See* grew

guerrilla *See* gorilla

guessed, guest

guessed *v.* past tense of guess, to give an approximate answer; to suppose or believe: 'I guessed that you would arrive late'

guest *n.* someone you invite to your house; a restaurant or hotel patron; a person appearing on a show for a single performance

Guiana, Guinea, guinea, Guyana

Guiana *n.* a region on the northern coast of South America

Guinea *n.* a nation in West Africa

guinea *n.* an English coin no longer in use; an amount used for certain fees and accounts

Guyana *n.* a South American country

guide, guyed

guide *n.* a person or thing that points you or leads you to a desired place: 'The guide on my tour was well trained'; a mask or symbol that draws your attention; a book with advice or instructions; the leader in a military formation guyed *v.* past tense of guy, to fasten with a rope or cable

guild *See* gild

guilt *See* gilt

guise, guys

guise *n.* a style of dress; an assumed appearance: 'That conservative will take on a liberal guise to be elected'

guys *n.* (pl.) more than one boy, man, or person: 'See what the guys in the back room want'

gulf *See* golf

gully *See* golly

gurgle *See* gargle

guy *See* goy

guyed *See* guide

H

hail, hale

hail *n.* frozen rain; a shower of any objects: 'A hail of rose petals greeted the newlyweds'

hail *v.* to call or summon: 'hail a taxi'; to come from or live in a certain place: 'We hail from Michigan'; to pour down hail; to shower down like hail

hail *interj.* a salute: 'Hail and farewell!'

hale *v.* to force to go: 'They'll hale him into court for nonpayment of child support'

hale *adj.* healthy, robust: 'hale and hearty'

hair, hare

hair *n.* a fine threadlike outgrowth from the body

hare *n.* a large rabbit

hare *v.* to run swiftly: 'Every time they see me they hare off'

haircut, haricot

haircut *n.* the shaping or cutting of a head of hair, usually done in a barber shop or beauty salon

haricot *n.* a thin stringbean; a lamb stew

hairless *See* airless

hairy, harry

hairy *adj.* with lots of hair; frightening: 'That's a hairy movie'

harry *v.* to harass, bother or pressure: 'He's going to harry me to get the work done on time'

half, halve, halves, have

half *n.* one of two equal parts: 'Half a loaf is better than none' halve *v.* to divide into two equal parts; to reduce by one half

halves *n.* (pl.) more than one half: 'two halves equal one whole'

have *v.* to possess, hold, contain, carry on; to sustain; to receive; to be obligated to: 'I have to go home by eight o'clock'; auxiliary used with another verb: 'I have seen that movie two times'

hall, haul

hall *n.* a large room used for functions: 'The orchestra sounds best in a smaller concert hall'; a corridor; a great estate house: 'They held receptions for 150 people in their country hall'

haul *n.* what you carry; what one has acquired: 'The thieves made off with a good haul'

haul *v.* to drag, or to pull

hallow, halo, hollow

hallow *[hal'•oh] v.* to make holy: 'We hallow these grounds'

halo *[hay'•lo] n.* a circle of light around a religious figure or the moon

hollow *n.* a hole inside an object: 'a tree hollow'; a valley or other low ground

hollow *v.* to remove matter from inside something: 'Let's hollow out the pumpkin'

hollow *adj.* nothing inside, just space: 'a hollow tube'; ideas of little value: 'Their views of her art are hollow'; slightly insincere: 'a hollow laugh'

handmade, handmaid

handmade *adj.* made by hand, not by machine

handmaid *n.* a female servant; a strong helper

handsome, hansom

handsome *adj.* good looking or attractive: 'She's a handsome woman'; 'That's a handsome building'

hansom *n.* a horse-drawn carriage

handyman, handy man

handyman *n.* a person who does odd jobs

handy man *n.* a man who can handle tools well

hang, hank

hang *v.* to support from above with a rope or other devices; to execute (kill) by suspending from a rope; to lower or let drop: 'Hang your head in shame'; for a jury, to deadlock a jury by one's vote; to depend: 'We all hang on your success'

hang *n.* the right way: 'I can't get the hang of using this machine'

hank *n.* a small piece of thread or hair

hangar, hanger

hangar *n.* a shelter for airplanes

hanger *n.* a curved frame that holds clothes; someone who hangs things

hangover, hang over

hangover, *n.* an ill feeling resulting from heavy consumption of alcohol

hang over *v.* to lean over: 'You may hang over a railing to throw up if you have a hangover'

hang-up, hang up

hang-up *n.* a problem, constraint, or inhibition: 'He has a hang-up about blind dates'

hang up *v.* to put one's clothes or other items on a hanger; to put a telephone receiver back in the holder; sometimes, to end a telephone conversation abruptly

hansom *See* handsome

hard, hart, heart

hard *adj.* tough, strong, difficult: 'That's a hard job'; strict; stubborn; definite: 'That's a hard commitment'; erect; durable

hard *adv.* with great force or effort: 'We worked hard on this project'; with unhappiness: 'He took the loss hard'; with much damage: 'This area was hit hard by crime'

hart *n.* a grown male deer

heart *n.* the bodily organ, central to life, that pumps blood; any person, object, or idea of greatest importance: 'That proposal gets to the heart of the problem'; the center of emotions: 'His heart ached when she left'; a personality or disposition: 'He has a soft heart for a sob story'; a suit in a deck of cards

hard-shell, hard shell

hard-shell *adj.* rigid, dogmatic, particularly in religious beliefs

hard shell *n.* an oyster with a hard shell

hare *See* hair

haricot *See* haircut

harry *See* hairy

haul *See* hall

haunch, hunch

haunch *n.* a part of the buttock, the hindquarter

hunch *n.* an intuitive sense or feeling: 'I had a hunch you would say that'

hunch *v.* to assume a bent, peculiar, or deformed posture

hauteur *See* auteur

have *See* half

haven, heaven

haven *n.* a safe place: 'This new project will be a haven for the homeless'; a port

heaven *n.* that other world where people are eternally happy; any place that provides pleasure: 'My new home is just heaven'; the sky

haws, hawse

haws *v.* 3d person, sing., present tense of haw, to speak in a round-about way: 'He hems and haws about this suggestion'

haws *n.* (pl.) animal membranes; hawthorn trees; shrubs or their fruits

haws *interj.* (pl.) commands to animals to turn left

hawse *n.* part of a ship's bow

See also hoars

hay, hey

hay *n.* grass used as feed; a small amount of money, chicken feed (slang)

hey *interj.* said to attract someone's attention or to express happiness or annoyance

hays, haze

hays *n.* (pl.) grasses used as feed

haze *n.* unclear air caused by fog, mist, or smog; mental dullness or fog: 'He's always in a haze due to drugs'

haze *v.* to harass or subject to repeated ridicule, as in fraternities or in the army; to become foggy or misty

head, he'd, heed

head *n.* the top of the body containing the brain, face, etc.: 'You wish that your heart would heed what your head is telling you'; the mind: 'She has a good head on her shoulders'; the main part or role: 'She's the head of this organization'; small bubbles in beer: 'the head on a glass of beer'; a distance equal to the size of a head: 'The horse won by a head'

he'd *contr.* he had or he would: 'He'd better heed my advice, or he'll go broke'

heed *[rhymes w. need]* *v.* to agree; to pay attention: 'Heed my words: he'll never amount to anything'

heal, heel, he'll, hell

heal *v.* to make one sound or healthy again: 'The cut will heal in a little while'; to cure: 'Doctors heal illness'; 'Time heals all wounds'

heel *n.* the back of the foot; a despicable person: 'That heel will never apologize'

heel *v.* to follow at the heels of someone: 'She is teaching the puppy to heel'

he'll *contr.* he will or he shall

hell *n.* the nether world, the opposite of heaven

hear, here
> hear *v.* to receive or recognize sounds with one's ears; to listen to: 'You can hear this music every night at 7:00', to get news about something: 'I hear that Jim was ill'; to try a case in court: 'Judge Jones will hear this case'
> here *adv.* at this place or point; hither; at this time
> here *interj.* present, as when answering a roll call

heard, herd
> heard *v.* past tense of hear
> herd *n.* a group of animals or a group of people; the common people (used contemptuously)
> herd *v.* to look after livestock; to form a herd; to go with a herd

heart *See* hard

hearth, heath
> hearth *[harth] n.* the floor of a fireplace; one's home: 'He was reluctant to leave his hearth and go off to war'
> heath *n.* a shrub; an open land area with poor soil

heaven *See* haven

he'd, heed *See* head

heinous *See* anus

heir *See* air

heirless *See* airless

he'll, heel *See* heal

hence, whence
> hence *adv.* away: 'Get thee hence'; future time: 'The budget should balance three years hence'; therefore or thus: 'Hence, he will speak at 5 P.M.'
> whence *adv.* from where: 'Whence did she come?'

herd *See* heard

here *See* hear

heritage, hermitage
> heritage *n.* property that you inherit; a nation's, society's, or family's traditions: 'Our heritage is freedom, embodied in the Bill of Rights'; what you possess by reason of birth
> hermitage *n.* a monastery where hermits live

heroin, heroine
>   heroin *n.* a drug
>   heroine *n.* a woman who is a hero; the female central
>   character in a story

hertz, hurts
>   hertz *n.* an electrical unit
>   hurts *v.* present tense of hurt, to suffer or inflict pain or
>   harm: 'My arm hurts'; 'He hurts her feelings when he
>   doesn't listen to her'

hew *See* ewe

hewer *See* ewer

hey *See* hay

hi, hie, high
>   hi *interj.* hello
>   hie *v.* to hasten, to go quickly: 'Hie yourself down to this
>   fabulous sale'
>   high *n.* a new level; a state of euphoria produced by being on
>   drugs; the top gear of a motor
>   high *adj.* a large amount: 'This food is high in cholesterol';
>   very good: 'That furniture is of high quality'; favorable or
>   well thought of: 'We have a very high opinion of her'; far
>   above the earth: 'The kite flew high'
>   high *adv.* in a high manner; extravagantly; 'She lives high'

hide, hied
>   hide *n.* animal skin or one's own skin (metaphorical),
>   particularly if you're trying to save it; a place of
>   concealment to view animals, birds, etc.
>   hide *v.* to conceal: 'I'll hide the presents until tomorrow';
>   'She'll always hide her feelings'
>   hied *v.* past tense of hie; to hasten

higher, hire
>   higher *adj.* comparative of high, above something or someone
>   else; greater in amount or quality, or more advanced:
>   'Rome's civilization was higher than that of the Franks'
>   hire *v.* to employ someone; to take a job; to rent: 'hire a
>   limousine'

high grade, high-grade

high grade *n.* a special animal breed; a high mark or score: 'He gets a high grade for his performance'

high-grade *adj.* top quality: 'These are high-grade components'; mineral or metal ores that yield a large amount of the metal sought

him, hymn

him *n.* objective form of he: 'I saw him yesterday'

hymn *n.* a religious song of praise

Hindi, Hindu

Hindi *n.* the official language of India

Hindu *n.* a follower of the principal religion of India

hippie/hippy, hippy

hippie *or* hippy *n.* an antiestablishment youth modeled on behavior characteristic of the 1960s, who dresses unconventionally, wears long hair, stresses free expression, and often uses drugs

hippy *adj.* large-hipped

historical, hysterical

historical *adj.* refers to history; from the past: 'This novel used actual historical figures'

hysterical *adj.* extremely emotional: 'They were hysterical after the fire'; very funny

ho, hoe

ho *interj.* an exclamation for good or bad events; also, Santa's laugh: 'Ho-ho-ho!'

hoe *n.* a flat-bladed tool: 'Use a hoe to weed your garden'

See also whoa

hoar, whore, who're

hoar *adj.* white, especially with frost or age

whore *n.* a prostitute

who're *contr.* who are

See also haws; hoars

hoard, horde, whored

hoard *n.* a well-protected stock of money or other valuables

hoard *v.* to accumulate and to store valuables, usually in a
secret place

horde *n.* a large crowd: 'The horde of customers jammed the
entrance, causing a near riot'; a tribe of nomads: 'The
Golden Horde was led by Genghis Khan'; a swarm: 'A
horde of wasps'

horde *v.* to gather in a horde

whored *v.* past tense of whore, to prostitute oneself

hoars, hoarse, horse, whores

hoars *n.* (pl.) frosts

hoarse *adj.* having a frog in your throat, unable to speak: 'He
was hoarse from yelling at the concert'

horse *n.* a four-legged animal you ride on; a piece of
gymnastic equipment that is vaulted over; slang for
heroin; a crib, an aid to students cheating on tests (slang)

whores *n.* (pl.) prostitutes

See also haws

hobby, hubby

hobby *n.* a spare-time recreation: 'Her hobby is chess, mine is
music'; a small falcon

hubby *n.* a husband: 'Her hubby's hobby is baseball'

hockey, hockey/hocky, hokey, hooka/houkah, hookey/hooky

hockey *n.* a team sport played on ice with sticks and a puck

hockey *or* hocky *n.* excrement; pretentious nonsense (slang)

hokey *adj.* corny; old-fashioned; false, phony (slang)

hooka *or* houkah *n.* a Middle Eastern water pipe with a long
tube or tubes

hookey *or* hooky *n.* a truant: 'They played hookey for 40 days
last term'

hold, holed

hold *v.* to keep something firmly in your grasp, in your hands
or arms; to contain: 'This bottle should hold one quart';
to occupy a position: 'He'll hold the president's job'; to
conduct: 'to hold a meeting or a party'; to make someone
accountable: 'I hold you responsible for the success of

this campaign'; to maintain a position: 'You hold the lead in this race'

holed *v.* past tense of hole, to put holes in an object

holdup, hold up

holdup *n.* a robbery: 'a holdup in the bank'; a delay: 'What's the holdup?'

hold up *v.* to rob; to keep something raised: 'He'll hold up his hands'

hole, whole

hole *n.* an opening; a gap: 'The fullback ran through the hole in their line'; a weakness: 'There's such a large hole in that argument that a six-year-old can win it'; an unpleasant place: 'Why do they stay in that hole?'; a difficult situation

hole *v.* to hide (slang): 'hole up'

whole *n.* the entire thing: 'The whole of America rejoiced at the peace'

whole *adj.* complete: 'That's the whole story'; the full amount, the entire structure; healthy: 'A whole person after the surgery'

holey, holly, holy, wholly

holey *adj.* containing holes

holly *[rhymes w. polly] n.* a shrub with bright red berries: 'Deck the halls with boughs of holly'

holy *adj.* religious, pertaining to God

wholly *[holy] adv.* altogether, completely: 'This meal was wholly satisfying'

holiday, holy day

holiday *n.* a nonworking day to vacation or to celebrate an event

holy day *n.* a major religious commemoration which might or might not be a day off work

hollow *See* hallow

hombre, ombre, ombré

hombre *[om'•bray] n.* a man, a term popularized in cowboy movies ombre [*om'•ber*] *n.* a card game

ombré [*om•bray'*] *adj.* a fabric with colors shading into one
another

home, hone

home *n.* where you live, where the hearth is; a group
residence for older, ill, disabled, or disturbed people: 'a
senior citizens' home'; in sports, a team's local,
permanent base: 'They play half of their games at home';
a place to keep something: 'I can't find a home for these
plants'; the base or end point in some sports: 'reach
home' (in baseball)

home *v.* to send or to put into a home; to pinpoint: 'The
missile is set to home in on its target with great accuracy'

hone *v.* to sharpen: 'hone one's skills'

homogeneous, homogenous, homogonous

homogeneous [*hoh•moh•jean'•ee•us*] *adj.* all members of a
group being roughly of the same type or at the same
level: 'They place students in homogeneous groups'

homogenous [*huh•ma'•jin•us*] *adj.* having similar biological
structures due to the same origin

homogonous [*hoh•ma'•gi•nis*] *adj.* pertaining to biological
similarities among different types of flowers

hone *See* home

honk, hunk

honk *n.* a short loud sound made by a horn or by a goose

hunk *n.* an attractive, well-built man or woman (slang); a
piece of something: 'I'll have another hunk of pie'

hooka/houkah, hookey/hooky *See* hockey

hoop, whoop

hoop *n.* a large ring used in recreation or sports: 'That
basketball player puts the ball through the hoop with
ease'; a band that holds a barrel together; a large circular
earring; a flexible series of circles used to expand a skirt

whoop [*hwoop'*] *n.* an exultant exclamation: 'You give a
whoop for joy when your team hits the hoop'

horde *See* hoard

horse *See* hoars

hostel, hostile

> hostel *n.* an inexpensive lodging usually used by traveling youth groups
>
> hostile *adj.* extremely unfriendly: 'I don't know why she's so hostile toward me'; strong opposition or disagreement: 'The party was hostile to the candidate's views'

hotdog, hot dog

> hotdog *v.* to show off: 'When he makes a touchdown, he loves to hotdog it'
>
> hot dog *n.* a frankfurter

hour, our

> hour *n.* sixty minutes; the time at which something happens: 'The clock strikes on the hour'; an important time: 'our hour of need'
>
> our *pron.* belonging to us: 'our country'

however, how ever

> however *adv.* in whatever manner; to whatever degree: 'I couldn't raise the money, however hard I tried'
>
> however *conj.* nevertheless: 'I notice, however, that the money was refunded'
>
> how ever *adv.* 'How ever did he get promoted to CEO?'

hubby *See* hobby

hue *See* ewe

human, humane

> human *n.* a human being, a person
>
> human *adj.* refers to the qualities or behavior of people: 'Human life is precious'; 'To err is human; to forgive, divine'; a nice person: 'She's very human'
>
> humane *adj.* kind, compassionate, or considerate of human or animal needs

humbles, umbles

> humbles *v.* 3d person, sing., present tense of humble; to abase, to bring low, to degrade: 'She humbles herself at his feet'

umbles *n.* (pl.) entrails (liver, heart, etc.), especially of a deer

humerus, humorous

humerus *n.* the bone of the upper arm

humorous *adj.* funny, amusing

hunch *See* haunch

hunk *See* honk

hunter, junta

hunter *n.* one who hunts

junta *[hoon'•ta] n.* a small group ruling a country, usually after a coup d'état

hurdle, hurtle

hurdle *n.* a low stand that runners jump over in a race; any obstacle: 'She had one more hurdle to overcome to reach that office'

hurtle *v.* to move quickly; to drive or move recklessly: 'He loves to hurtle along the country road at 90 miles an hour in his fancy car'

hurts *See* hertz

hymn *See* him

hyperbola, hyperbole

hyperbola *[high•pur'•boh•la] n.* a curve in mathematics

hyperbole *[high•pur'•bi•lee] n.* an exaggeration: 'It's hyperbole to say that you'd go to any length to stop him'

hypercritical, hypocritical

hypercritical *[high•per•cri'•ti•kul] adj.* overly critical or fault-finding: 'They are hypercritical of everything the new person does'

hypocritical *[hip•oh•krit'•i•kul] adj.* insincere, phony: 'It would be hypocritical of me to thank him after such rude behavior'

hysterical *See* historical

I

I *See* aye/ay

I'd, id, ide/id *See* eyed

idle, idol, idyll/idyl

    idle *adj.* shiftless, lazy; unemployed; not worth doing, useless: 'It's idle to study this when it won't be of use'; not in use: 'The machines were idle due to a lack of parts'; in sports, not due to play: 'The Browns were idle this week'

    idle *v.* to let a car's motor run without moving the car; to cause to be unemployed: 'The recession will idle millions of workers'

    idol *n.* an image of a god; someone you hero-worship; a false god

    idyll *or* idyl *n.* a poem about a carefree, romantic episode; a delightful, peaceful experience, often in the countryside

ileum, ilium

    ileum *n.* a part of the small intestine

    ilium *n.* a large pelvic bone

I'll *See* aisle

illapse *See* elapse

illation *See* elation

illegible, ineligible

    illegible *adj.* unclear writing: 'You can't read a doctor's illegible handwriting'

    ineligible *adj.* not qualified or entitled: 'You're ineligible for the job because you lack experience'

illicit *See* elicit

illiterate *See* alliterate

illusion *See* allusion

illusory *See* elusory

illuvium *See* alluvion

imbrue, imbue

    imbrue *v.* to stain or drench in liquid

    imbue *v.* to color something completely; to absorb or fill with feeling or ideas: 'He imbued the scientific papers with unusual feeling'

immanent *See* eminent

immerge *See* emerge

immersed *See* emersed

immigrant *See* emigrant

immigrate *See* emigrate

imminent *See* eminent

immunity, impunity

    immunity *n.* the state of being protected, untouchable: 'The shot gave him immunity from measles'; the state of being exempt: 'He has diplomatic immunity and doesn't have to pay taxes'

    impunity *n.* the state of exemption from deserved punishment: 'He violates the housing laws with impunity'

immure, inure

    immure *v.* to bury something in a wall; to imprison someone: 'They can immure you for years for using a gun to commit a crime'

    inure *v.* to get used to something, often unpleasant: 'I have to inure myself to his erratic behavior'; to become beneficial: 'The new law will inure to the inner city'

impartable, impartible

    impartable *adj.* capable of being transmitted: 'His views were readily impartable'; able to be shared

    impartible *adj.* not divisible

impassable, impassible, impossible

impassable *adj.* blocked; incapable of being passed; in bad shape: 'That road is impassable since the storm'

impassible *adj.* incapable of feeling pain or emotion

impossible *adj.* incapable of being done or of existing: 'It's impossible to finish that in one day'; hard to handle: 'that child is impossible'

impatience, impatiens

impatience *n.* lack of patience; annoyance because of delay

impatiens *n.* a flowering plant

important, impotent

important *adj.* vital, valuable, essential: 'The important point to remember is to double-check all results'; having influence or power: 'The important people are all here'

impotent *adj.* powerless, ineffective: 'They were impotent to stop the use of crack'; incapable of performing sexual intercourse

impostor, imposture

impostor *n.* one who takes on someone else's identity fraudulently: 'The imposter's imposture went undetected for five years'

imposture *n.* the act of assuming a false identity

impracticable, impractical

impracticable *adj.* incapable of being accomplished at all or with the methods being used

impractical *adj.* unrealistic: 'The proposal to double taxes is impractical'; incapable of handling sensibly or prudently: 'He's too impractical to organize this office'

impressed, imprest

impressed *v.* past tense of impress, to try to win admiration: 'I tried hard but never impressed my boss'; to mark something with force; to emphasize the importance of an act or idea: 'I impressed on them the need for action'; to force someone to do something: 'They were impressed into military service' imprest *n.* a loan

impunity *See* immunity

imputation *See* amputation

in, inn

in *n.* power or favor: 'I have an in with the top brass'

in *adj.* arriving: 'The train's not in yet'; fashionable: 'the in restaurant or club'

in *adv.* toward the inside, placing something into, refers to a place, location, or condition: 'Please come in'; 'We're staying in'

in *prep.* during, at that time: 'The Declaration of Independence was signed in 1776'; refers to a certain state or condition: 'He's in a bad mood'; 'I'm in love'; refers to a general area: 'I like to play in the yard'; where you live or work: 'I teach in a high school'; 'I live in the city'

inn *n.* a place to eat, sleep, or both, less formal and usually smaller than a hotel

inane, insane

inane *adj.* silly: 'His suggestions about the homeless were inane'; 'an inane comic farce'

insane *adj.* mad, abnormal: 'Insane people were let out of institutions with no provisions for aftercare'

inapt/unapt, inept

inapt *or* unapt *adj.* inappropriate; not apt; not suitable

inept *adj.* foolish; incompetent

incest, insect

incest *n.* sexual relations between close relatives who can't be legally married, e.g., a father and a daughter, a mother and a son

insect *n.* a bug, a very tiny animal

incidence, incidents

incidence *n.* the rate at which something occurs: 'The incidence of serious crime is rising' incidents *n.* (pl.) events or happenings; dangerous occurrences: 'The series of armed incidents could lead to war'

incipient, insipient

incipient *adj.* emerging, developing: 'Preventive measures are needed to tackle the incipient spread of typhoid'

insipient *adj.* foolish

incite, insight, in sight

incite *v.* to stir up: 'That speech will incite people to take strong action'

insight *n.* the ability to see the inner nature of people or situations: 'Reading has helped me acquire greater insight into alcoholics' behavior'

in sight *n.* in view. 'The guard kept the prisoner in sight at all times'

incompetence, incompetents

incompetence *n.* inability to perform capably or adequately

incompetents *n.* (pl.) people who can't perform capably or adequately

inculcate, inculpate, inoculate

inculcate *v.* to teach via repetition

inculpate *v.* to incriminate, blame

inoculate *v.* to introduce an organism into a situation suitable for growth; to inject substances that produce immunity to disease: 'You should inoculate your child against measles, whooping cough, and mumps'; to imbue people with ideas

indelible, inedible

indelible *adj.* unable to be removed or washed away: a mark, impression, or stain

inedible *adj.* unable to be eaten: 'That inedible meal will leave an indelible impression on us'

indict, indite

indict *v.* to charge someone with a crime through legal proceedings

indite *v.* to write: 'You have to indite something to get an
 indictment'

indiscreet, indiscrete

indiscreet *adj.* careless or unwise: 'They were indiscreet
 about their office affair'

indiscrete *adj.* not separated or divided into parts: 'They sent
 us an indiscrete mass of papers that took hours to sort
 out'

inedible *See* indelible

ineligible *See* illegible

inept *See* inapt/unapt

inequity, iniquity

inequity *n.* unfairness or an injustice: 'The new tax rate was
 an inequity for the middle-class taxpayer'

iniquity *n.* evil, or an act of wickedness: 'The son is punished
 for the iniquity of the father'

infection, inflection

infection *n.* a disease, often communicable; ideas or
 behaviors that can influence others, viewed negatively

inflection *n.* a change in tone or volume of voice: 'His
 inflection told us he was upset'; the act of bending as in
 a mathematical curve; a change in word form to show
 gender, number, or other distinctions

infest, invest

infest *v.* to invade or damage: 'Every summer ants infest the
 neighborhood'

invest *v.* to put money or time into something for a future
 return: 'I'd prefer to invest my money in bonds'; to
 furnish with authority or honor: 'We invest our
 legislators with the power to pass laws'; to besiege in
 warfare

in-flight, in flight

in-flight *adj.* during an airplane flight: 'You watch an in-flight
 movie on long plane trips'

in flight *adj.* running away: 'The losing troops were in flight'

influx, in flux

> influx *n*. an inflow: 'There has been a massive influx of
> foreign investment into the United States'
> in flux *n*. a state of change or uncertainty: 'After the war
> everything was in flux'

ingenious, ingenuous

> ingenious *[in•jeen'•yus] adj*. intelligent, clever, resourceful,
> original: 'That idea for saving gas is ingenious'
> ingenuous *[in•jen'•yoo•us] adj*. innocent, simple, trusting:
> 'He was so ingenuous that he believed everything his
> friend told him'

inmate, innate

> inmate *n*. one who inhabits a prison or hospital
> innate *adj*. a quality that exists at birth, or an inherent trait:
> 'Many still believe that intelligence is innate'

inn *See* in

innervate *See* enervate

inoculate *See* inculcate

insane *See* inane

insect *See* incest

insert, inset

> insert *v*. to put something inside something else: 'Insert the
> letters in these envelopes'
> inset *n*. a small object, usually a drawing or piece of cloth,
> placed within a larger one

insidious, invidious

> insidious *adj*. stealthy; dangerous but enticing; treacherous,
> deceitful: 'They spread insidious rumors about his
> alleged affairs'
> invidious *adj*. envious; negative: 'Their invidious comparison
> of Jack to his brother hurt Jack all his life'

insight, in sight *See* incite

insipient *See* incipient

insolate, insolent, insulate, isolate

> insolate *v*. to expose to the sun: 'They insolate those fruits for
> several days to help them ripen'

insolent *adj.* rude, insultingly contemptuous: 'He was
punished for his insolent behavior'

insulate *v.* to protect a person, group or object; to keep
separate; to prevent a transfer of heat or of ideas: 'They
tried to insulate their people from the people and views
of other nations'

isolate *v.* to set apart people, words, or objects: 'His arrogance
will isolate him from his peers'

install, instill

install *v.* to put in place or set up; to hold a ceremony
marking a person's appointment to office: 'They will
install the college president tomorrow'

instill *v.* to educate or influence gradually: 'They try to instill a
respect for reading in their children'

instance, instants

instance *n.* an example: 'That was an instance of his failure'; a
step or stage of a process or series

instance *adv.* refers to an example: 'for instance'

instants *n.* (pl.) short time intervals: 'There were only a few
instants in which to shoot the photo'

insure *See* ensure

intense, intents

intense *adj.* strong, to a great degree: 'She had intense
feelings about women's rights'; highly concentrated: 'The
summer course was intense'

intents *n.* (pl.) purposes or aims

intension, intention

intension *n.* a great degree; strong mental exertion

intention *n.* resolve, purpose, or aim: 'Her intention was to
win the tennis championship'

intercession, intersection, intersession

intercession *n.* an effort to resolve a conflict between two
parties by intervention; an effort to help the weaker party
in a conflict: 'His intercession for the poor was well
known'

intersection *n.* a meeting of two or more streets or other objects: 'His house is at the intersection of Main and Bridge streets'

intersession *n* 'he time between two school terms

interment, internment

interment *n.* burial: 'The interment took place on Sunday at Woodlawn Cemetery'

internment *n.* a form of imprisonment: 'The internment of the prisoners violated the rules of war'

intern/interne, in turn

intern *or* interne *[in'•turn] n.* an advanced student gaining practical experience in a professional field, such as a medical student working in a hospital

intern *[in•turn'] v.* to imprison, especially in a war

in turn *adv.* in order or sequence: 'You will be served in turn'

interpellate, interpolate

interpellate *[int•ur•pul'•ate] v.* to formally question an official concerning an official action or policy

interpolate *[in•ter'•pu•late] v.* to insert new material into a text or discussion; to estimate or understand missing material through surrounding known material

interstate, intestate, intrastate

interstate *adj.* between states: 'Interstate highways are badly in need of repairs'

intestate *adj.* having died without leaving a will

intrastate *adj.* within a particular state: 'Congress does not regulate intrastate commerce'

into it, intuit

into it *prep.* slang for a strong involvement or attachment, for example, to a kind of music; 'She's into rock and roll'

intuit *v.* to grasp through feeling or insight: 'She can always intuit the real feelings behind his words'

inure *See* immure

invade, inveighed

> invade *v.* to enter a nation or body with injurious intent or effect: 'They plan to invade enemy territory in June'; to enter in force, not with force, encroach, permeate: 'Teenagers invade shopping malls'
>
> inveighed *v.* past tense of inveigh, to complain bitterly: 'He inveighed against the evils of society, but did nothing about them'

invest *See* infest

invidious *See* insidious

ion, iron

> ion *n.* an electrically charged atom
>
> iron *n.* a heavy metal; a device used to smooth or press clothing; a golf club; a device used to shackle a person

irascible *See* erasable

irredeemable, irremeable, irremediable

> irredeemable *adj.* hopeless; incapable of getting something back: 'Those coupons are irredeemable after June 30th'
>
> irremeable *adj.* unable to return to a former place or state
>
> irremediable *adj.* can't be corrected or cured: 'They did irremediable damage to their cause with that unsupported charge'

irregardless *See* regardless

irrelevant, irreverent

> irrelevant *adj.* not applicable: 'Your remarks about taxes are irrelevant to our discussion of ecology'; having little value: 'What they taught me was irrelevant'
>
> irreverent *adj.* disrespectful: 'The students made irreverent remarks about their teachers'

irruption *See* eruption

isle *See* aisle

islet *See* eyelet

isolate *See* insolate

its, it's

    its *adj.* possessive belonging to: 'The nation shook off its malaise'; 'The animal cleaned its fur'; 'The flower opened its petals'

    it's *contr.* it is: 'It's late, let us leave'; 'It's not over till the fat lady sings'; 'It's time for its (the dog's) meal'

    [Confusion arises because possessive nouns normally take an apostrophe: 'the man's size,' 'the coat's look,' but 'its look' refers to the look of the coat.]

J

jalousie, jealousy

jalousie *[jal'•i•see] n.* a slanted window shutter or a set of blinds

jealousy *[jell'•i•see] n.* the state of resentment or envy of one who is a rival: 'His jealousy of his brother's achievements led him to drink'

jam, jamb

jam *n.* a sweet preserve; a mass of people or things causing a blockage: 'a traffic jam'; in trouble (slang): 'in a jam'

jam *v.* to block or obstruct; to wedge something in a tight position; to interfere: 'jam a radio signal'; to cause to lock: 'jam the keyboard'; to overcrowd: 'Too many people tried to jam into the small room'; to improvise in music, especially jazz

jamb *n.* a post that forms the side of a door or window

jean *See* gene

jell *See* gel

jellied *See* gelid

jerkin *See* gherkin

jest *See* gest

jester *See* gesture

jewel, joule, jowl

jewel *[joo'•il] n.* a precious stone; a valued person or object: 'That new worker is a jewel'

joule *[jool] n.* a measure of energy in physics

jowl *[jowl (*jow *rhymes w.* cow*)] n.* the jaw; a cheek; loose
skin on the throat

jewelry, Jewry, jury

jewelry *n.* precious stones and metals worn for adornment

Jewry *n.* the Jewish people or culture

jury *n.* a body of citizens that decides a legal case: 'The jury
debated its verdict for ten days'; a committee judging a
contest

jib *See* gib

jibe *See* gibe

jinks, jinx

jinks *v.* 3d person, sing., present tense of jink, to make quick
erratic moves; to avoid being a target

jinx *n.* bad luck; something that brings bad luck: 'He wears
the same hat every day to ward off a jinx'

joule *See* jewel

joust, just

joust *n.* medieval combat on horses between knights using
lances; any conflict or competition

just *adj.* fair or impartial: 'a just decision'; moral: 'a just cause';
legitimate: 'a just case'

just *adv.* very recently; exactly; only: 'We just arrived and our
vacation seems almost over'

jowl *See* jewel

juggler, jugular

juggler *n.* one who entertains by keeping several objects in
the air at once; one who can handle many duties at a
time; someone engaged in deception or manipulation:
'The new accountant is a good juggler of the books'

jugular *n.* a major vein going to the brain; the most vital and
vulnerable part; engaging in a vicious attack: 'goes for the
jugular'

juice, jus

juice *n.* a liquid from a vegetable, fruit, or plant; electricity;
the interest paid on a usurious loan; liquor; a narcotic
(slang)

jus *[rhymes w.* use*] n.* the whole body of law

junta *See* hunter

jury *See* jewelry

just *See* joust

K

kabala/kabbala *See* cabal

Kaddish, kiddish, Kiddush

Kaddish *[cod'•ish] n.* a Hebrew prayer said by mourners after the death of a close relative

kiddish *adj.* like a child

Kiddush *n.* a blessing said over bread or wine on the eve of a Jewish sabbath or holiday

kain *See* cane

kaki *See* cocky

karat *See* carat

karma *See* coma

karting *See* carting

kayak, kyack

kayak *[kie'•ack] n.* an Eskimo canoe

kyack *[kie'•ack] n.* a pack sack on either side of a saddle

keratin *See* carotene

kernel, colonel

kernel *n.* a part of an ear of corn; the edible part of a nut; the core of something

colonel *n.* the military rank between lieutenant colonel and brigadier general

ketch *See* catch

ketchup/catchup/catsup, catch up

ketchup or catchup or catsup *n.* a tomato-based sauce

catch up *v.* to work on projects that are late: 'I have to catch up on these overdue reports'; to draw level and sometimes overtake: 'I will catch up to him in this game'

key, quay

key *[rhymes w. see]* *n.* a device to open a door; a fact or idea that helps solve a problem, a clue: 'Affordable housing is the key to solving homelessness'; the tone of a musical scale or voice pitch: 'She sang in the key of F'; 'She spoke in a low key'; a button or lever on a musical instrument or typewriter; the tone of a campaign: 'The ad campaign was carried out in a low key'

key *v.* to form a target: 'The ad campaign will key in on 25 to 40 year olds'; to place symbols on a text to denote or highlight changes; to enter information into a computer via a keyboard

key *adj.* referring to the main or most important aspect: 'This is the key answer to this question'

quay *[kee* or *kway]* *n.* part of a boat dock

khaki *See* cocky

khat *See* cat

kibbutz, kibitz

kibbutz *[ki•boots']* *n.* a collective settlement in Israel

kibitz *[kib'•bets]* *v.* to watch and offer often unwanted comments

kiddie/kiddy, kitty

kiddie *or* kiddy *n.* a child

kitty *n.* a kitten; the pool or pot of money in a card game (slang)

kiddish, Kiddush *See* Kaddish

kill, kiln

kill *v.* to murder; to exert major effort to accomplish something: 'She will kill herself to finish that project'; to pass time doing little: 'we have some time to kill before the movie begins'; to extinguish: 'Kill the lights'; to exhaust: 'That 12-hour shift killed me'; to finish off (slang): 'Let's kill the bottle of wine'

kiln *[kill]* *n.* an oven or furnace for hardening pottery

Klan *See* clan

klatch/klatsch *See* clatch

klister *See* clyster

klomp *See* clomp

knag, nag

> knag *n.* a wood knot; a wart
>
> nag *n.* someone who is constantly complaining; an old horse

knap, nap, nape, nappe

> knap *n.* to strike or rap sharply
>
> nap *n.* a short sleep; the surface or woolly part of a rug
>
> nape *n.* the back part of the neck
>
> nappe *[nap] n.* a sheet of water falling over a dam; a sheet of rock

knave, nave

> knave *n.* a tricky, deceitful, dishonest person
>
> nave *n.* the central hall of a church

knead, kneed, need

> knead *v.* to work material with one's hands: 'knead dough for bread'
>
> kneed *v.* past tense of knee, to hit with one's knees: 'That dirty player always kneed his opponent'
>
> need *n.* poverty: 'A world without need'; a requirement: 'Take care of your first need before spending on luxuries'; a duty or obligation

kneel, knell

> kneel *v.* to get on one's knees, particularly in prayer
>
> knell *n.* the tolling of a bell on someone's death; any mournful sound; a sign of impending failure

knew *See* gnu

knickers, nickers

> knickers *n.* short, loose trousers
>
> nickers *v.* 3d person sing., present tense of nicker; to neigh or whinny

knight, night

> knight *n.* a medieval nobleman, or, today, an honored or titled Englishman
>
> night *n.* the dark period after sunset

knit, nit

knit *v.* to make fabric or clothing using alternating loops; to mend easily: 'The broken bones should knit well'; to bring people or ideas together: 'She'll knit the disorganized department into a tight working group'

nit *n.* a parasite's egg; a trivial detail, hence, to nitpick

knob, nob

knob *n.* a rounded lump; a round handle: 'door knob'

nob *n.* the head (slang)

knobby, nobby

knobby *adj.* full of lumps

nobby *adj.* chic, stylish

knock, nock

knock *v.* to strike: 'knock on the door'; 'knock over the display' 'knock down his opponent'; to insult or criticize (slang): 'He likes to knock the new TV shows'; for a car to make a rattling noise

nock *n.* a notch in a bow or arrow

knockdown, knock down

knockdown *n.* a blow, particularly in boxing, that causes an opponent to fall; furniture that you can assemble easily

knockdown *adj.* overwhelming; offered at a reduced price: 'A knockdown price'

knock down *v.* to hit the one who falls, to cause someone to fall: 'He can knock down his opponents, but he can't knock them out'; to demolish: 'They will knock down the vacant building'; to sell an item at an auction; to earn (slang): 'She'll knock down $250 a week at her new job'

knorr *See* gnaw

knot, not

knot *n.* a fastening of a tie, lace, or cord; a tangle or a problem; a group of people staying close: 'a knot of spectators at the accident'; a small hard spot in a tree; a muscle cramp; a nautical unit of speed; a close tie: 'matrimonial knot'

not *adj.* in no manner; expressing the idea of *no:* 'He'd better not do that!'

knotty, naughty

knotty *adj.* full of knots; complex: 'a knotty problem'

naughty *adj.* lacking in propriety or disobedient: 'a naughty boy'

know, no

know *v.* to be sure: 'I know the answer'; to understand, to remember, to be familiar with: 'I know John well'; to have essential skills: 'I know how to build houses'; to agree: 'She'll perform well. Yes, I know'

no *n.* a vote against something

no *adj.* negative; refusal, rejection; forbidden: "no smoking; none

knows, noes, nose

knows *v.* 3d person, sing., present tense of know, to understand; to be certain; to be familiar with

noes *n.* (pl.) of no: 'On this vote, the noes have it'

nose *n.* the organ of smell; a sense of smell; the front of a vehicle; the ability to detect or track developments: 'She has a nose for news'; a symbol for meddling: 'Please keep your nose out of our business'

koala *See* coaler

koan *See* cone

kob *See* cob

koi *See* coy

koko *See* cacao

kola *See* coaler

kraal *See* crawl

kraft *See* craft

kyack *See* kayak

L

laager *See* lager

label, labial, labile

    label *n.* a means of identifying something or someone: 'I'd certainly give him the label of radical'; a brand name for clothing; a record brand or name used by a recording company

    labial *[lay'•bee•ul] n.* a sound articulated with the lips

    labial *adj.* pertaining to the lips or to female genitalia

    labile *[lay'•bile] v.* flexible; unstable

laboratory, lavatory

    laboratory *n.* a room equipped for scientific research or medical tests

    lavatory *n.* a room or equipment used for washing or toiletry

laches, latches

    laches *[latch'•iz] n.* negligence in asserting a legal right or duty

    latches *n.* (pl.) devices for fastening, but not locking, gates or doors

lacks, lax

    lacks *v.* 3d person, sing., present tense of lack, not to possess what one needs or wants: 'He lacks the qualities needed for that office'

    lax *adj.* careless; slack or loose; not rigid: 'Their lax rules resulted in people coming to work at all hours'

ladder, lather, later, latter

ladder *n.* a piece of equipment that is climbed in order to reach a high place; the stages or levels of any group or organization or of society at large: 'She's lower on the social ladder than her cousins'

lather *n.* foam produced by mixing water and soap, usually for shaving or bathing; the moisture produced by excessive sweating, notably on horses; a state of excitement or anxiety: 'He gets into a lather over even small mistakes'

later *adj.* comparative of late, after a usual time: 'She was always later than he to appointments'

later *adv.* after a designated time; in a while: 'I'll see you later'

latter *adj.* pertaining to the second of two people or groups previously referred to; the second part of a time period: 'The latter part of the year'

laddie, lady

laddie *n.* a lad or a young boy

lady *n.* a woman; a socially prominent or titled woman

lade, laid

lade *v.* to load, as onto a ship: 'They usually lade the boats at night'

laid *v.* past tense of lay, to put down (*not* to lie down): 'He laid the matter to rest'

See also lay

lager, laggard, larger, logger, laager

lager *[lah'•ger] n.* a light beer

laggard *n.* one who loiters or falls behind

larger *adj.* comparative of large, bigger

logger *n.* one who engages in lumbering

laager *[lah'•ger] n.* a circle of wagons

lain, laine, lane

lain *v.* past participle of lie, to recline: 'He has lain in bed too long' laine *n.* woolen cloth

lane *n.* a small passageway

See also lay

lair, layer

lair *n.* a den; a refuge

layer *n.* a substance that you put on top of or between another substance or substances: 'a layer of bricks'; a hen that lays eggs

lam, lamb

lam *v.* to beat, thrash, or strike: 'She will lam her son if he uses foul language again'; to flee quickly, especially from the law (slang): 'on the lam'

lamb *n.* a young sheep

lama, llama

lama *n.* a Buddhist monk or priest

llama *n.* a South American animal related to the camel

lame, lamé

lame *n.* a square (slang)

lame *adj.* having a disabled limb that impairs movement

lamé *[la•may']* *n.* a clothing fabric

lane *See* lain

laps, lapse

laps *n.* (pl.) lap, the position of the thighs of a seated person; a complete length or turn in sports

laps *v.* 3d person, sing., present tense of lap, to ingest food or drink with the tongue; to touch gently: 'The wave laps against the shore'

lapse *n.* a small mistake caused by inattention; a more serious failing or misjudgement: 'She criticized his lapse in manners at the party'; a major decline: 'A lapse into a depression'; a termination, as of an insurance policy, due to nonpayment; a time period, usually long: 'After a lapse of several years, they called us'

large, lodge

large *adj.* big, great, more than average size or quantity

lodge *n.* a country house; a branch of an organization, society, or fraternal order

larger *See* lager

largess/largesse, largest

largess or largesse *[lar•zhes']* *n.* generosity or gifts: 'Their largess in supporting the opera surprised the cast'

largest *adj.* superlative of large; the biggest, having the greatest size or quantity

larva, larvae, lava

larva *n.* the immature form of an insect which hatches from the egg, becomes a pupa, and changes structurally into an adult: 'The larva in the cocoon emerged as a beautiful monarch butterfly'

larvae *n.* (pl.) more than one larva

lava *n.* molten rock from a volcano

laser, lazar

laser *n.* a device that produces powerful visible, ultraviolet, or infrared light beams from energy

lazar *[laser]* *n.* a leper; a person afflicted with a disease

latches *See* laches

later *See* ladder

lath, lathe

lath *n.* a thin strip of wood used as a base for plaster

lathe *n.* a machine that forms metal

lather, latter *See* ladder

lattice, lettuce, let us

lattice *n.* a framework of crossed strips; a geometrical arrangement

lettuce *n.* a green, leafy vegetable

let us *v.* allow us: 'Let us go, you and I'

lava *See* larva

lavatory *See* laboratory

lawn, lorn

lawn *n.* a level green area around a house or estate; a material used for clothing lorn *adj.* forsaken, desolate:'love lorn'

lax *See* lacks

lay, lei

lay *v.* to put something down; past tense of lie, to recline

[Lay, lie, lain, and laid are often confused. Let's clear this up once and for all. *Lay*, in the *present* tense, means to put something down or in a particular place (an action done *to* an object): 'Lay the book on the table.' *Laid* is the *past* tense of lay, to put something down: 'He laid his head on the pillow.' *Lie* means to recline (an action): 'He needs to lie down.' Here's the confusing part: The past tense of lie, to recline, is also *lay* (the past tense of lie, to tell an untruth, is lied): 'He lay in bed all morning.' *Lain* is the *past participle* of lie, to recline: 'He has lain in bed all day.']

lay *n.* the way something is placed relative to another position or point: 'The lay of the land'; a ballad; a partner in sexual intercourse (slang)

lay *adj.* referring to nonreligious persons who work with religious centers or groups: 'a lay brother'; the general public as opposed to specialists or professionals: 'The lay public opposes the medical profession on the issue of preventive medicine'

lei *[lay] n.* a Hawaiian decorative floral necklace

See also lie

layer *See* lair

layoff, lay off

layoff *n.* a temporary discharge of employees due to reduced business or model changeovers: 'The annual auto layoff will take place soon'

lay off *v.* to discharge; to stop bothering someone: 'Lay off him, he's okay'

lays, laze

lays *v.* 3d person, sing., present tense of lay, to put something down laze *v.* to lie around doing nothing, idly

lazar *See* laser

lea, lee

lea *n.* an open space

lee *n.* a shelter

leach, leech

leach *v.* to remove materials from soil or metals by pouring a special liquid into them

leech *n.* a bloodsucking worm once used to remove poison from humans' blood; a person who exploits another's resources: 'He's a leech who sponges off all his relatives'

lead, led

lead *[led] n.* a heavy, gray, malleable metal that is harmful if ingested

led *v.* past tense of lead: 'As of yesterday, the Bears led the NFL'

lead, lied

lead *[rhymes w.* feed*] n.* an advantage, as in sports or in business or technology: 'This player has the lead after two sets'; an important part in a show: 'He just got the lead role in the new TV show'; the most important part of a news story; a clue: 'The scientists followed his lead in investigating UFOs'

lead *v.* to influence others to follow you: 'He'll lead his unit into battle'

lied *[rhymes w.* feed*] n.* a German art song

leader, lieder, liter

leader *n.* the head of a group

lieder *[rhymes w.* feeder*] n.*(pl.) German songs

liter *n.* a metric measure equivalent to slightly less than a quart

leaf, lief

leaf *n.* a part of a tree or plant; foliage; a foldable table extension

lief *[leaf] adj.* gladly: 'I would lief give my life for my beloved'

leak, leek

leak *n.* an act that occurs when a substance escapes from a container accidentally; a crack or defect that causes the escape; a deliberate release of information in order to damage someone: 'He might leak the story to a favorite reporter'

leek *n.* a root vegetable with an onionlike flavor

lean, lien

lean *adj.* thin or sparse; less fatty; spare, lacking richness (often in relation to the economy): 'Drought brought us lean years'

lean *v.* to move one's body in a certain way or direction: 'I often lean back on my chair'; to hold certain ideas: 'He seems to lean in the direction of a liberal trade policy'; to rest against: 'I like to lean against the fence'

lien *[lean] n.* a legal hold on someone's property in payment of a debt

leaper, leper

leaper *n.* one who leaps or jumps; suicide jumper (slang)

leper *[rhymes w. pepper] n.* one who has the disease of leprosy; someone who is shunned or ostracized: 'After his speech calling for increased taxes, he was treated like a leper'

leased, least, lest

leased *v.* past tense of lease, to pay for the use of property without owning it: 'He leased new cars every year instead of buying'

least *adj.* the smallest in size or degree; the lowest quantity or quality: 'He has the least athletic ability of anyone I met'

least *adv.* a very small degree: 'One of the least expected happenings'

lest *conj.* unless

led *See* lead

lee *See* lea

leech *See* leach

leek *See* leak

legation, ligation

> legation *n.* the offices of a diplomatic mission
>
> ligation *n.* a special knot or stitch such as surgeons use; any means of binding something

lei *See* lay

lends, lens

> lends *v.* 3d person sing., present tense of lend, to give money or property that must be repaid or returned: 'Dad lends me the car every weekend'; to provide or add a quality: 'The plant lends the room a festive air'
>
> lens *n.* a specially curved optical glass to improve or enhance eyesight; the part of the eye that focuses light from objects

lentil, lintel

> lentil *n.* a bean
>
> lintel *n.* a wood or stone cover above a door or other opening

leopard, leotard

> leopard *[lep'•ard] n.* a large spotted feline animal
>
> leotard *[lee'•o•tard] n.* a one-piece garment (bodysuit) worn by dancers and gymnasts

leper *See* leaper

less, loess

> less *adj.* fewer, smaller: 'I want less meat and more potatoes'
>
> less *adv.* to a smaller extent: 'After what she did, I am less inclined to like her'
>
> less *prep.* in math, minus: 'Six less two is four'
>
> loess *[less] n.* a windblown yellowish brown loamy deposit

lessen, lesson

> lessen *v.* to make something smaller in size or importance
>
> lesson *n.* a learning unit or concept; a special experience that serves as a model: 'I learned my lesson about drinking after that party'

lesser, lessor

> lesser *adj.* smaller in size or significance: 'I chose the lesser of two evils'

lessor *n.* one who holds a lease

lest *See* leased

lettuce, let us *See* lattice

liable, libel

>liable *adj.* legally obligated: 'I am liable for my son's debts';
>>probable: 'The deficit is liable to lead us into a
>>depression'

>libel *n.* a written or published lie that damages one's
>>reputation: 'I'll sue them for libel for calling me an
>>alcoholic'

liar, lier, lyre

>liar *n.* one who lies or tells falsehoods

>lier *n.* a person or thing that lies in ambush

>lyre *n.* an ancient string instrument

lichen, liken

>lichen *[liken] n.* a plant that grows on trees or rocks

>liken *v.* to indicate a resemblance, to compare: 'I liken him to
>>a skunk'

licker, liqueur, liquor

>licker *n.* a person or animal that licks or laps with the tongue

>liqueur *[lih•ker'] n.* a sweet alcoholic drink usually taken
>>after a meal

>liquor *[lih'•ker] n.* an alcoholic beverage

lickerish, licorice

>lickerish *adj.* greedy; fond of fancy foods

>licorice *n.* a sweet black candy with flavoring from the
>>licorice plant

lie, lye

>lie *n.* a falsehood; the location of an object, such as the
>>position of a ball in golf; an animal's usual lair

>lie *v.* to tell a falsehood; to be or become horizontal: 'to lie
>>down'; to stay hidden; to await: 'We don't know what will
>>lie ahead in this crisis'; situated or found: 'Both cities lie
>>100 miles north of Paris'

>lye *n.* a strong alkaline washing solution

>*See also* lay

lied *See* lead

lieder *See* leader

lief *See* leaf

lien *See* lean

lier *See* liar

lieu, loo

> lieu *[loo] n.* in place of: 'I'm taking long weekends in lieu of a week's vacation'
>
> loo *n.* a card game

life, live

> life *n.* the capacity of a functioning object to grow and move, as distinct from inanimate objects like rocks; the opposite of death; the time that people are alive: 'He spent his life trying to prove his theory'; the useful period of operation: 'This car's life is ten years'; the duration of an institution or activity: 'The agreement's life is one year'; animation or excitement: 'He was the life of the party'
>
> live *[rhymes w. give] v.* to be or remain alive; to dwell or reside: 'I live in Chicago'; to conduct oneself a certain way: 'He prefers to live like a hermit'
>
> live *[rhymes w. hive] adj.* alive: 'That is a live snake he has in that box'; pertaining to a TV or radio show that is being performed as one watches or hears it: 'They enjoy live shows more than taped shows'

lifelong, livelong

> lifelong *adj.* continuous or lasting for a lifetime: 'A lifelong affection for red roses'
>
> livelong *adj.* very long or whole: 'I've been working on the railroad all the livelong day'

ligation *See* legation

lightening, lightning

> lightening *v.* present participle of lighten, to make something less heavy; to relieve or ease a burden: 'By adding staff, you are lightening our workload'; to make something brighter

lightning *n.* a powerful electric flash in the sky

lightning *adj.* happening very quickly: 'With lightning speed the students took over the administration building'

liken *See* lichen

limb, limn

limb *[rhymes w. him] n.* an arm or leg; the branches of a tree, hence, to 'go out on a limb' is to take a big risk of falling or failing

limn *v.* to draw a picture; to describe a person or object

linage, lineage

linage *[line'•ij] n.* the number of lines in printed matter: 'She was charged for the advertisement according to the linage'

lineage *[lin'•ee•ij] n.* ancestry, line of descent: 'He could trace his lineage to the 12th century'

lineament, liniment

lineament *[lin'•ee•uh•mint] n.* a facial or bodily outline or distinguishing feature: 'Her lineaments were most pleasing'

liniment *[lin'•i•mint] n.* an ointment that helps ease body aches

lineup, line up

lineup *n.* a special line formed for observation: 'a police lineup'; the team members who will play in a game

line up *v.* to stand in a row: 'You can line up for theater tickets'

links, lynx

links *n.* a golf course; (pl.) the connections between things or people: 'The links between the U.S. and Britain remain strong'

links *v.* 3d person, sing., present tense of link, to connect or to show a causal relationship: 'This study links cancer to certain foods'

lynx *n.* a catlike wild animal; a wildcat

lintel *See* lentil

lion, loin

> lion *n.* a giant catlike animal found mainly in Africa; a person of importance or ferocity
>
> loin *n.* a cut of meat; a part of the human torso

liqueur, liquor *See* licker

liter *See* leader

literal, littoral

> literal *adj.* the basic or physical meaning of a word or term, as opposed to the figurative, or derived meaning. For example, the literal meaning of price is the amount of money you pay for something; its figurative meaning can be the nonmonetary cost of doing something: 'Cancer is the price one pays for ignoring admonitions against smoking'
>
> littoral *adj.* pertaining to the seashore: 'Littoral plants and animals have been endangered by oil spills'

live *See* life

livelong *See* lifelong

lively, livery

> lively *adj.* animated, enthusiastic, active: 'They are a lively crew'
>
> lively *adv.* vigorously: 'Please step lively, folks'
>
> livery *n.* a company that hires out vehicles; a place that keeps and cares for horses; a servant's uniform
>
> livery *adj.* a possible liver ailment

llama *See* lama

lo, low

> lo *interj.* an expression of surprise
>
> low *adj.* down; below average: 'Too many people try to get by on very low incomes'; the opposite of high; vulgar: 'I don't like that kind of low humor'; depressed; weak: 'The battery is low'; soft or quiet: 'She always speaks in a low voice'
>
> low *v.* to moo

load, lode, lowed

> load *n.* something that is carried; the amount or weight that is carried; the amount of work performed by a person or a machine: 'Since the layoffs, my load is much heavier'
>
> load *v.* to fill up; to put material onto a truck, boat, or other vehicle; to slant or bias a discussion: 'He tends to load the argument in favor of taxes by leaving out key information'
>
> lode *n.* a metal deposit; any rich source
>
> lowed *v.* past tense of low, to moo

loam, loan, lone

> loam *n.* very rich soil
>
> loan *n.* money or property given out that must be repaid or returned
>
> lone *adj.* alone: 'the Lone Ranger'

loaner, loner

> loaner *n.* something given to you for temporary use while the original is being fixed
>
> loner *n.* someone who prefers to be by him- or herself

loath/loth, loathe

> loath *or* loth *[rhymes w. both] adj.* reluctant: 'I am loath to lend him any more money, since he rarely repays his debts'
>
> loathe *[loath but th as in bathe] v.* to despise: 'I loathe his arrogance'

local, lo cal, locale

> local *adj.* coming from a particular or limited area: 'She's a local resident'
>
> lo cal *adj.* low calorie, a food with fewer calories than its normal version
>
> locale *[lo•kal'] n.* the place where something is happening, such as a scene in a play or a movie

loch, lock

> loch *n.* a lake, in Scotland

lock *v.* to secure or fasten; to put away objects in a secured place; to join firmly: 'Lock arms and march together'

lochs, lox, locks

lochs *n.* (pl.) more than one loch; lakes

locks *n.* (pl.) more than one lock, a means of securing a door or other object

locks *v.* 3d person, sing., present tense of lock

lox *n.* smoked salmon

locus, locust

locus *n.* in mathematics, a set of points; the center of an activity: 'The locus of power has shifted from the military to the civil authorities'

locust *n.* a type of grasshopper that swarms and destroys plants and vegetation

lode *See* load

lodge *See* large

loess *See* less

logger *See* lager

loin *See* lion

lone *See* loam

loner *See* loaner

loo *See* lieu

lookout, look out

lookout *n.* one who keeps watch; a guard or a partner in crime who watches for police during a robbery

look out *v.* to pay attention or to protect oneself: 'You have to look out for yourself'; to observe: 'You can look out of your window to see what's happening outside'

loom, loon, lune

loom *n.* a weaving device

loom *v.* to appear suddenly or dangerously in an exagerrated or large form: 'Fog on that road makes oncoming cars loom like trucks'; to impend: 'More losses of those species loom in the future as a result of environmental destruction'

loon *n.* a bird with long legs and a distinctive cry; a crazy
person

lune *n.* a mathematical figure formed by two intersecting arcs

loop, loup, loupe

loop *n.* a figure created by curving a material back on itself;
an electrical circuit

loup *v.* to leap

loupe *n.* a jeweler's or photographer's special magnifying
glass

loose, lose, luce

loose *[rhymes w. moose] adj.* not firmly held; unrestrained or
unfettered, the opposite of tight; relaxed; immoral; not
packaged: 'loose fruit'; imprecise: 'a loose translation of
the Dead Sea Scrolls'

lose *[rhymes w. whose] v.* to fail to attain a goal in
competition; the opposite of win

luce *[rhymes w. moose] n.* a species of fish, a pike

loot, lute

loot *n.* what is taken from an enemy or from unprotected
houses; stolen property (slang)

loot *v.* to plunder or steal

lute *n.* a musical instrument similar to a guitar

lorn *See* lawn

loth *See* loathe

loud, louse, lout

loud *adj.* marked by high volume; very noisy; easy to hear;
ostentatious: 'He wore a loud jacket'

louse *n.* a tiny wingless parasitic insect; a detestable person:
'That louse constantly undermines his peers and friends'

lout *n.* a clumsy or brutish man

loup, loupe *See* loop

louver/louvre, lover

louver *or* louvre *[loo'•ver] n.* a set of window slats or
protectors that allow air and light in but permit privacy

lover *n.* one who loves

low *See* lo
lowed *See* load
lox *See* lochs
luce *See* loose
lucks, lux, luxe

> lucks *v.* 3d person, sing., present tense of luck, to have good luck
>
> lux *n.* a unit of ilumination
>
> luxe *n.* a high-quality object or place; luxury: 'That hotel offers luxe at low prices'
>
> luxe *adj.* luxurious

lumbar, lumber

> lumbar *adj.* referring to the lower back
>
> lumber *n.* timber that has been cut down and sawed into boards
>
> lumber *v.* to move ponderously

lune *See* loom
lute *See* loot
luxuriance, luxuriant, luxurious

> luxuriance *n.* a state of profuse growth: 'I'm proud of the luxuriance of my garden'
>
> luxuriant *adj.* relating to plants, healthy and growing, fertile, lush
>
> luxurious *adj.* expensive and high quality: 'She owned a luxurious estate in Palm Springs'

lye *See* lie
lynx *See* links
lyre *See* liar

M

maar, mar

maar *n.* a volcanic crater

mar *v.* to damage, to spoil

Mach, mock

Mach *[mock] n.* speed of an object relative to the speed of
sound: 'An airplane traveling at Mach 2 is going at twice
the speed of sound'

mock *v.* to ridicule: 'They mock my dress, which is years
ahead of its time'; to mimic

maco, mako

maco *[mah•koh'] n.* Egyptian cotton

mako *[mah'•koh] n.* a species of shark

madam, Madame/Madam

madam *n.* a bawd; a woman in charge of a brothel

Madame *or* Madam *n.* a respectful or polite term of address
to a woman, especially a married woman

made, maid

made *v.* past tense of make, to produce: 'He made a suit of
clothes'; to cause: 'That made me sad'; to appoint: 'We
made her chairperson of the organization'; to equal: 'In
the budget, two billion plus two billion made four
billion'

maid *n.* a girl; a young unmarried woman; a female
household servant

magnate, magnet

> magnate *n.* a very influential or powerful person: 'He's a banking magnate'
>
> magnet *n.* a piece of steel or iron that attracts iron or steel; anything, including a person, that attracts

mail, male

> mail *n.* letters or other items delivered by the post office; metal-chain body armor
>
> male *n.* a boy or man

mailer, malar

> mailer *n.* an advertising flyer; one who mails something
>
> malar *n.* the cheek bone

main, mane

> main *n.* a pipeline; the ocean
>
> main *adj.* chief in size or importance: 'What's the main cause of war?'
>
> mane *n.* the long hair of a horse, lion, or person

maize, maze

> maize *n.* corn; the color of corn
>
> maze *n.* a labyrinth: 'The British lord prides himself on his elaborate garden maze'

make-believe, make believe

> make-believe *n.* a particularly imaginative act of pretending: 'Children often are better at make-believe than are adults'
>
> make believe *v.* to pretend, not necessarily imaginatively

makeup, make up

> makeup *n.* cosmetics: 'She put on her makeup before going to the prom'; the way something is organized: 'the makeup, or layout, of a printed page'; a retest for students who missed an earlier exam
>
> make up *v.* to reconcile after a fight: 'kiss and make up'; to apply cosmetics: 'to make up with makeup'; to decide: 'Make up your mind'; to pay back for an error: 'She'll have to make up for her mistakes'

mako *See* maco

malaise, Malays, Malaysia

malaise *[muh•laze']* *n.* vague mental or physical discomfort

Malays *[muh•laze'* or *may'•laze]* *n.* (pl.) the inhabitants of
Malaysia

Malaysia *n.* a Southeast Asian country

malar *See* mailer

male *See* mail

mall, maul, mole, moll

mall *n.* a promenade; a site for a number of retail stores:
'Another new shopping mall is going up nearby'

maul *n.* a heavy hammer used to drive stakes

maul *v.* to beat or batter: 'The park ranger warned that the
bear might maul people who were in its way'

mole *n.* a dark skin spot; a burrowing animal; an enemy
agent planted inside one's intelligence service: 'The CIA
operations chief remained convinced that there was a
mole in the organization'

moll *n.* a prostitute; a gangster's girlfriend

mamba, mambo

mamba *n.* an African venomous snake

mambo *n.* a rhythmic Latin dance

manage, manege, ménage

manage *v.* to control an organization; to succeed; to cope: 'I'll
manage, even without her help'

manege *[ma•nej']* *n.* a school for horsemanship

ménage *[may•nahj']* *n.* a household; a domestic
establishment

mandatary, mandatory

mandatary *n.* the recipient of a mandate or special authority

mandatory *adj.* compulsory: 'It's mandatory for all students to
maintain a C average'

mandrel/mandril, mandrill

mandrel *or* mandril *n.* a spindle; a metal bar

mandrill *n.* a baboon

mane *See* main

maniac, manic, manioc

> maniac *n.* a mad person, usually with specific fixations; a person who acts in an extreme manner: 'He drives like a maniac'
>
> manic *adj.* relating to a condition of high excitement and craze, both physical and psychological
>
> manioc *n.* a starchy root used in making tapioca

manifest, manifesto

> manifest *n.* a ship's or plane's passenger list
>
> manifest *v.* to demonstrate clearly: 'The audience may manifest its appreciation with loud cheers'
>
> manifesto *n.* a strong statement of principles and intentions: 'The rebels' manifesto called for the confiscation of all large estates'

manikin, mannequin

> manikin *n.* a dwarf
>
> mannequin *n.* a model of a human body used by window dressers, artists, and tailors; a person who models clothes in a store

manner, manor, manure

> manner *n.* a method or way in which something is done: 'I never liked his manner of making last-minute requests'; a person's behavior: 'She had a courteous manner, but could be abrupt on occasion'; a particular creative style: 'He's trying to write in the manner of Hemingway'
>
> manor *n.* a feudal estate; the main house on a large estate
>
> manure *[muh•noor']* *n.* dung used as fertilizer

mantel, mantle

> mantel *n.* a shelf or slab, often above a fireplace
>
> mantle *n.* a sleeveless outer garment; the earth's inner layer, the movement of which often causes earthquakes; the responsibilities that come with an important job: 'He assumed the mantle of the presidency with complete confidence'

mantle *v.* to conceal or cover

maqui, maquis, marquee, marquis, marquise

maqui *n.* a Chilean medicinal plant

maquis *[ma•kee']* *n.* a zone of shrubbery; evergreen plants; the French resistance in WWII

marquee *[mar•kee']* *n.* a rooflike projection, often featuring a theatre's name; an outdoor tent

marquis *[mar•key' or mar'•kwis]* *n.* a nobleman

marquise *[mar•keez']* *n.* a pointed oval-shaped gem cut or ring setting

mar *See* maar

marc, mark, marque

marc *n.* the residue remaining after a fruit, such as grapes, has been pressed

mark *n.* a sign; symbol; discoloration: 'Don't get a finger mark on the paper'; a school grade: 'His highest mark was in science'; an imprint; a level: 'The city's population reached the three-million mark'; a distinguishing feature; the monetary unit of Germany and Finland

marque *n.* an automobile identifying emblem or brand name

mare, mayor

mare *n.* a female horse or donkey

mayor *n.* the chief official of a city

marina, marine

marina *n.* a small-boat harbor: 'That marina holds over 200 boats'

marine *n.* a soldier serving in one of the naval forces trained to land from water

marine *adj.* relating to the sea: 'The seal is a marine mammal'

marital, marshal, martial

marital *adj.* referring to marriage: 'a marital squabble'

marshal *n.* the highest ranking officer in many armies; an official who executes court orders; one who leads ceremonial events: 'She was the first woman elected as marshal of the St. Patrick's Day parade' marshal *v.* to organize or arrange; to line up people or events; to usher

martial *adj.* warlike: 'that nation's martial behavior frightened its neighbors'

marque *See* marc

marquee, marquis, marquise *See* maqui

marriage, mirage

marriage *n.* a close union; a relation between a wife and a husband; a wedding; a joining of different elements or parts: 'The marriage of theme and style in his writing'

mirage *[mi•rahzh']* *n.* an optical phenomenon that creates an illusion; something illusory

marry, merry

marry *v.* to join as husband and wife; to combine elements or parts

merry *adj.* full of laughter and fun: 'Everyone at the marriage was in a merry mood'

marshal *See* marital

marten, martin

marten *n.* a weasellike mammal

martin *n.* a bird; a swallow

martial *See* marital

mascle, muscle, mussel

mascle *n.* a mark used in heraldry

muscle *n.* body tissue that creates movement or strength; power: 'political muscle'

mussel *n.* an edible mollusk

mask, masque, mosque

mask *n.* a facial disguise; an air filter for the face; a molded facial caricature; a cosmetic skin covering

mask *v.* to conceal; to cover or disguise one's feelings or thoughts: 'She'll always mask her true feelings toward him'

masque *n.* a masquerade party; a Renaissance performance

mosque *n.* a Muslim temple

mason, meson

mason *n.* a person who lays brick or stone

meson *[mez•on']* *n.* an unstable atomic particle

massage, message

massage *[mi•sahzh']* *n.* a body rub

message *[mess'•ij]* *n.* a communication sent to or left for someone: 'I left a message on her answering machine'; an important idea conveyed by a film, a story, or a series of public communications: 'His message was that free speech could never be restricted'; a formal communication to a legislative body: 'The President's annual message on the State of the Union'

massed, mast

massed *v.* past tense of mass, to gather into a mass or large group: 'The troops massed at the border'

mast *n.* a metal structure to support a ship's sails; a pole that transmits radio or TV signals: 'A television mast sits on top of the Empire State Building'

material, materiel

material *n.* a textile fabric; the basic matter used to make things: 'Building material'; information or background for articles, plays, etc.: 'He gathered a good deal of material on LBJ before writing'; one's potential: 'He's not good material for this program'

material *adj.* refers to the physical or practical as opposed to the spiritual or psychological: 'I work mainly to meet my material needs'; important: 'Her contribution will make a material difference'

materiel *[mi•teer•ee•el']* *n.* the weapons and supplies used by the military

maul *See* mall

maw, moire

maw *n.* the stomach, gullet, or jaws

moire *[maw•ray' or mwahr]* *n.* a fabric having a wavy pattern

See also moor, morays

maybe, may be

maybe *adj.* possibly or perhaps: 'Maybe you'll have better luck next time'

may be *v.* to be possible or probable: 'He may be the next president'

mayor *See* mare

mayoral, mayoralty

mayoral *adj.* refers to the mayor: 'His mayoral performance failed to fulfill his promise'

mayoralty *n.* the office or term of office of a mayor

maze *See* maize

me, mi

me *pron.* objective case of I: 'She told me to get lost'

mi *n. [mee]* a musical note in a scale

mean, mesne, mien

mean *n.* a statistical measure, an average

mean *v.* to have in mind as one's intent or idea: 'What does the term colonialism mean?'; to be important: 'His gifts mean a lot to me'; to have consequences: 'If I move, it will mean a loss of income'; to convey or signify: 'I mean what I say: don't do that again'; to act deliberately: 'I did mean to insult him, and I won't apologize'

mean *adj.* bad tempered; low in quality; good or great (slang)

mesne *[mean] adj.* in law, intermediate, middle, or intervening

mien *[mean] n.* one's way of conducting oneself, or one's appearance: 'He always wore such a mournful mien'

meat, meet, mete

meat *n.* the flesh of animals

meet *n.* a sports competition: 'a track meet'; a meeting

meet *v.* to come together: 'They meet every week to discuss books'; to make someone's acquaintance: 'I'd like to meet that actor'; to greet an arrival: 'I'll meet your plane at three o'clock'; to satisfy one's requirement or to conform: 'That salary can't meet my needs'; to compete: 'The teams meet next Saturday' mete *v.* to distribute, apportion, allot: 'to mete out punishment'

meatier, meteor

meatier *adj.* comparative of meaty; containing more meat or more substance: 'That's a meatier article'

meteor *n.* a bright, moving, small heavenly body

See also meeter

medal, meddle, metal, mettle

medal *n.* a decoration or award, usually a small metal disc

meddle *v.* to interfere: 'Please don't meddle in our business'

metal *n.* any of a group of opaque, conductive substances such as iron, gold, silver

mettle *n.* inherent character or courage: 'She was given the chance to show her mettle'

meddler, medlar

meddler *n.* a person who involves him- or herself with other people's affairs in an objectionable manner

medlar *n.* a small tree; a lark

mediation, medication, meditation

mediation *n.* intervention by a third party to resolve a dispute

medication *n.* medicinal products or the act of providing medicines: 'The doctor told us to take this medication every four hours'

meditation *n.* quiet and deep reflection, spiritual contemplation: 'She practiced yoga and other forms of meditation daily'; an author's thoughts and writing about a religious or philosophical issue

meet *See* meat

meeter, meter

meeter *n.* one who meets or greets people

meter *n.* an instrument that measures quantity, cost, or duration: 'a taxi meter' or 'a postage meter'; the basic unit of measure in the metric system that is a bit more than a yard; a regular beat or rhythm in poetry or music

See also meatier

memoir, memory

memoir *[mem'•wahr] n.* a biography or autobiography

memory *n.* the mind's ability to retain and recall events or ideas; the event or experience you recall; the part of a computer that stores information

ménage *See* manage

mendacity, mendicity

mendacity *n.* falsehood; the quality of being dishonest: 'His tale of his exploits was an example of his mendacity'

mendicity *n.* the act of begging or the condition of being a beggar

merry *See* marry

mesne *See* mean

meson *See* mason

message *See* massage

metal *See* medal

mete *See* meat

meteor *See* meatier

meteorology, metrology

meteorology *n.* the study or science of weather

metrology *n.* the science of weights and measures or measurement

mettle *See* medal

mewl, mule

mewl *v.* to whimper; to cry weakly

mule *n.* the offspring of a horse and a donkey; a stubborn animal or person; a person who transports illegal drugs or guns (slang)

mews, muse

mews *n.* a street of stables or carriage houses with living quarters

muse *n.* the spirit presiding over the arts and sciences; a source of inspiration

muse *v.* to meditate; to lose oneself in one's thoughts

mho, mot, mow

mho *[rhymes w.* flow*] n.* an electrical unit, the reciprocal of the ohm mot *[rhymes w. flow] n.* a witty or pithy saying

mow *[rhymes w. flow] adj.* to cut, as grass or grain: 'mow the lawn'; to knock down mercilessly: 'The troops hope to mow down the enemy'

See also moat

mi *See* me

middy, midi

middy *n.* a midshipman in a naval academy; a blouse with a sailor collar

midi *[rhymes w. seedy] n.* a short coat or skirt with a hem that comes to mid calf

midst, missed, mist

midst *n.* the central part; the middle; a position of proximity or nearness: 'We have several notables in our midst'

midst *prep.* in the middle, during: 'In the midst of the crisis, he resigned'

missed *v.* past tense of miss, to fail, to omit, to barely or narrowly avoid: 'He missed that car by six inches'; to regret the absence of: 'I missed my family, and called them often'; to slip up: 'I missed the plane and missed my meeting'; not to catch or see: 'I missed the excitement, what happened?'

mist *n.* a haze, a fog, a cloud, smog

mien *See* mean

might, mite

might *n.* power, strength, or vigor: 'They have to give in to our might'

might *v.* used as an auxiliary with another verb expressing possibility: 'It might happen or be true, but I'm not certain'; may: 'I thought you might be offended by his remarks'; expressing contingency: 'Hard as it might be, you still should go for it'; expressing advisability: 'You might try this approach to the problem'; used as a polite query: 'Might I ask what you intend to do with your money?'

mite *n.* a small parasite; a small bit of help; a small child

mil, mill

mil *n.* one-thousandth of an inch

mill *n.* a building where grain is ground; a factory: 'We worked in that steel mill for twenty years until it closed'

mill *v.* to grind flour; to cut metals; to move around in disarray: 'The people mill around for hours at the fair'

milch, milk

milch *adj.* giving milk: 'milch cows are kept for milk, not for meat'

milk *n.* a white fluid produced by a female mammal's mammary glands used as food or nourishment

milk *v.* to draw milk from a cow; to get or draw what you can from an institution, person, or situation, often through an exploitative act: 'He milked the naive investors for all they were worth'

milk toast, Milquetoast

milk toast *n.* buttered toast served in hot milk

Milquetoast *[milk toast] n.* a timid, meek, apologetic person

millenary, millinery

millenary *n.* a group of 1,000 units or 1,000 years

millinery *n.* women's hats; the business of one who makes women's hats

millileter, millimeter

milliliter *n.* one one-thousandth of a liter; a metric measurement

millimeter *n.* one one-thousandth of a meter; a metric measurement

milline, million

milline *n.* an advertisement which runs in a publication selling more than 1,000 copies

million *n.* a thousand thousands, written as 1,000,000

mina, myna

mina *[my'•nuh] n.* a unit of weight used in ancient Greece

myna *[my'•nuh] n.* a bird

See also miner

mince, mints

mince *v.* to chop finely; to move in an affected or effeminate manner; to speak frankly (in the negative): 'I won't mince my words; this work is no good'

mints *n.* (pl.) places where coins are made; aromatic plants or candies

mints *v.* 3d person, sing., present tense of mint, to produce money; to invent: 'He mints a new word in almost every article he writes'

mind, mined

mind *n.* the center of thought, perception, and reason; the process of thinking or deliberating; intellect as opposed to emotion; opinion, view: 'She has a liberal mind'; memory: 'That put me in mind of an old war story'; one's intellectual ability: 'She has a good mind' or 'She has a mind for science'; attention or concentration: 'He can't keep his mind on anything for more than ten minutes'

mind *v.* to object to: 'Yes, I do mind your smoking'; to obey: 'He won't mind his parents' orders'; to notice; to take care of someone or something: 'Mind the children while I'm out'

mined *v.* past tense of mine, to excavate or to dig in the earth; to use or extract information: 'She mined every reference source for her book'; to plant explosives: 'U.S. forces mined the channel approaches'

miner, minor

miner *n.* a person who works in a mine

minor *n.* a person under legal age: 'Bars are not supposed to serve a minor'; a musical scale

minor *adj.* unimportant: 'That's a minor mistake, don't worry'; not serious or dangerous: 'It was just minor surgery'

See also mina

minion, minyan

minion *n.* a servant or a subordinate

minyan *n.* a group of ten males, 13 years or older, necessary for conducting Jewish public worship

minks, minx
>   minks *n.* (pl.) weasellike animals or coats made from their
>   fur
>   minx *n.* a flirtatious or pert young woman

mints *See* mince

mirage *See* marriage

miserly, misery
>   miserly *adj.* stingy; relating to one who hoards his wealth
>   misery *n.* extreme unhappiness; a state of suffering resulting
>   from poverty: 'Four-fifths of the world's population lives
>   in misery'

mishap, misshape
>   mishap *n.* misfortune or bad luck; an accident: 'Dad, I had a
>   slight mishap with the car'
>   misshape *v.* to provide a wrong or poor shape or form to an
>   object; to distort facts or ideas: 'His article will misshape
>   thinking about her art'

missal, missel, missile
>   missal *n.* a book of prayer that contains all forms of worship
>   for the year
>   missel *n.* a bird; a European thrush
>   missile *n.* a self-propelled bomb or rocket; any object that is
>   thrown, shot, or hurled

missed, mist *See* midst

mite *See* might

mix-up, mix up
>   mix-up *n.* a mistake or confusion
>   mix up *v.* to confuse; to blend thoroughly: 'Mix up the olive
>   oil with the vinegar'

moan, mown
>   moan *n.* a painful sound that is a sign of suffering; a complaint:
>   'There goes the usual moan about my cooking'
>   mown *v.* past participle of mow, to cut grass or grain: 'The
>   grass was mown'

moat, mote, motte

moat *n.* a deep ditch: 'The moat in front of the castle was filled with water'

mote *n.* a speck of dust

motte *[rhymes w.* lot*] n.* a group of small prairie trees; a prehistoric mound

See also mho

mock *See* Mach

modal, model, module

modal *[mode'•al] adj.* pertaining to a manner or mode; in grammar, the mood

model *n.* a small reproduction of a product; a particular product design or version: 'this year's car model'; an example to be imitated: 'a role model'; one who displays designer's clothes; a theoretical or mathematical description of a process; one who poses for an artist or photographer

model *adj.* exemplary, outstanding: 'a model husband'; 'a model farm'

module *n.* a standard part or subassembly of a product that can be fixed or replaced separately

mode, mowed

mode *n.* a manner of doing something; a way of living; a style or fashion: 'a new artistic mode'; a statistical measure of frequency

mowed *v.* past tense of mow, to cut down grass or grain

mohr *See* moor

moire *See* maw

moires *See* morays

mole, moll *See* mall

mood, mooed

mood *n.* one's frame of mind or disposition: 'He's in a bad mood'; a bout of temper or anger; in grammar, changes in verb inflection to depict different types of action or feeling mooed *v.* past tense of moo, the sound made by a cow

moolah, mullah

moolah *n.* money (slang)

mullah *[mu'•la] n.* a Muslim teacher of dogma and law

moor, Moor, mhorr, more

moor *n.* an open, relatively barren stretch of land; a peat bog

moor *v.* to attach floating objects like boats to a secure object on land

Moor *n.* an Arab from North Africa

mhorr *n.* an African gazelle

more *adj.* greater; bigger in number, quality, or degree; the comparative of many or much; an additional amount: 'Do you have more bananas?'

more *adv.* in addition, besides, or to a greater degree: 'He was more surprised than she when he proposed'

See also maw

moose *See* mouse

moot, mute

moot *n.* a debate; an assembly which deliberates and administers justice: 'The law students practiced their arguments for the next moot court'

moot *adj.* debatable or meaningless: 'a moot point'

mute *[myoot] n.* a person who cannot or does not speak

mute *v.* to soften or weaken: 'I will mute my criticism if he will change'

mop, mope

mop *v.* to clean using a long-handled device with an absorbent material attached; to dry one's face: 'I'll mop my face with this towel to remove the sweat'

mope *v.* to act sluggish, listless; to be inactive; to brood

moped, mopped, moppet

moped *[moe'•pehd] n.* a motorized bicycle

moped *v.* past participle of mope, to be listless, down, or sad

mopped *v.* past tense of mop, to clean with a mop

moppet *[mop'•pet] n.* a young child

moral, morale, morel, morral, mural

> moral *n.* a lesson taught by a story or fable: 'The moral of this fable is: 'Don't count your chickens before they're hatched'; in the plural, principles or standards; ethics
>
> moral *adj.* showing good or a correct behavior: 'He's a very moral person'; relating to broad principles of right and wrong: 'The president's veto was hardly moral'; psychic, as opposed to material satisfaction: 'They lost 12-10, but it was a moral victory'
>
> morale *[more•al']* *n.* a group's degree of confidence and enthusiasm when entering a contest or battle: 'After two victories, their morale rose'; a sense of common purpose
>
> morel *[mi•rehl']* *n.* an edible mushroom
>
> morral *[mi•ral']* *n.* a bag for feeding horses
>
> mural *[myoo'•ril]* *n.* a painting or drawing on a wall

morays, mores, moires

> morays *n.* giant, dangerous eels
>
> mores *[rhymes w. forays]* *n.* a society's customs, conventions, or moral attitudes: 'Our sexual mores have changed drastically in the past twenty years'
>
> moires *n.* (pl.) cloths with a wavy pattern

more *See* moor

morn, mourn

> morn *n.* daybreak or morning (often poetic)
>
> mourn *v.* to express sorrow or to grieve, usually for a death: 'They will always mourn the loss of their parents'

morning, mourning

> morning *n.* the first part of the day; dawn; the period from sunrise to noon
>
> mourning *n.* the act of grieving; an outward sign, such as clothing, of grieving

morral *See* moral

morro, morrow

> morro *n.* a rounded hill
>
> morrow *n.* the following day (often poetic)

Moslem *See* Muslim

mosque *See* mask

mot *See* mho

mote *See* moat

motif, motive

> motif *[moh•teef']* *n.* the main element or idea of a literary work; a figure in a design: 'My wallpaper has a floral motif'; a repeating thematic element in a work of art or music
>
> motive *[moh'•tiv]* *n.* the inner drive that causes one to act: 'His motive for going to college is to gain wealth'
>
> motive *adj.* relating to something producing action, motion, or energy

motte *See* moat

mourn *See* morn

mourning *See* morning

mouse, mousse, moose

> mouse *[rhymes w. house]* *n.* a rodent; a dark swollen bruise under an eye; a handheld device to move a computer's cursor
>
> mousse *[moose]* *n.* a creamy gelatinous dessert usually flavored by whipped cream or chocolate; a foamy hair styling aid
>
> moose *n.* a large antlered mammal

mow *See* mho

mowed *See* mode

mown *See* moan

mucus, mucous

> mucus *n.* a slimy secretion which is produced by, protects, and moistens the mucous membranes in the nose, mouth, or throat
>
> mucous *adj.* containing or secreting mucus; slimy or like mucus

mule *See* mewl

mullah *See* moolah

mural *See* moral

muscle *See* mascle

muse *See* mews

musical, musicale

> musical *n.* a theatrical production with music: 'a musical comedy'
>
> musical *adj.* related to music: 'musical instruments'; relating to one who is adept at music
>
> musicale *n.* an event featuring a musical program

Muslim/Moslem, muslin, Islam

> Muslim *or* Moslem *n.* a person who adheres to the Islamic faith
>
> muslin *n.* cotton cloth
>
> Islam *n.* the religious faith to which Muslims adhere; the group of nations in which the Islamic faith is dominant

mussed, must

> mussed *v.* past tense of muss, to rumple or ruffle: 'He mussed her hair when he embraced her'
>
> must *n.* something not to be missed, such as a play, novel, or exhibit: 'This concert is a must for all Beethoven lovers'
>
> must *v.* to have to, to be obliged: 'You must cross only at the light'; to be determined: 'I must go to that concert'; probable or likely: 'This must be the warmest summer in ten years'

mussel *See* mascle

mustard, mustered

> mustard *n.* a plant; a spicy seasoning made from the mustard plant's seeds: 'He put mustard on his hot dog'
>
> mustered *v.* past tense of muster, to assemble or to gather: 'He mustered 10,000 troops in a fortnight'; to rouse

mute *See* moot

myna *See* mina

mystic, mystique

> mystic *[mist'•ic] n.* a person claiming contact with God or access to basic truths through time spent in contemplation

mystic *adj.* relating to the occult, the mysterious; having hidden symbolism; inducing awe or mystery

mystique *[mis•teek'] n.* a sense of special power; an air of mystery, reverence, or success surrounding a person: 'I never could understand his mystique'

N

nacre, naker
>nacre *n.* the shellfish which yields mother-of-pearl
>naker *n.* a kettledrum

nag *See* knag

nap, nape, nappe *See* knap

natty *See* gnatty

naughty *See* knotty

naval, navel
>naval *adj.* referring to a navy: 'The naval engagements off
>>Guadalcanal were bloody'
>navel *n.* the small mark on the abdomen to which the
>>umbilical cord was attached

nave *See* knave

naw *See* gnaw

nay, née, neigh
>nay *n.* a negative answer or vote: 'As there was one more nay
>>then yea, the bill failed to pass'
>nay *adv.* not merely but also: 'I'd be happy, nay thrilled, to
>>work late with you'
>née *[rhymes w.* bay*] v.* originally or formerly called; used to
>>introduce the family maiden name of a married woman
>>who assumed her husband's name: 'Mrs. John Thomas,
>>née Smith'
>neigh *n.* the cry of a horse
>neigh *v.* to utter such a cry

neat, neath
> neat *adj.* clean, orderly: 'My son never kept his room neat';
> great (slang): 'That song is neat'
> neath *prep.* of beneath: 'Neath the starry skies, I fell in love
> with her'

nebula, nebulae
> nebula *n.* a galaxy; a cloudlike patch in the sky consisting of
> gas or dust; a spot on the cornea causing defective vision
> nebulae *n.* plural of nebula

née *See* nay

need *See* knead

neigh *See* nay

nemesis, nemeses
> nemesis *n.* a person who seeks vengeance or retribution on
> another; a formidable and usually victorious rival: 'That
> pitcher is my nemesis: he always strikes me out'
> nemeses *n.* plural of nemesis

neurosis, neuroses
> neurosis *n.* an emotional disorder manifested by
> unreasonable anxieties, obsessions, fears, and physical
> complaints without presence of disease or physical
> causes
> neuroses *n.* plural of neurosis

new *See* gnu

nibble, nybble
> nibble *n.* a small bite or morsel of food
> nybble *n.* a computer term for a string of binary digits
> consisting of four bytes

nice *See* gneiss

nickers *See* knickers

nicks, nix
> nicks *v.* 3d person, sing., present tense of nick, to cut, dent,
> or scar: 'He nicks himself with his razor every time he
> shaves'
> nix *n.* a water sprite; nothing (slang)

nix *v.* to veto (slang)

niece *See* gneiss

night *See* knight

nit *See* knit

no *See* know

nob *See* knob

nobby *See* knobby

nock *See* knock

nocturn, nocturne

nocturn *n.* a division in the Roman Catholic service of matins

nocturne *n.* a dreamy, pensive musical composition: 'That Chopin nocturne is most romantic'; a painting of a night scene

noes *See* knows

none, None, nun

none *n.* no part: 'I want none of that.'

none *pron.* no one, nobody: 'None were admitted without a ticket'; not any: 'None of my children went to college'

none *adv.* in no way, not at all: 'She was none the worse for wear'

None *n.* the fifth canonical hour in church

nun *n.* a woman belonging to a religious order which accepts vows of poverty, chastity, and obedience

nor *See* gnaw

nose *See* knows

not *See* knot

nozzle, nuzzle

nozzle *n.* the end of a hose through which liquid pours

nuzzle *v.* to rub gently with the nose; to lie close and snug, to nestle

nuke, nuque

nuke *v.* to destroy, using nuclear weapons: 'The general thought that we ought to nuke them back into the stone age'

nuque *n.* the back of the neck

nybble *See* nibble

O

O, oh, owe

O *n.* the 15th letter of the English alphabet

O *interj.* used in direct address: 'O Lord have mercy on us'

oh *interj.* an expression of pain, surprise, or fear: 'Oh! that hurts!'

owe *v.* to be indebted: 'I owe the landlord two months rent'; to be obligated: 'You owe me a favor'

oar *See* aw

oasis, oases

oasis *n.* a fertile spot in a desert; a refuge

oases *n.* plural of oasis

object *See* abject

obsequies, obsequious

obsequies *[abb'•si•kwees] n.* (pl.) funeral rites

obsequious *[ob•see'•kwee•us] adj.* fawning, bootlicking, excessively obedient: 'His obsequious aides offended the other employees'

obstruct *See* abstract

obtuse *See* abstruse

ocher/ochre, okra

ocher *or* ochre *n.* a yellowish color; earth of that color

okra *n.* a vegetable of the mallow family, often used in soups or stews

ode, owed

ode *n.* a lyric poem usually celebrating a hero

owed *v.* past tense of owe, to be indebted

O'er *See* aw

oeuvre, over

oeuvre *[erv'•ruh] n.* an artist's or writer's complete works

over *prep.* above, higher: 'They live over me' 'The moon is rising over those trees'; 'She wore a beautiful coat over her suit'; throughout: 'He showed me all over the town'; during: 'She saw him two times over the past week'; more than: 'The shirt cost over $75.00'

over *adv.* expresses movement from one side to another: 'He moved over from the Democratic party to the Republican party'; downward movement: 'He was knocked over by the car'; remaining: 'We have some food left over'; at an end: 'That awful movie is finally over!'

of, off

of *prep.* used with numbers or to indicate contents: 'three cups of tea'; 'five pairs of socks'; possessing or characteristic: 'a woman of great beauty'; 'the mores of this community'; involved with or belonging to: 'He's a member of this union'; ' "I wouldn't be a member of a club that would have me as a member." ' (Groucho Marx); size or quantity: 'the number of people'; denotes cause: 'He died of pneumonia'

off *prep.* away: 'My son lives off campus'; removed: 'I fell off the chair when I heard the news'; 'You'll be off this treatment soon'; near: 'He lives off the main highway'; inactive or free: 'I'll be off at 5 P.M.'; reduced: 'He was able to get it for 10 percent off the list price'

off *adj.* imperfect, poor, or inferior: 'That meat is off'; unwell: 'I'm a bit off today'; canceled: 'The deal is off'

off *adv.* movement away: 'They drove off'; descending: 'They got off the train'; removing: 'Take off your wet clothes'; stopping or ceasing: 'Turn the light off'

offal *See* aweful

oh *See* O

ohm, om

>   ohm *n.* a unit of electrical resistance

>   om *n.* a mystical word or mantra chanted during meditation
>   and contemplation

okra *See* ocher/ochre

older *See* elder

oldest *See* eldest

oleo, olio

>   oleo *n.* oleomargarine, a butter substitute

>   olio *n.* a miscellany, a hodgepodge, a medley; a spicy stew

ombre, ombré *See* hombre

oncology, ontology

>   oncology *n.* the branch of medical science dealing with
>   tumors

>   ontology *n.* the branch of philosophy dealing with the nature
>   of existence

one, wan, won

>   one *n.* a single thing or person; the number between zero
>   and two

>   one *pron.* anyone or people in general: 'One can do well in
>   that school'

>   wan *adj.* pale, faint: 'After his long illness, he looked wan and
>   haggard'

>   won *v.* past tense of win, to gain a victory

onetime, one time, on time

>   onetime *adj.* former: 'He does not box anymore but he was a
>   onetime champion'

>   one time *n.* just once: 'If you make a serious blunder even
>   one time, you're out'

>   on time *adv.* according to schedule: 'The train arrives at 7
>   P.M.; it is always on time'

onion, union

>   onion *n.* a pungent vegetable; an edible bulb of the lily family

>   union *n.* a joining together: 'The merger created a union of
>   two disparate companies'; a labor organization: 'The
>   garment workers' union'

onto, on to

> onto *prep.* refers to a position on top of something or someone: 'The cat jumped onto the table'; aware of: 'The cops are onto us'
>
> on to *prep.* continuing: 'I'm going on to California after I go to Washington'

ontology *See* oncology

opposition *See* apposition

oppressed *See* appressed

oracle *See* auricle

or *See* aw

oral *See* aural

orator, oratorio

> orator *[or'•i•ter] n.* a competent and powerful public speaker: 'Martin Luther King was a great orator'
>
> oratorio *[aw•ruh•tor'•ee•oh] n.* a lengthy musical piece for chorus and orchestra

orbiter *See* arbiter

order, ordure

> order *n.* a state of peace: 'law and order'; a fixed or definite plan: 'the order of battle'; a religious group: 'an order of nuns'; a command: 'The captain gave us the order to march 30 miles'; an item to be received and paid for: 'a restaurant order'; 'an order for books'; stability: 'We put this place in order and kept it that way'; the nature of society: 'The president talked of a new world order'; rank, class; degree: 'A problem of this order needs a quick solution'
>
> order *v.* to request something: 'I always order steak, not chicken'; to command: 'He should order his secretary to retype the letters'
>
> order *conj.* because: 'I went there in order to see my family'
>
> ordure *n.* filth, excrement, dung

ordinance, ordnance

> ordinance *n.* a law, a decree, or a regulation
>
> ordnance *n.* military arms, supplies, or artillery

ore *See* aw

oriel, oriole

oriel *n.* an upper-story bay window

oriole *n.* a species of bird.

See also areola

oscillate, osculate

oscillate *[ah'•si•late] v.* to swing back and forth physically or conceptually: 'They oscillate between liberalism and conservatism'

osculate *[ahs'•kyoo•late] v.* to kiss

ought *See* aught

our *See* hour

ova, ovum

ova *n.* (pl.) more than one egg

ovum *n.* one egg

over *See* oeuvre

overall, over all, overalls

overall *adj.* including everything, general: 'The overall behavior of the group was good'; from one end to the other: 'The overall length of this room is 20 feet'

over all *adv.* above, superior to: 'He was appointed over all the generals'

overalls *n.* one-piece work clothes covering the chest and lower part of the body

overdo, overdue

overdo *v.* to do something to excess: 'He will overdo the roast if he keeps it in the oven for three hours'; 'Don't overdo it!'

overdue *adj.* not on time: 'The library books were overdue as they were returned three days late'

overlay, overlie

overlay *v.* to spread over or to cover; to superimpose

overlie *v.* to lie on

overseas, oversees

>overseas *adj.* across the sea, often referring to foreign
>countries: 'They tried to build up their overseas sales by
>sending salesmen to Europe'

>overseas *adv.* abroad: 'About 5 million Americans travel
>overseas annually'

>oversees *v.* 3d person, sing., present tense of oversee, to
>supervise, watch over: 'She oversees the job to ensure
>that it is done correctly'

ovoid *See* avoid

ovum *See* ova

owe *See* O

owed *See* ode

owl, aoul, aul

>owl *n.* a nocturnal bird of prey; a person with nocturnal
>habits

>aoul *n.* a gazelle

>aul *[rhymes w.* owl*] n.* a felt tent used in central Asia; a
>settlement in the Caucusus

>*See also* all

oxeyed, oxide

>oxeyed *adj.* very round; having eyes like an ox

>oxide *n.* a combination of oxygen and another chemical

P

pac, PAC, pack, peck

pac *n.* a moccasin boot liner; a waterproof boot; a sheepskin
boot lining

PAC *n.* acronym for Political Action Committee, a group
through which a corporation or union distributes money
to a political candidate

pack *v.* to put items inside a container; to cram a large
amount into a small space: 'She was going to pack the
suitcase till it would not close'; to possess power or
force: 'These missiles pack a heavy load of firepower'; to
ensure success in a group by influencing its composition:
'They will try to pack the meeting just before the
balloting starts'

peck *v.* to make quick, sharp strokes: 'The birds continued to
peck at the food'

paced, paste

paced *v.* past tense of pace, to stride back and forth at a
measured step; to regulate the speed of something: 'She
paced her speech to provide for the greatest impact'

paste *n.* a food or other substance reduced to a smooth,
creamy mass so that it is easily spreadable; artificial gems
made of glass: 'The jewel was just paste, but it looked
real'; an adhesive; 'I put paste on the stamp to make it
stick on the envelope'; a blow (slang): 'I'll paste you in
the mouth if you don't shut up'

See also passed

packed, pact

packed *v.* past tense of pack, to put items into a container

packed *adj.* full of people or things: 'Yankee Stadium was packed with more than 50,000 people'

pact *n.* a solemn agreement or a treaty: 'The two countries agreed to a nonaggression pact'

packs, pax, pox

packs *n.* (pl.) more than one pack

packs *v.* 3d person, sing., present tense of pack, puts or bundles items into a container or package

pax *n.* an embrace of peace during Mass; a period of peace imposed by a dominant nation: 'After the victory in Iraq, the pundits began to talk of Pax Americana'

pox *n.* a disease characterized by pustules on the skin; syphilis

paean, paeon, peon, pion

paean *[pee'•on] n.* a hymn of thanksgiving

paeon *[pee'•on] n.* a special metrical foot of four syllables

peon *n. [pee'•on]* anyone bound in servitude; a member of the landless class; a menial or orderly

pion *[pie'•on] n.*a subatomic particle

pail, pale

pail *n.* a bucket or a container

pale *n.* an enclosure; an area with limits or boundaries

pale *v.* to lose color or importance: 'Their crimes pale into insignificance compared to the other gang's'

pale *adj.* light in color: 'She was pale after I gave her the bad news'; weak: 'That was a pale excuse'

pain, pane

pain *n.* physical or mental suffering or distress; deep unhappiness: 'His departure caused her much pain'; an unpleasant sensation

pane *v.* a section of window glass

pair, pare, pear

> pair *n.* a couple; two matched items: 'a pair of shoes'; a team: 'a pair of horses'; two people or things joined or close together
>
> pare *v.* to remove the outer covering: 'You must pare apples with a sharp knife'
>
> pear *n.* an edible fruit

palate, palette, pallet

> palate *n.* the roof of the mouth
>
> palette *n.* a thin board used by an artist to mix paints
>
> pallet *n.* a bed; a wooden platform used for loading heavy materials

pale *See* pail

pall, pawl

> pall *n.* a cloth used to cover a coffin; an overhanging smoke cloud; any gloomy or depressing atmosphere or mood
>
> pall *v.* to become boring or unpleasant: 'Those three-hour pieces always pall'; to become satiated; to lose strength; to cover with a shroud
>
> pawl *n.* a mechanical device, a special lever attached to a machine to permit movement in only one direction

paltry, poultry

> paltry *adj.* trivial, measly, worthless: 'You expect me to knock myself out for this paltry sum?'
>
> poultry *n.* domestic fowls used for food

pamper, pampre

> pamper *v.* to spoil, to coddle, to treat indulgently
>
> pampre *n.* a vine or grape ornament on buildings

pan, panne

> pan *n.* a container used in cooking; the turning motion of a camera to produce a panoramic effect; a critical comment, often as a review of a movie or play
>
> panne *n.* a type of cloth

pandit, pundit

> pandit *n.* the title of a wise man in India

pundit *n.* a learned person; one who knows a lot about a particular subject and serves as an authority in public commentary: 'That television opinion show tends to use the same pundit each week'

pane *See* pain

pantheon, Parthenon

pantheon *n.* a building in which the famous of a country are entombed; a group of famous people: 'Einstein deserves a special place in the pantheon of scientists'; a building for housing all the gods, especially in Greek mythology

Parthenon *n.* the temple of Athena in Athens, Greece

par, parr

par *n.* a standard: 'His golf game was three above par'; equal standing: 'He's on a par with her as a speaker'; the nominal or face value of stocks or bonds

parr *n.* a young salmon

parade, prayed, preyed

parade *n.* a celebratory or military procession by large groups; a display of objects or beliefs

prayed *v.* past tense of pray, to entreat God or life's fortunes

preyed *v.* past tense of prey, to seize and devour animals; to have an injurious effect on: 'That problem preyed on his mind'

pare *See* pair

parish, perish

parish *n.* a governmental or church administrative unit or area, or the people in that area

perish *v.* to die; to be wiped out, destroyed, or ruined: 'The entire crop will perish without more water'

parity, party

parity *n.* equality: 'The women demanded parity with the men: equal pay for equal work'

party *n.* a social get-together; an organized political group: 'The Republican party threw a gigantic party for the newly elected senators'

parlay, parley

parlay *[pahr'•lay] v.* to bet one's winnings again: 'He let his winnings ride, hoping to parlay them into a fortune'; to gain wealth from a small initial stake: 'He aimed to parlay his small inheritance into a great fortune'

parley *[pahr'•lee] n.* a conference to resolve a war or dispute

parley *v.* to confer, especially with an opponent: 'The commanders of both armies will parley under a flag of truce'

parol, parole, payroll

parol *[par'•il] n.* oral, by word of mouth, used in legal cases as 'parol evidence'

parole *[puh•role'] n.* the conditional release of a prisoner before the sentence is entirely served

payroll *n.* a list of employees to be paid and their salaries; the total amount paid employees: 'My payroll is 10 percent below last year's'

parr *See* par

Parthenon *See* pantheon

participial, participle

participial *adj.* relating to the grammatical form of a participle

participle *n.* a verbal form that functions as an adjective but has characteristics, such as tense and mood, of a verb. (For example, the present participle of *run* is *running*: 'The clock is running'; 'running water.' Examples of a past participle are *write, written*: 'a written contract'; *type, typed*: 'a typed letter.'

partition, petition

partition *n.* an act of dividing; something that separates, such as a wall: 'The desk is behind that partition'

petition *n.* a request, often as a formal written or legal document

party *See* parity

passable, passible

passable *adj.* able to be crossed or passed: 'Despite the rise in the river's level, the road was still passable'; barely satisfactory: 'That restaurant serves passable meals' passible *adj.* capable of feeling or emotion; impressionable

passé, posse

passé *[pass•ay']* *adj.* out of date, old-fashioned

posse *[pah'•see]* *n.* a volunteer group formed to aid law enforcement officers; a street gang (slang)

passed, past

passed *v.* past tense of pass, to go by: 'We passed his house'; to allow entry: 'The maitre d' passed us through the ropes'; to succeed: 'She passed the bar exam'; to be approved: 'Congress passed the farm bill'

past *n.* time gone by; an earlier part of one's life: 'Her past is catching up with her'

past *adj.* pertaining to former times: 'Jimmy Carter is a past president of the United States'

past *prep.* after: 'It's ten past three'; beyond: 'I walked past that shop'; beyond a stage, level, or condition: 'My children are past the crawling stage'

passibility, possibility

passibility *n.* the state of being passible, or able to feel

possibility *n.* the condition of being possible, or having the potential to occur

Passover, pass over

Passover *n.* A Jewish holiday celebrating the exodus from Egypt

pass over *v.* to go by: 'The airplane will pass over New York City at 2 P.M. on its way to Washington'; to fail to consider: 'They will pass over him when it comes to promotion'

paste *See* paced

pastoral, pastorale

pastoral *[pass'•ti•ruhl]* *adj.* pertaining to shepherds or rural life; serene

pastorale *[pass•ti•ral']* *n.* a musical composition based on a pastoral theme

paten, patten, pattern

paten *n.* a metal plate, especially one used to hold the bread of the Eucharist

patten *n.* a wooden shoe or clog

pattern *n*. an organized, regular way of doing things or of behaving: 'Their work pattern was drastically changed by the installation of computers'; a model, sample, or design

pattern *v*. to produce an item using a model; to simulate other forms or another's behavior or personality: 'She wants to pattern her life after Susan B. Anthony'

patent, patient

patent *n*. an official grant of exclusive rights to an inventor

patient *n*. a person receiving medical treatment

patient *adj*. able to wait or to withstand pressure without complaining or becoming annoyed: 'The teacher was very patient with the unruly students'; steadfast despite opposition

pathetic *See* bathetic

pathos *See* bathos

patience, patients

patience *n*. the quality of uncomplaining endurance

patients *n*. (pl.) people receiving medical treatment

patrol, petrel

patrol *n*. the act of moving to secure an area; the person who performs this act; a military unit that checks out a forward area

petrel *n*. a sea bird

paunch, punch

paunch *n*. a fat belly

punch *n*. a drink of fruit juices; a tool used to make holes; power or force: 'That book on the Iran-contra crisis packs a punch'; a blow struck: 'That last punch knocked out his opponent'

pause, paws, pores, pours

pause *v*. to halt temporarily or to rest briefly

paws *n*. (pl.) the feet of certain animals

paws *v*. 3d person, sing., present tense of paw, to draw one's paws over: 'The dog paws the ground'; to embrace or touch clumsily or offensively: 'Every time he sees me he paws me, so I slap him' pores *n.* (pl.) minute openings in the skin

pores *v.* studies closely: 'He pores over his textbooks in preparation for the exam'

pours *v.* 3d person, sing., present tense of pour, to cause a liquid to flow: 'She pours the milk from the container into the glass'; to rain heavily or to flood; to gush or to talk incessantly

pawky, porky

pawky *adj.* shrewd, lively, bold, canny

porky *n.* a porcupine

porky *adj.* fat; piglike

pawl *See* pall

pawn, porn

pawn *n.* a chess piece of low value, and thus, quickly sacrificed; a person who is easily used or manipulated; an item placed as a pledge of repayment with a pawnbroker

porn *n.* pornography

paws *See* pause

pax *See* packs

payroll *See* parol

pea, pee

pea *n.* a small round legume

pee *n.* a passing grade in school; urine (slang)

peace, piece

peace *n.* a state of tranquility or calm; the absence of war or conflict

piece *n.* a portion: 'She gave him a piece of pie'; a coin: 'I used the 50-cent piece that I found on the sidewalk to pay my fare on the bus'; a specific length or quantity: 'Our goods are sold by the piece'; a figure or object used in a board game: 'a chess piece'; one part of a set: 'a piece of furniture'; an example: 'That's a fine piece of sculpture'

piece *v.* to add to or complete: 'I'll piece out the collection by adding this drawing'; to combine facts into a significant pattern

See also peas

peak, peek, peke, pique, piqué

peak *n.* the top of a mountain; the front part of a cap; the
maximum amount or degree; the highest level: 'He is at
the peak of his career'

peek *n.* a glimpse or glance

peke *n.* a Pekinese dog

pique *[peek] n.* displeasure, anger, or resentment: 'After he
insulted her, she left in a fit of pique'

piqué *[pee•kay'] n.* a durable ribbed fabric

peal, peel

peal *n.* a loud series of sounds or notes: 'a peal of thunder'; a
loud ringing of bells

peel *n.* the skin of a fruit

peel *v.* to strip off layers: 'He should peel the apple before
eating it'

pealer, peeler

pealer *n.* one who peals or rings bells

peeler *n.* one who strips off layers; a strip tease dancer (slang)

pear *See* pair

pearl, purl

pearl *n.* a precious gem; any precious item or person

purl *n.* a knitting stitch

peasant, pheasant

peasant *n.* a person who works the land; a person of the
lower class

pheasant *n.* a large game bird

pecan, piquant

pecan *[pi•con'] n.* an oval-shaped nut

piquant *[pee'•cahnt] adj.* interesting and intriguing; having a
pleasantly spicy taste

peck *See* pac

pedal, peddle, petal, piddle

pedal *n.* a lever pressed by the foot to increase or decrease
the speed of a vehicle: 'Go easy on the pedal, you don't
want to crash the car'; a lever pressed by the foot on a
musical instrument

peddle *v.* to travel from place to place selling things: 'He tried to peddle Bibles from door to door'; to attempt to sell things or ideas generally: 'He hoped to peddle his ideas about tax reform'

petal *n.* the colored outer part of a flower

piddle *v.* to waste time: 'Don't piddle around on foolish things'

pedigree, perigee

pedigree *n.* lineage or descent; a distinguished ancestry; an animal's record of pure breeding: 'The dachshund had a registered pedigree'

perigee *n.* an astronomical position, the point at which the moon or other earth satellite is nearest to the earth

pee *See* pea

peek *See* peak

peeking, Pekin

peeking *v.* present participle of peek, to glance: 'The woman was unaware that he was peeking at her'

Pekin *n.* a type of duck; a type of cloth

peel *See* peal

peeler *See* pealer

peepul/pipal, people

peepul *or* pipal *n.* a fig tree

people *n.* a group of persons; human beings; average persons; those who are part of a particular country, race, or region: 'The French people'

peer, pier

peer *n.* an equal in status, age, or ability: 'He has no peer as a speaker'; a noble: 'He's an English peer'

peer *v.* to look carefully at something difficult to discern: 'Just peer closely at this faded manuscript'

pier *n.* a wharf; a structure extending out into the water and used as a landing place or a promenade

See also per

peke *See* peak

pekoe, picot

pekoe *[pee' • koh] n.* a high quality tea made from the
youngest leaves

picot *[pee' • koh] n.* an embroidered loop on lace or ribbon

pelisse, police, polis

pelisse *[puh • lees'] n.* a long fur or a fur-trimmed coat

police *v.* to keep order through the police; to patrol an area;
in the army, to clean up an area

polis *[pol' • is] n.* a Greek city-state; a community

penal, penile

penal *adj.* relating to legal punishment: 'Penal codes are laws
covering crime'; liable to punishment

penile *adj.* relating to the penis: 'He discussed with his
doctor the possibility of a penile implant'

penance, pennants

penance *n.* a church rite which involves confession,
repentance, and absolution; a punishment for one's sins:
'She did penance for her transgressions'

pennants *n.* (pl.) narrow flags used as symbols for military
units, ships, or governments; awards to victors: 'The
Yankees won two pennants'

See also penitence

pencil, pensile

pencil *n.* a writing instrument of graphite

pensile *adj.* hanging, as a pendant

pend, penned, pent

pend *v.* to remain undecided; to await; to hang

penned *v.* past tense of pen, to write: 'He penned a short
word to her'; to keep confined: 'The cattle were penned
in tiny corrals'

pent *adj.* confined or kept in: 'His pent-up feelings exploded
in a tirade against his boss'

pendant, pendent

pendant *n.* a piece of jewelry that hangs on a chain; an
ornament that hangs free

pendent *adj.* undecided, pending; suspended; overhanging

penile *See* penal

penitence, penitents

penitence *n.* the state of being regretful for one's sins

penitents *n.* (pl.) people who regret or repent their sins

peon *See* paean

people *See* peepul/pipal

per, purr

per *prep.* for each: 'She earns ten dollars per hour'; according
to: 'We'll build this per your instructions'

purr *v.* to make soft vibrating sounds: 'Listen to the engine purr'
See also peer

peremptory, preemptory

peremptory *adj.* decisive; precluding debate, admitting no
contradiction: 'A peremptory challenge is a lawyer's
request to unseat a juror without need of a reason';
showing urgency: 'a peremptory call'; haughty

preemptory *adj.* establishing a prior claim or right;
supplanting: 'That network puts on many preemptory
news reports to interrupt my favorite show'; heading off,
forstalling: 'Their preemptory air strike prevented the
enemy from firing its missiles'

perfect, prefect

perfect *[per'•fict] adj.* without blemish or defect, flawless:
'perfect weather'; 'a perfect answer'; 'He's always a
perfect gentleman'; right or appropriate: 'He's perfect for
that job'; a musical interval

perfect *[per'•fict] n.* a verb tense

perfect *[per•fect'] v.* to improve to the point of perfection:
'They will perfect the new computer model in less than a
year'

prefect *[pree'•fect] n.* a government or church official

perfecta, perfector

perfecta *n.* a bet that picks the first and second winner, in
order, in a race

perfector *n.* one who perfects

perform, preform

perform *v.* to do or carry out; to fulfill an obligation: 'This car will perform as promised'; to act in a play, movie, or concert: 'She will perform at this club all month';

preform *v.* to shape or decide in advance: 'They preform their opinions without hearing the other side'

perigee *See* pedigree

perish *See* parish

perquisite, prerequisite

perquisite *n.* a benefit above and beyond one's salary, a perk: 'One of her perquisites is a chauffeured limousine'

prerequisite *n.* a precondition; a condition or act that is necessary before taking the next step or before one can reach a certain level: 'A medical degree is a prerequisite for practicing medicine'

persecute, prosecute

persecute *v.* to oppress; to harass; to maltreat: 'The upperclassmen persecute their underlings'

prosecute *v.* to bring into court; to conduct the government's court action; to pursue to the end: 'They will prosecute the war to final victory'

persona, personal, personnel

persona *[pur•soe'•nuh] n.* one's outward manner or appearance, particularly of public personalities: 'His persona was that of a slick politician'

personal *adj.* refers to an individual, not a group: 'a personal service'; 'a personal opinion'; a private matter; done face to face: 'a personal interview'

personnel *[per•son•ell'] n.* a body of employed persons; persons in the armed forces; an organization's department that deals with its employees

personality, personalty

personality *n.* the distinctive characteristics of a person: 'She has a wonderful personality'; a celebrity: 'That actress is a well-known personality' personalty *n.* personal property in law

perspective, prospective

perspective *n.* in art, the impression of distance, depth, and conflict; point of view; the ability to view things in context or balance

prospective *adj.* anticipated or expected in the future: 'She is a prospective mother'

perspicacious, perspicuous

perspicacious *adj.* shrewd, keen, discerning

perspicuous *adj.* clear, lucid, precise: 'It doesn't take a perspicacious person to understand a perspicuous argument'

pervade, purveyed

pervade *v.* to spread throughout: 'I've seen sloppiness pervade this entire organization'

purveyed *v.* past tense of purvey, to provide food or other items, usually by selling; to provide information: 'TV purveyed the news to him'

perverse, perverts, preserve

perverse *[per•vers'] adj.* corrupt; improper, incorrect; obstinate, wrongheaded: 'He takes a perverse delight in saying no to his mother'

perverts *[per'•verts] n.* (pl.) people who are corrupt or engage in sexual perversion

perverts *v.* 3d person, sing., present tense of pervert, to corrupt or undermine: 'That bill perverts everything our country stands for'; debase; turn from what is morally right

preserve *n.* an area where animals or the land are protected: 'Hunting is forbidden on this wildlife preserve'; a protected type or sector of activity: 'Accounting is her preserve'

preserve *v.* to maintain; to protect; to keep from damage or spoiling: 'Salting food will preserve it'

petal *See* pedal

peter, pita

>peter *v.* to become gradually smaller or diminish: 'The candle will peter out in fifteen minutes'; to become exhausted

>pita *[pee'•tuh] n.* a Middle Eastern flat pocket bread; a fiber-yielding plant

petit, petite, petty

>petit *[petty] adj.* a legal term meaning small or minor: 'a petit jury'

>petite *[puh•teet'] adj.* having a small or tiny figure

>petty *adj.* insignificant; lower level; trifling; narrow-minded; mean; spiteful: 'It's petty of you to quarrel about such a minor purchase'

petition *See* partition

petrel *See* patrol

pharaoh *See* faro

phare *See* fair

phase *See* faze

phat *See* fat

pheasant *See* peasant

phenomenon, phenomena

>phenomenon *n.* any perceived event or process: 'Crime is increasingly an urban phenomenon'; an exceptional person or thing: 'Willie Mays was a baseball phenomenon from the start of his career'

>phenomena *n.* plural of phenomenon

phew *See* few

phial *See* file

philter *See* filter

phlox *See* flocs

phosphene, phosphine

>phosphene *n.* a luminous image produced by exerting pressure on the eyeball

>phosphine *[fos' feen] n.* a poisonous gas; a yellow dye

phosphorous, phosphorus

>phosphorous *adj.* referring to the element phosphorus: 'phosphorous bombs'

phosphorus *n.* a nonmetallic element that shines or glows in
the dark

phrase *See* fraise

phreak *See* freak

physic, physique, psychic

physic *[fi'•zik] n.* the art or practice of medicine; a
medication; a medical purge: 'The doctor prescribed a
physic for constipation'

physique *[fi•zeek'] n.* the body's appearance or form:
'Exercise has given him a fine physique'

psychic *[sy'•kick] adj.* pertaining to the mind; spiritual in
origin; sensitive to supernatural forces; referring to
someone with visionary powers

physical *See* fiscal

pi, pie

pi *n.* a letter in the Greek alphabet; the ratio of a circle's
circumference to its diameter or the number expressing
that ratio

pie *n.* a dessert, a pastry shell with a sweet or savory filling; a
total sum or count that can be divided: 'He wants a
bigger piece of the firm's pie'

pica, pika, piker

pica *[pie'•kuh] n.* a size of typeface; an abnormal appetite for
bizarre nonfood items

pika *[pee'•kuh] n.* a tailless hare

piker *n.* an insignificant bettor; a cheapskate: 'That piker
never picks up a check'

picaresque, picturesque

picaresque *adj.* characteristic of rogues and their adventures: 'He
wrote a picaresque novel about a scoundrel's escapades'

picturesque *adj.* having a striking appearance; charming or
quaint; beautiful; vivid or colorful: 'They spent the day in
a picturesque Mexican village'

picks, pics/pix, pyx

picks *n.* (pl.) heavy tools with pointed ends used to crack or
break things

picks *v.* 3d person, sing., present tense of pick, to choose or
   select; to take; to collect; to clean: 'He picks his teeth'
pics *or* pix *n.* (pl.) motion pictures (slang)
pyx *[picks] n.* a vessel used in church services

picnic, pyknic

picnic *n.* an outdoor outing with food; an easy task: 'That job
   was no picnic'
pyknic *[picnic] n.* a person with a stocky build or with a
   broad girth

picot *See* pekoe

picture, pitcher

picture *n.* a visual representation; a movie; a memory; a
   verbal description; a situation: 'The picture on the island
   looks shaky; trouble is likely soon'
picture *v.* to visualize: 'Picture this room with new furniture
   and drapes'; to describe vividly and colorfully
pitcher *n.* a container with a spout used to hold and pour
   liquids; one who throws the ball to the batter in baseball

picturesque *See* picaresque

piddle *See* pedal

pidgin, pigeon

pidgin *[pigeon] n.* a spoken language that is a simplified
   mixture of two other languages: 'pidgin English'
pigeon *n.* a bird; a potential victim (slang)

pie *See* pi

piece *See* peace

pieced, piste

pieced *v.* past tense of piece, to form or put together: 'We
   pieced together the mystery'
piste *n.* a hard-packed downhill ski course

pier *See* peer

pika, piker *See* pica

pileup, pile up

pileup *n.* a multicar collision

pile up *v.* to amass: 'If the market continues, she will pile up
a fortune'; to cause a ship or other vehicle to crash; to
form a heap or pile: 'She'll pile up all her clothes on the
floor'

Pilipino *See* Filipina

pinion, piñon

pinion *n.* the outer edge of a bird's wings; a gear or shaft
with small teeth: 'This car has rack and pinion steering'

pinion *v.* to clip a bird's wings; to forcibly restrain someone

piñon *n.* a pine tree or its nut

pinnacle, pinochle

pinnacle *[pin'•a•cul] n.* a small turret with a spire; the
highest point of achievement: 'He's at the pinnacle of his
career'

pinochle *[pee'•nok•ul] n.* a card game

pion *See* paean

pipal *See* peepul

piquant *See* pecan

pique, piqué *See* peak

piste *See* pieced

pistil, pistol, pistole

pistil *n.* the part of a plant that produces seeds

pistol *n.* a small handheld firearm

pistole *[pis•toll'] n.* an early Spanish or other European gold
coin

pita *See* peter

pitcher *See* picture

pix *See* picks

pixie, pyxie

pixie *n.* a mischievous sprite; a cute small person or child

pyxie *n.* an evergreen shrub

place, plaice

place *n.* a particular location: 'We lived in that place for many
years'; a relative position: 'I took my place in line'

place *v.* to set, to finish: 'The Yankees often place last in their division'; to appoint; to arrange to publish: 'to place an article on the op-ed page'; to remember: 'I could not place her at first'

plaice *n.* a type of flounder

plaid, played

plaid *[plad] n.* a woolen cloth with a tartan pattern; a pattern of lines crossing at right angles

played *[playd] v.* past tense of play, to have fun, to take part in a game or drama; to perform on an instrument: 'She played the piano'; to compete; to occupy a particular position on a team: 'She played guard in basketball'; to use someone in a sports event: 'The coach played her for only a few minutes'

plain, plane

plain *n.* a prairie; a treeless expanse of land

plain *adj.* simple: 'I prefer plain food'; ordinary; clear; candid: 'plain talk'

plane *n.* an airplane; a flat surface; a tool for smoothing a surface; a tall tree; a level or type of behavior: 'His remarks were always on a low plane'

plane *adj.* flat

plaintiff, plaintive

plaintiff *n.* one who brings charges in court: 'The case of the plaintiff was very strong'; the complaining party

plaintive *adj.* sad, mournful: 'The child sent plaintive cries throughout the house'

plait, plat, plate

plait *n.* a braid of hair, rope, or other material

plat *n.* a town plan or map; a small parcel of ground

plate *n.* an eating utensil, a dish; a metal covering on a machine; an auto license marker: 'a license plate'; utensils made of precious metals: 'Church plate should be protected'; a special book illustration; the home base in baseball plate *v.* to cover with metal, especially silver or gold

plantar, planter

plantar *adj.* pertaining to the sole of the foot: 'plantar warts'

planter *n.* one who plants; a container for plants

plater, platter

plater *[play'•tur] n.* one who applies metal layers; an inferior racehorse

platter *[pla'•tur] n.* a large serving plate

played *See* plaid

play-off, play off

play-off *n.* continued play to resolve a tie in a regular game or match

play off *v.* to set one person or group against another for personal gain: 'The dictator tries to play off the peasants against the small business owners'

plead, pleat

plead *v.* to offer a plea or argue a case in a court; to make a strong emotional request for help or support: 'He will plead for her forgiveness'; to offer an excuse: 'Don't plead ignorance; I'm sure you know who did it'

pleat *n.* the sharp fold made by doubling cloth

pleas, please

pleas *n.* (pl.) appeals: 'Her pleas for help went unanswered'

please *v.* to give pleasure; to do as one wishes: 'I'll do anything that you please'

please *adv.* a polite request: 'Please come with me'; polite acceptance: 'Yes, I'll take three, please'

pledger, pledgor

pledger *n.* one who makes a pledge or a solemn promise or commitment to carry out an action; one who agrees to deliver or accept goods

pledgor *n.* the legal term for a pledger in a business transaction only; one who provides personal property as a guarantee in a deal, as opposed to other types of commitment

pleural, plural

> pleural *adj.* pertaining to the membranes that cover the lungs
>
> plural *adj.* relating to more than one; relating to the grammar form that denotes more than one

plié, ply

> plié *[plee•ay']* *n.* a ballet movement where the knees are bent
>
> ply *v.* to work diligently; to carry on a trade or occupation

pliers, plyers

> pliers *n.* a tool used to grasp an object or bend a wire
>
> plyers *n.* (pl.) people who work diligently or carry on a trade

plots, plotz

> plots *n.* (pl.) small pieces of earth: 'burial plots'; conspiracies: 'The CIA engaged in successful plots to overthrow regimes'; the essence of a play or novel; 'Her twisting plots were always hard to follow'
>
> plots *v.* 3d person, sing., present tense of plot, to mark one's course on a plane or ship; to conspire; to make a plan; to develop the organization of a play or book
>
> plotz *v.* to be overcome with emotion; to burst or collapse from exhaustion, excitement, or surprise (slang)

plum, plumb, plume

> plum *n.* a fruit
>
> plumb *n.* a lead weight at the end of a line used in checking the water's depth
>
> plumb *v.* to get to the bottom of a problem or matter: 'That story told how she started to plumb the depths of her emotions in order to recover'
>
> plumb *adv.* very: 'You're plumb crazy to say that'
>
> plume *[rhymes w.* doom*]* *n.* an ornamental feather

plural *See* pleural

pogrom, program

> pogrom *n.* an organized looting or massacre, especially of Jews

program *n.* a schedule; a list of items: 'The program
contained several calypso songs'; a computer's set of
instructions; a curriculum; a performance aired on TV or
radio

program *v.* to plan a program; to put data into a computer

point, pointe, pointy

point *n.* a tip, a tiny dot; a fact or idea cited in a discussion;
the main idea: 'My point is that we have to cut costs'; a
particular location: 'Turn to the right at that point'

point *v.* to aim; to direct or show, particularly with one's
finger or with a sign: 'I'll point you in the direction of
London'

pointe *[pwant] n.* a ballet position on the tip of the toe

pointy *adj.* coming to a sharp tip

poise, pose

poise *n.* a self-possessed manner; grace; a way of carrying
oneself: 'She has the poise of a much older woman'

pose *n.* a stance or look assumed for a photograph or
painting; an affectation

pose *v.* to adopt that stance or look; to pretend; to ask (pose)
a question; to put forth or to cause: 'His actions pose a
threat to their marriage'

polar, poler, poller

polar *adj.* pertaining to the north or south poles: 'The polar
ice is melting'; relating to a magnetic pole; diametrically
opposed: 'polar opposites'

poler *n.* one who poles or propels a boat with a long pole

poller *n.* one who conducts opinion surveys; one who
canvasses; one who records votes

pole, poll, pol

pole *n.* the extremity of an axis, such as the north or south
pole; a long cylindrical piece used to push or pull; the
inside position in a race; the positive or negative part of
a battery; either of two opposites: 'You're at the opposite
pole from me on the issue of abortion'

poll *n.* a survey of people's opinions or preferences; the nape of the neck; the casting or recording of votes; the place where votes are cast

pol *[pahl] n.* a politician (slang)

police *See* pelisse

policy, polity

policy *n.* a written contract: 'an insurance policy'; a course or plan of action: 'It is the policy of the government to provide a safety net for everyone'

polity *n.* a form of political organization; the form of government of a nation, church, state, etc.

polis *See* pelisse

pommel, pummel

pommel *n.* a knob on a saddle; the hilt of a sword

pummel *v.* to beat, to hit, or to pound

pomp, pump

pomp *n.* a show of magnificence, splendor; a ceremonial or festive display; an ostentatious act

pump *n.* a device that pushes air, liquid, or other substances into or out of an object: 'a tire pump'; 'a gasoline pump'; a low cut shoe that grips the foot at the toe and heel without ties

pump *v.* to force a substance through a conductor; to pressure or question someone in order to obtain information; to move up and down vigorously: 'The heart must pump continuously'; to put or infuse money or energy into a project or activity: 'He was asked to pump a million dollars into that company to keep it alive'

pom-pom, pompon/pom-pom

pom-pom *n.* an anti-aircraft gun

pompon *or* pom-pom *n.* a flower, such as a chrysanthemum, with small, closely packed petals; decorations like small floral balls used on hats, shoes, or wrists: 'Each cheer leader wore a giant pompon at the homecoming game'

pooch, putsch

> pooch *n.* a dog: 'They will never let that pooch into the
> Westminster show'
>
> putsch *n.* a suddenly executed plan to overthrow a
> government

poodle, puddle

> poodle *n.* a curly-haired dog
>
> puddle *n.* a small pool of water, left after a rain or a shower

pool, pull

> pool *n.* an enclosed body of water used for swimming; a
> small pond; a group sports bet: 'a football or baseball
> pool'; a game played on a billiards table; a joint
> investment fund; an available supply; an illegal business
> combine; a shared facility: 'a car pool'
>
> pool *v.* to combine resources: 'They will pool their money to
> buy the store'
>
> pull *n.* influence: 'I have pull with my Congress member'; the
> act of drawing something or someone toward you; heavy
> effort: 'The long pull up the mountain'; a device used to
> draw something: 'a drawer pull'
>
> pull *v.* to remove something from the skin: 'Pull out that
> splinter'; to draw something toward you with force; to
> injure oneself due to straining: 'to pull a muscle'; to hold
> back: 'He'll pull the horse so that another horse will
> win'; to commit a crime: 'They tried to pull off a
> robbery'; to take out a weapon: 'Watch out, he's going to
> pull a knife'; to support: 'I'll pull for the Cubs to win the
> pennant'

poor, pore, pour

> poor *adj.* having little means of support; lacking resources for
> reasonably comfortable living; low quality: 'They did a
> poor repair job on my car'; incompetent: 'He's a poor
> manager'; inadequate or meager: 'The meeting had poor
> attendance'
>
> pore *n.* a small opening in the skin or in a membrane

POP, POPE

pore *v.* to look at or study intently: 'He can pore over his
texts for hours'
pour *v.* to cause to flow: 'I'll pour you a glass of milk'; to talk
incessantly: 'He'll pour forth his complaints about his
new job'
See also pure

pop, pope

pop *v.* to hit: 'Pop him in the mouth'; to create an explosion;
to burst open: 'The corn will soon pop'; to shoot drugs
(slang); to shoot someone with a gun; to enter or leave
suddenly: 'I'll just pop in for a few minutes'; to protrude:
'News of their divorce made my eyes pop'
pop *adj.* popular: 'pop music'; 'pop art'
pope *n.* the head of the Roman Catholic Church

poplar, popular

poplar *n.* a kind of tree
popular *adj.* well liked, widely held: 'popular beliefs'; easily
understood: 'a popular book on astronomy'

popped, poppet, puppet

popped *v.* past tense of pop, to hit or burst open; cooked
popcorn; took drugs; entered suddenly
poppet *n.* a valve used in machines that rises perpendicularly;
a wooden brace used in ships; an affectionate term for a
young child, akin to moppet (British usage)
puppet *n.* a type of doll or figure that fits over the hand and
is moved and manipulated for entertainment; a group or
person under another's control or influence

populace, populist, populous

populace *n.* the common people, the masses
populist *n.* a politician claiming to represent the 'common
people'
populous *adj.* thickly settled, crowded, having many people:
'That area has become less populous due to
environmental hazards'

pore *See* poor

pores *See* pause

porky *See* pawky

porn *See* pawn

porpoise, propose, purpose

porpoise *n.* an aquatic mammal, a kind of whale or dolphin

propose *v.* to suggest or to offer a plan: 'We propose to resolve this dispute peacefully'; to nominate someone for membership or for an office; to make an offer of marriage

purpose *n.* an aim; a plan; determination: 'Our purpose was to win all the games'

portend, pretend

portend *v.* to bode or foreshadow: 'The hot weather may portend a major drought'

pretend *v.* to feign: 'He'll pretend to be angry, but he really isn't'; to display a false image; to lay claim: 'He'll pretend to the throne'

portent, potent

portent *n.* an omen

potent *adj.* powerful, effective: 'That's a potent anticancer drug'

portion, potion

portion *n.* a part of a whole; a food serving; a share; one's destiny: 'Their portion was ever to remain.poor'

potion *n.* a mixture of liquids; a medicine; a mixed drink

pose *See* poise

poser, poseur

poser *n.* a puzzle; one who asks questions or puts problems; one who poses

poseur *[poe•zer']* *n.* one who puts on airs or acts for effect

posse *See* passé

possibility *See* passibility

postulant, postulate

postulant *n.* a candidate for a religious order

postulate *v.* in philosophy or mathematics, to take a claim or idea as true or fact, or as a necessary condition

poultry *See* paltry

pour *See* poor

pours *See* pause

pox *See* packs

praise, prase, prays, preys

praise *v.* to comment favorably or commend; to glorify: 'Praise God'

prase *n.* a light green variety of quartz

prays *v.* 3d person, sing., present tense of pray, to entreat; to address God humbly

preys *v.* 3d person, sing., present tense of prey, to raid; to make someone a victim

pray, prey

pray *v.* to address a deity; to make an earnest request

prey *n.* a victim; an animal taken as food

prey *v.* to make a victim: 'Drug dealers prey on the community'; to raid: 'Pirates still prey on shipping in the Indian Ocean'; to be disturbing: 'His remarks still prey on my mind'

prayed *See* parade

prayer, preyer

prayer *[pray•er] n.* one who prays or offers such a plea

prayer *[prair] n.* a plea to a deity

preyer *[pray•er] n.* one who preys or victimizes

precede, proceed

precede *v.* to go before in rank, time, place, or quality: 'Age should precede beauty'

proceed *v.* to advance or to continue: 'We will proceed with the plan'

precedence, precedents, presidents

precedence *n.* order or priority in a formal or ceremonial setting: 'The precedence at this meeting is that the chair speaks first' precedents *n.* earlier acts used as guides or examples; legal decisions that are used as rules in deciding similar cases: 'The lower court judge based his decision on the precedents of the Supreme Court'

presidents *n.* (pl.) heads of republics, corporations, or organizations

precedential, presidential

precedential *adj.* serving as a precedent

presidential *adj.* having the qualities of or relating to a president

précis, precise

précis *[rhymes w. lacy] n.* a concise summary of essential points of a book or document

precise *adj.* strictly accurate: 'He gave a precise account of the accident to the police'; exact or rigid: 'Everyone must observe precise dress codes'

precisian, precision

precisian *n.* one who adheres strictly to the standards of a religion or moral code; a puritan

precision *n.* the quality of being strictly accurate: 'She sawed the board with precision'

predication, prediction

predication *n.* an affirmation, assertion, or declaration; a grammatical statement using a predicate, which tells about the subject of a sentence

prediction *n.* a prophecy or a forecast: 'His prediction of victory came true'

preemptory *See* peremptory

prefect *See* perfect

prefer, proffer

prefer *v.* to value more, to like better: 'I prefer my meat rare'; to put forth a legal claim: 'To prefer charges'; to give priority to someone or something

proffer *v.* to offer

preform *See* perform

premier, premiere

premier *[pri•meer']* *n.* a prime minister

premier *adj.* the first or the most important: 'She's the premier actress of her time'

premiere *[pri•meer']* *n.* the first public showing of a theatrical, musical, or artistic work

preposition, proposition

preposition *n.* a word that combines with a noun or pronoun to form an adverbial or adjectival phrase. Examples of such words are: by, for, into, on, since, with, in, and to

proposition *n.* a proposal, a statement: 'Let's consider the proposition that Columbus did not discover America'; a formal statement in philosophy or mathematics to be proved or disproved; a request for sexual relations

prerequisite *See* perquisite

prescribe, proscribe

prescribe *v.* to dictate; to order: 'The doctor will prescribe an exercise regimen for her patient'

proscribe *v.* to prohibit: 'The new regime aims to proscribe any public criticism of its leaders'; to denounce; to banish; to condemn

presence, presents, prescience

presence *n.* being in a particular place: 'He explained that his presence was due to his receiving a subpoena'; manner or bearing: 'She has great physical presence'; economic or military power: 'The U.S. presence in Europe'

presents *[preh'•zints]* *n.* (pl.) gifts: 'Santa Claus brought presents for all the children'

presents *[pree•zents']* *v.* 3d person, sing., present tense of present, to make a gift; to afford; to allow: 'This action presents the possibility of saving the company'; to exhibit: 'This theater presents a new play in May'; to offer or produce: 'Now, when it's too late, she presents her plan for dealing with this crisis'; to introduce: 'May I present my niece?'

prescience *[pree'•she•ins] n.* foresight; the ability to predict
presentiment, presentment
>   presentiment *n.* a foreboding, a sense that something bad is
>   going to occur
>   presentment *n.* the act or state of presenting or showing; a
>   representation; the act of providing a note or bill as in a
>   financial settlement; the act of providing a formal legal
>   statement: 'The grand jury delivered its presentment to
>   the judge'

preserve *See* perverse
presidential *See* precedential
presidents *See* precedence
pressed, prest
>   pressed *v.* past tense of press, to apply force; to squeeze; to
>   urge: 'They pressed him for payment'; to smooth or
>   flatten: 'The cleaner pressed the clothes'
>   prest *n.* an advance or loan of money

pretend *See* portend
prey *See* pray
preyed *See* parade
preyer *See* prayer
preys *See* praise
pride, pried
>   pride *n.* self-respect; excessive self-esteem, conceit, or
>   arrogance; satisfaction with an achievement: 'We take
>   great pride in our clean streets'; the best of a group: 'The
>   pride of this year's graduating class'; a group of lions
>   pried *v.* past tense of pry, to look carefully or slyly; to probe
>   someone's private concerns inappropriately; to open
>   something using leverage: 'The police pried open the
>   window'; to get something, such as information, with
>   great difficulty

prier, prior
>   prier *n.* a snoop; one who pries, or opens with force
>   prior *n.* a church official

prior *adj.* previous; preceding in time or in order: 'He had a prior claim on the proceeds of the sale'

pries, prize

pries *v.* present tense of pry, to be overly inquisitive: 'He pries into everyone's affairs'; to use leverage to open or separate someone or something

prize *n.* an award; something that is won; anything of great value; an enemy ship captured in a war

prize *v.* to value highly: 'I prize all my children equally'

prima, primo

prima *[pree'•muh] adj.* first or principal (used for women): 'She's the prima ballerina of the Bolshoi ballet'

primo *[pree'•mo] adj.* first or principal (used for men)

primo *adv.* in the first place

primer, primmer

primer *[pry'•mer] n.* a device used to detonate explosives; a material used to prepare a surface for painting

primer *[rhymes w.* dimmer] *n.* a basic level textbook

primmer *[rhymes w.* dimmer] *adj.* more formal; more uptight or prudish

prince, prints

prince *n.* a male member of a royal family; the son of the king; a ruler of a principality

prints *n.* (pl.) printed impressions; art reproductions

prints *v.* 3d person, sing., present tense of print, to produce a newspaper or magazine; to make printed impressions; to write letters similar to print: 'I will read his handwriting if he prints'; to produce computer data; to fingerprint

principal, principle

principal *n.* a person in charge of a school; the main part of a loan (as opposed to the interest); any head or key person in an organization; the main part of a financial estate

principal *adj.* first in importance, chief: 'His principal interest in life was to make money' principle *n.* a high level or code of conduct: 'He was an unusual politician, a man of high moral principle'; basic belief or idea: 'A cardinal Christian principle'; a basic conceptual law: 'The principle of one person one vote'; the mode of organization or operation of an entity: 'This nation operates on the principle of participatory democracy'

prize *See* pries

proceed *See* precede

prodigal, prodigy, protégé

prodigal *[prod'•i•gul] adj.* wastefully extravagant: 'His prodigal spending ruined them'; profuse or abundant

prodigy *[prod'•i•gee] n.* a gifted or highly talented child; an extraordinary deed

protégé *[pro'•tuh•zhay] n.* a person whose career proceeds under the guidance of another, usually older, person of prominence

proffer *See* prefer

profit, prophet, Prophet

profit *n.* an advantage or gain; any monetary gain from invested capital, such as the amount received minus cost

prophet *n.* one who foretells the future; an Old Testament figure; one gifted with spiritual insight

Prophet (the) *n.* Muhammad, the founder of Islam

program *See* pogrom

prophecy, prophesy

prophecy *[prof'•ah•see] n.* a prediction; a divine revelation

prophesy *[prof•e•sigh'] v.* to predict; to speak with divine inspiration

propose *See* porpoise

proposition *See* preposition

pros, prose

pros *n.* (pl.) short for professionals

prose *n.* ordinary discursive writing, in contrast to poetry; dull expression

proscribe *See* prescribe

prosecute *See* persecute

prospective *See* perspective

prostate, prostrate

prostate *n.* a gland that secretes reproductive fluids in males

prostrate *v.* to throw oneself on the ground in submission; to reduce to helplessness

protean, protein

protean *[proh'•tee•in] adj.* changeable or able to assume diverse forms or roles: 'All the Barrymores were protean actors'; versatile

protein *[proh'•teen] n.* an organic compound essential to all life forms

protégé *See* prodigal

Psalter, salter, psaltry

Psalter *[sawl'•ter] n.* a biblical book of Psalms

salter *n.* one who applies salt to cure fish or meat

psaltry *n.* an ancient musical instrument

psora, sora

psora *[sore'•uh] n.* scabies; an itchy skin disease; psoriasis

sora *n.* a marsh bird

psychic *See* physic

psychosis, psychoses, sycosis

psychosis *n.* a serious mental illness characterized by loss of contact with reality

psychoses *n.* plural of psychosis

sycosis *n.* an inflammation of the hair follicles

ptarmic, tarmac

ptarmic *[tar'•mik] n.* a substance, such as a gas, that causes sneezing

tarmac *n.* a road surface made of broken stones and tar

pubic, public

pubic *adj.* pertaining to the front arch of the pelvis

public *n.* the populace; the overall community; a particular audience: 'the moviegoing public'

public *adj.* belonging or relating to the people: 'a public official'; 'a public hearing'; generally known: 'His crime became public'

puddle *See* poodle

puffin, puffing

puffin *n.* a seabird with a brightly colored bill

puffing *v.* present participle of puff, to blow out repeatedly: 'He was puffing as he ran up the stairs'

puisne, puny

puisne *[puny] adj.* younger; of junior or inferior rank

puny *adj.* unimportant; weak; of feeble development: 'He is a puny little runt'

pull *See* pool

pullover, pull over

pullover *n.* a sweater pulled over the head

pull over *v.* to move to the side and stop, said of a vehicle

pummel *See* pommel

pump *See* pomp

punch *See* paunch

pundit *See* pandit

pupal, pupil

pupal *adj.* relating to the development of an insect larva

pupil *n.* a student; a part of the eye that is the black circle in the middle of the colored iris

puppet *See* popped

pure, puree

pure *adj.* not mixed with anything; unmixed ancestry: 'a pure breed dog'; sheer: 'to play for pure fun or joy'; innocent, stainless, untainted: 'pure in heart'

puree *[pyoo•ray'] n.* a thick pulp of strained food such as vegetables

purl *See* pearl

purpose *See* porpoise

purr *See* per

purveyed *See* pervade

push-up, push up

push-up *n.* a strengthening exercise performed by using the arms to raise and lower the prone body

push up *v.* to raise something with upward force: 'He should push up the window to get fresh air'

put, putt

put *n.* a special hand toss, as in track and field events; an option to sell stock at a later date at a fixed price

put *v.* to place: 'I put the plate and saucer on the table'; to express or state: 'It's hard to put my feelings into words'; to classify: 'I would put Ravel in a class with Tschaikovsky'; to use or apply something: 'I couldn't put pen to paper for weeks'

putt *[rhymes w. but] n.* a short golf stroke made near the hole

put-on, put on

put-on *n.* a joke or a hoax

put on *v.* to clothe oneself; to present or show: 'Our school put on *Macbeth* this year'

putout, put out

putout *n.* an out by a defensive player in baseball

put out *v.* to extinguish: 'She put out the fire'; to place: 'He put out the cat for the night'

putsch *See* pooch

put-up, put up

put-up *adj.* prearranged in order to deceive: 'That was not a real fight he won; it was a put-up job'

put up *v.* to erect; to fasten to a wall; to allow: 'They put up with his atrocious behavior for years'; to provide capital; to deliver or produce: 'Put up or shut up'

pyknic *See* picnic

pyric, pyrrhic, Pyrrhic

pyric *[pie'•rik] adj.* caused by burning

pyrrhic *[pir'•ick] n.* in poetry, a meter of two unaccented syllables

Pyrrhic *adj.* pertaining to or similar to the Greek king Pyrrhus, who won a battle at great cost: 'a Pyrrhic victory'

pyx *See* picks

pyxie *See* pixie

Q

quack, couac

quack *n.* a charlatan; the cry of a duck

couac *[kwack] n.* a strident tone produced by a slightly defective reed instrument

quail, quale

quail *n.* a game bird

quail *v.* to display fear or to flinch: 'He will quail at the prospect of arguing with the boss'

quale *n.* in philosophy, an abstract quality experienced as an independent essence from a thing, e.g., blackness, softness

quark, quirk

quark *n.* a hypothetical particle of matter

quirk *n.* odd behavior or an idiosyncrasy; an accident: 'a quirk of fate'

quarts, quartz

quarts *n.* (pl.) vessels or measurements of liquids with a specific volume

quartz *n.* a mineral that appears as a clear crystal

quay *See* key

quean, queen

quean *[queen] n.* a brazen woman; a prostitute

queen *n.* a female monarch; the wife of a king

queerest, querist

queerest *adj.* superlative of queer, the most unnatural; strangest, or oddest querist *[kwi'•uh•rist] n.* one who questions or inquires

queue *See* cue

quiet, quit, quite

quiet *adj.* making little noise; still; peaceable or calm

quit *v.* to stop or leave: 'He quit his job after the first day'

quit *adj.* free, released from obligation: 'By signing this, I am quit of all further responsibility'

quite *adv.* completely; to a great extent: 'I'm quite sure he's quite young'

quire *See* choir

quirk *See* quark

quitter, quittor

quitter *n.* one who gives up too readily, a defeatist: 'They dropped him from the team because he's a quitter'

quittor *n.* a serious foot inflammation in horses or similar animals

quoin *See* coign

quota, quote

quota *n.* a share or proportion required of or due an entity or person: 'They set a quota for each contributor'; a share or number permitted to enter or participate: 'The law sets a quota on the number of immigrants from each country'

quote *n.* a quotation, a repetition of exact words; the price of a stock or bond

R

Ra *See* ray

rabbet, rabbit, rabid, rarebit, Rabat

rabbet *n.* a groove in a piece of wood

rabbit *n.* a small long-eared animal with long hind legs

rabid *adj.* infected with rabies; mad or fanatic: 'She is a knee-jerk liberal and he is a rabid conservative'

rarebit *[rare'•bit] n.* a dish of seasoned melted cheese over toast, also known as Welsh rabbit

Rabat *n.* one of the four capitals of Morocco

rabbi, rabi, rebbe

rabbi *[ra'•bye] n.* a Jewish religious leader; the title of the official leader of a Jewish congregation

rabi *n.* the spring grain harvest in Pakistan and India

rebbe *[reb'•uh] n.* a title of respect for a leader of any of a number of Jewish sects; a teacher in a Hebrew school

rabble, rebel

rabble *n.* a mob; the lower class

rebel *[reb'•uhl] n.* one who fights authority or flouts convention; a Confederate soldier in the Civil War

rebel *[ree•bell'] v.* to oppose authority; to show contempt or dislike; to engage in armed revolt

rack, wrack

rack *n.* a shelf for luggage; a framework to hold objects: 'He took a bottle from his wine rack'; a torture device; a triangular ball holder in billiards; a state of intense pain or suffering; a rod with teeth: 'They bought a car with rack and pinion steering'

rack *v.* to cause agony or pain; to strain: 'He tried to rack his brains for an answer and couldn't find one'; to store or accumulate (slang): 'He tries to rack up credits with his boss'

wrack *n.* seaweed on the shore

racked, racket, racquet/racket

racked *v.* past participle of rack, to cause agony: 'The nation is racked by unemployment.'

racket *n.* a commotion: 'What's all that racket?'; a fraudulent scheme: 'Their racket was selling plots of land in swamps'; an occupation (slang): 'What's his racket?'

racquet *or* racket *n.* a bat with netting set in an oval frame used in playing tennis, squash, and badminton

radical, radicle

radical *adj.* extreme: 'Although she was thought to be quite conservative, she held radical views on the question of women's rights'; basic or fundamental; pertaining to extreme changes

radicle *n.* a small plant root

raggee/ragi, reggae

raggee *or* ragi *[rag'•ee] n.* a cereal grain

reggae *[reg'•ay] n.* a style of Jamaican music

raid, rayed

raid *n.* a sudden surprise attack or visit: 'The police conducted a raid on the suspected drug base'; a competitive business move to lure another's employees or influence stock prices

rayed *v.* past tense of ray, to emit rays, or to treat with X rays

raider, rater, ratter

raider *n.* a person, aircraft, ship, or business that makes a surprise attack

rater *n.* one who sets standards or values: 'The rater evaluated all the candidates before announcing her choice for the job' ratter *n*. an animal that catches rats: 'That terrier is an excellent ratter'

rail, rale

rail *n*. a bar of wood or metal used as a support or barrier: 'Hold on to the rail as you go down the the stairs to the railroad track'; the steel track used by trains; transportation by railroad; a short-winged bird

rail *v*. to complain: 'He would rail against fate'; to enclose with a rail

rale *n*. a sound heard at times in labored respiration

rain, reign, rein

rain *n*. condensed water drops; a downpour or shower; a series of unpleasant happenings or blows: 'a rain of losses'

rain *v*. to shower, to fall like rain: 'I'm watching her tears rain from her face'; to abundantly bestow: 'He promised to rain jewelry and money on her'

reign *n*. sovereignty or dominion: 'The reign of Queen Elizabeth II has lasted more than forty years'; the time such sovereignty lasts

rein *v*. to check or restrain: 'He was so wild they had to rein him in'

raise, rays, raze

raise *v*. to lift; to increase; to bring up: 'raise children'; to incite; to erect; to sound or utter: 'raise an alarm'; to cultivate; to collect: 'raise an army'

rays *n*. (pl.) more than one light beam

raze *v*. to level to the ground, to demolish: 'When will they raze that empty building?'

raiser, razer, razor

raiser *n*. one who increases: 'She is the principal raiser in their poker game'

razer *n*. one who razes, one who demolishes

razor *n*. an instrument to shave or cut hair

raisin, raising

raisin *n*. a sweet dried grape

raising *v.* present participle of raise, to increase: 'It seems that they are raising their prices almost daily'

rajah, roger

rajah *n.* a Hindu ruler

roger *interj.* OK, all right!: 'Roger and out'

rale *See* rail

ranch, raunch

ranch *n.* a farm for raising horses, cattle, or sheep

raunch *n.* slovenly or obscene speech or objects; vulgarity

rancor, ranker

rancor *n.* malice; bitter enmity; resentment: 'He felt considerable rancor toward the firm that fired him'

ranker *n.* a person who decides on the order or position of others, one who ranks

rap, wrap

rap *n.* a chat: 'Let's rap'; a sharp blow; a tap; blame: 'He took the rap for my error'; a type of music characterized by sharp rhythms and rhymes

rap *v.* to tap or to strike a series of times or blows; to talk things over; to criticize

wrap *n.* a cloak or coat; a wrapping or covering

wrap *v.* to cover or protect; to package: 'Please wrap these items in biodegradable paper'; to obscure; to complete: 'We're about to wrap up the job'

rapped, rapt, wrapped

rapped *v.* past tense of rap, to tap; to talk

rapt *adj.* intent, absorbed, or engrossed: 'They listened to the symphony with rapt attention'

wrapped *v.* past tense of wrap, to cover up; to complete

rappel, repeal, repel

rappel *[ruh•pehl']* *v.* to descend a mountain using a technique that involves wrapping one's rope in a special way around the body

repeal *[ri•peel']* *v.* to revoke: 'This act would repeal the right of free speech'; to renounce

repel *[ri•pehl']* *v.* to drive back: 'We must repel their attacks';
to reject; to upset someone: 'He'll repel you with his
constant sexist remarks'

rapper, wrapper

rapper *n.* a person who talks in rhyme and rhythm in popular
vocal groups

wrapper *n.* a person or thing that wraps or encloses: 'In a
plain brown wrapper'

rarebit *See* rabbet

rasse, wrasse

rasse *n.* a small civet or mammal

wrasse *n.* a brightly colored fish

rater *See* raider

rath, wraith, wrath

rath *n.* a prehistoric hill fort; a cave temple in India

wraith *n.* a specter; a thin and pale person

wrath *n.* anger: 'the wrath of God'

rational, rationale

rational *[rash'•un•uhl]* *adj.* sane; capable of reasoning: 'He
usually makes very rational decisions based on facts';
mathematical properties: 'rational numbers.'

rationale *[rash•un•al']* *n.* the basic reason or explanation for
something: 'The rationale for the cutbacks was the
decline in revenue'

ratter *See* raider

raucous, ruckus

raucous *adj.* unpleasantly loud: 'That was a raucous party'

ruckus *n.* a fight: 'Crowds that get raucous frequently engage
in a ruckus'

raunch *See* ranch

ravage, ravish

ravage *v.* to plunder, destroy, or damage severely

ravish *v.* to rape: 'Pirates were said to ravish prisoners'; to
seize by force; to overcome with delight: 'She'll ravish
him with her beauty'

ravel, reveal, revel

ravel *n.* a tangle; a complication; a loose thread

reveal *v.* to disclose; to display; to uncover: 'He will finally reveal his true feelings about me when I confront him'

revel *v.* to enjoy or to delight in: 'He'll often revel in gossip about his fellow workers'

ray, re, Ra/Re

ray *n.* a light beam

re *[ray] n.* the second note in the musical scale

re *[ree] prep.* with regard to, à propos: 'In re: your letter of the 15th'

Ra/Re *[ray] n.* the Egyptian sun god

rayed *See* raid

rays, raze *See* raise

razer, razor *See* raiser

read, reed

read *[rhymes w. need] v.* to look at a written source and understand it: 'read a book' 'read a foreign language'; to recite something written: 'read a story to a child'; to understand someone or something: 'I read you'; to register: 'The thermometers read over 90 degrees'; to obtain and store computer data

reed *n.* a tall grass growing in wet areas; a musical wind instrument; a part of a musical instrument set on the mouth and caused to vibrate

read, red

read *[red] v.* past tense of read, to look at a written source

red *n.* a primary color resembling blood; a political leftist; a 'downer' pill (slang)

real, reel

real *adj.* true, actual, not imaginary: 'He was in real pain after being shot'; genuine: 'real diamonds'; in law, fixed property such as land or buildings: 'real property'; utter: 'She's a real brain' reel *v.* to wind on a reel or to pull in something with a reel: 'He'll reel in the trout'; to walk unsteadily; to turn in circles

reality, realty

reality *[ree•al'•i•tee] n.* what is real or genuine, or that which exists: 'Stop being a baby and face reality'

realty *[ree'•il•tee] n.* real estate: 'I consulted a broker who handles realty'

realize, relies

realize *[ree'•i•lize] v.* to understand: 'I realize that we can't afford to take that trip'; to gain: 'She will realize a substantial profit on the deal'; to achieve: 'By working hard we'll realize our hopes for a house'; to fulfill: 'He'll soon realize his potential as an artist'

relies *[ri•lize'] v.* 3d person, sing., present tense of rely, to trust or to depend on: 'She relies on his help in this crisis'

realtor, relater, relator

realtor *n.* one who is authorized by the National Association of Realtors to be in the business of real estate

relater *n.* a narrator, one who tells a story

relator *n.* one who institutes a specialized legal proceeding; a narrator

rebait, rebate

rebait *v.* to put bait on again when fishing

rebate *v.* to reduce a price; to give a partial refund

rebbe *See* rabbi

rebel *See* rabble

rebound, redound

rebound *v.* to regain a normal or former state: 'It is hoped that his health will rebound now that he is under the care of a new doctor'; to bounce back from a hard surface; to recover a ball off the backboard in basketball

redound *v.* to affect poorly or well; to reflect upon a person's status: 'The size of his contribution will redound to his credit'

recite, re-cite
recite *v.* to relate; to declaim; to give answers to a teacher; to provide details; 'She'll soon recite her usual list of grievances'; to repeat from memory

re-cite *v.* to mention or refer to again

reck, wreck
reck *v.* to take care; to pay attention: 'We were too preoccupied to reck the dangers on the road'

wreck *n.* the remains of something ruined; a person who is exhausted, unhappy, or destroyed: 'After that hearing I'm a wreck'

wreck *v.* to destroy; to dismantle; to bring to ruin: 'That story will wreck his reputation.'

See also reek

reclaim, réclame
reclaim *v.* to restore: 'They will reclaim the arid land by installing irrigation pipes'; to recover: 'We reclaim valuable metals from garbage'; to reform: 'AA can reclaim this alcoholic'; to demand the return of something that belongs to you

réclame *[ray•klahm']* *n.* public recognition or notoriety

recluse, recuse
recluse *n.* one who leads a solitary life

recuse *v.* to challenge the qualifications of a judge or a juror or to disqualify

recoil, re-coil
recoil *v.* to rebound; to flinch; to shrink from: 'He'll recoil at the thought of having to speak before the entire school'

re-coil *v.* to coil again: 'She'll re-coil the hose after washing the car'

recollect, re-collect
recollect *[reh•kuh•lehkt']* *v.* to remember

re-collect *[ree•kuh•lehkt']* *v.* to collect again; to recover or rally

recover, re-cover

recover *v.* to regain something lost or stolen; to come back from bad health, damage, weakness, or loss; to reclaim useful materials from waste; in football, to get the ball back after a fumble

re-cover *v.* to cover again: 'She decided to re-cover the sofa'

recreate, re-create

recreate *v.* to play or to relax

re-create *v.* to create again, to form anew

recuse *See* recluse

red *See* read

redound *See* rebound

reed *See* read

reek, wreak

reek *v.* to give off a strong, unpleasant odor: 'Those clubs reek of smoke'; to emit steam or smoke

wreak *[reek] v.* to inflict: 'They will wreak havoc on the city' *See also* reck

reel *See* real

referee, reverie

referee *n.* a person who supervises a sport or settles a dispute; a court appointee who takes special testimony

reverie *n.* a daydream; the condition of being lost in thought

reform, re-form, Reform

reform *v.* to improve morally or to make better: 'They hope to reform the party after the next election'

re-form *v.* to form again: 'The battalion must re-form quickly after the defeat'

Reform *n.* a branch of Judaism

refuse, re-fuse

refuse *v.* to decline; to deny a request: 'I refuse to put out the garbage all the time'

refuse *[ref'•yoose] n.* rubbish

re-fuse *v.* to set a fuse again: 'Since the bomb failed to explode, they decided to re-fuse it'

regal, regale, regalia

regal *[ree'•gul] adj.* royal, kingly, splendid: 'They held a regal reception for their guests'

regale *[re•gayl'] v.* to entertain lavishly; to feast; to amuse: 'They loved to regale their guests with fascinating anecdotes about their trip'

regalia *[re•gayl'•ya] n.* symbols of royalty; fancy dress; ceremonial clothes worn by holders of office or members of an order: 'The Knights of Pythias don ancient regalia for their meetings'

regardless, irregardless

regardless *adj.* negligent, failing to give proper or adequate care; heedless: 'His regardless statement crushed her spirit'

regardless *adv.* in spite of: 'Regardless of what she says, I still will not do it'

irregardless *adv.* regardless: not a standard word in the English language

reggae *See* raggee

regime, regimen, regiment

regime *[re•zheem'] n.* the ruling government or the length of its rule

regimen *n.* a systematic plan, often to improve health: 'The players were put on a strict regimen of diet and exercise'

regiment *n.* a military unit

regiment *v.* to exercise strict control to insure conformity: 'The Chinese rulers took steps to regiment the nation after the student demonstrations'; to form into a regiment

reign, rein *See* rain

relater, relator *See* realtor

release, re-lease

release *v.* to set free; to make known: 'They will release the news to the press tonight'; to grant rights to publish or sell something

re-lease *v.* to lease once more

relic, relict

> relic *n.* a religious memento: 'The church saved the relic of one of its saints and martyrs'; a leftover from an ancient civilization; an out-of-date custom
>
> relict *n.* a plant or animal species that has survived from an earlier time

relies *See* realize

relieve, relive

> relieve *v.* to soothe; to ease one's pain; to provide aid to a troubled group or person: 'They sent troops to relieve pressure on the Third Division'; to provide variety: 'That colorful hanging should relieve the monotony of this room'; to substitute for someone: 'She'll relieve me at 8 P.M. so I can go to dinner'
>
> relive *v.* to imagine a previous experience or part of one's life; to live again: 'If I could relive my life, I'd become a doctor'

remark, remarque

> remark *v.* to comment briefly; to observe; to mark again: 'The teacher will have to remark the test papers'
>
> remarque *n.* a sketch made on the edge of an engraving plate and removed before the printing

repeal, repel *See* rappel

repertoire, repertory

> repertoire *[rep'•er•twar] n.* the collection of songs, plays, or dances that a performer or group can perform: 'The magician's repertoire comprised 1,000 tricks'; the total works or skills in an artistic field or occupation
>
> repertory *n.* a set of plays that a theatrical company performs periodically; such a theatrical company; a storehouse

represent, re-present

> represent *v.* to act for: 'They will represent the United States in the Olympics'; to depict, or to portray in a play or movie; to serve as a symbol for
>
> re-present *v.* to present again

repress, re-press

> repress *v.* to keep down or subdue: 'The Romanian
> government continues to repress its Hungarian minority';
> to control or suppress: 'Psychologists say it's not healthy
> to repress one's feelings'

> re-press *v.* to press again: 'I asked the tailor to re-press my
> trousers'

residence, residents

> residence *n.* a dwelling place; a place or duration of
> occupancy: 'during my residence in Japan'; the legal site
> of a large business

> residents *n.* (pl.) persons who live in a place as distinguished
> from visitors; doctors serving their last training years in a
> hospital: 'They are residents in psychiatry'

resign, re-sign, resin

> resign *[ree•zine']* *v.* to give up a position: 'Nixon had to
> resign the presidency'; to abdicate; to quit; to surrender a
> claim or right

> re-sign *[ree•sine']* *v.* to sign again

> resin *[reb'•zin]* *n.* a substance used in making plastics or in
> medicines

resister, resistor

> resister *n.* a person who offers opposition, especially to
> government: 'The leading war resister called on the
> president to end the war'

> resistor *n.* an electrical device used for current control in a
> circuit

resort, re-sort

> resort *n.* a vacation recreation center; a person, thing, or
> agency one reaches to for help: 'He turned to her as a
> last resort when he lost his job'

> resort *v.* to make use of as an expedient: 'He's sure to resort
> to crying whenever he does not get his way'; to turn to
> an extreme option: 'If his threats failed, he would resort
> to war'

re-sort *v.* to sort again; 'After the entire basket of envelopes fell on the floor, they had to re-sort them by zip code'

rest, wrest, wrist

rest *n.* remainder: 'After you take your piece of pie, I want the rest'; a period of inactivity or sleep: 'Take a rest before you start hammering again'; a place for people to stay or stop: 'A rest for the mountain climbers'; free from anxiety or problems: 'My mind's at rest'

rest *v.* to stop work; to lie down; to relax; to lie still or quiet; to avoid further action: 'Let the matter rest'; to be based on: 'His argument will rest on the following points'; to fix one's eyes on: 'Her eyes rest fondly on her new daughter'; in court, to finish one's presentation: 'I rest my case'

wrest *v.* to get something with much effort or great force; to wrench or gain by wrenching; to usurp: 'The army tried to wrest power over the weekend, but failed'

wrist *n.* the joint between the hand and arm; the part of clothing covering the wrist

resume, résumé

resume *v.* to take up again after interrupting

résumé *[ray'•zu•may] n.* a summary of one's employment record and qualifications

retch, wretch

retch *v.* to try to vomit or to vomit

wretch *n.* a vile and despised person

retinal, retinol

retinal *[ret'•i•nil] adj.* pertaining to the lining of the eyeball

retinol *[ret'•in•awl] n.* vitamin A

reveal *See* ravel

reveille, revelry

reveille *[rev'•ell•ee] n.* a call to soldiers or campers to awake, often sounded by a bugle

revelry *n.* noisy merriment: 'Their late-night revelry disturbed the other guests'

revel *See* ravel

reverend, reverent

> reverend *n.* the title of a member of the clergy: 'The priest, rabbi, minister, and reverend attended the ecumenical service'

> reverent *adj.* worshipful; characterized by or expressing respect or awe: 'As they entered the cathedral, they became very reverent'

reverie *See* referee

review, revue

> review *n.* a reexamination or reconsideration: 'The task force started to review the city's health programs'; an evaluation of a book, play, or film; a ceremonial display of troops

> revue *n.* a theatrical production, usually of musical comedy acts

rheum, room

> rheum *[room]* *n.* a nasal discharge or a cold

> room *n.* an enclosed or partitioned space for living or working; available space: 'There's enough room for two people'; the people in a particular space: 'The whole room got quiet'

> room *v.* to share living space: 'He'll room with two friends next semester'

rho *See* roe

rhumb, rum

> rhumb *n.* a point on a compass

> rum *n.* an alcoholic beverage distilled from sugar cane

rhyme/rime, rime

> rhyme *or* rime *n.* a set of words that sound similar, for example: 'hit, bit'; 'height, light'; poetry which uses rhyming words at the ends of lines

> rime *n.* icy crystals, or frost

riffle, rifle

> riffle *n.* a shoal; an underwater sand bed; a shuffle of cards

riffle *v.* to flip through pages of a publication rapidly; to
shuffle cards

rifle *n.* a gun held at the shoulder

rifle *v.* to search someone's belongings in order to steal; to
ransack

rig, rigg

rig *n.* a frolic; a prank; special equipment: 'a rig to help
remove people from wrecks'; oil-drilling equipment; a
ship's setup of sailing gear

rig *v.* to fit; to manipulate dishonestly; to clothe; to build a
temporary facility: 'We'll rig an assembly line in the living
room until the factory is opened'

rigg *n.* a type of fish

rigger, rigor

rigger *n.* a person who rigs or prepares a ship for sailing

rigor *n.* hardship: 'They barely survived the rigor of war';
difficulty; strictness; precision: 'She loved the rigor of
mathematics'

right, rite, wright, write

right *n.* what one is entitled to: 'My right to justice cannot be
taken away'; correct or moral behavior: 'I know right
from wrong'; a group of political conservatives: 'The
Right advocates less government intervention'; on the
right, referring to location or direction

right *v.* to correct: 'to right a wrong'; to return to normal:
'The loud noises in your car should right themselves in
time'

right *adj.* correct; moral; normal; politically conservative; most
desirable or preferable: 'He knew all the right people'

right *adv.* in the proper way; immediately: 'Go right home
after the party'

rite *n.* a special, prescribed form of ceremony; a church liturgy

wright *n.* a woodworker, a carpenter; one who constructs or
creates, often used in combination: 'He is a shipwright
married to a playwright'

write *v.* to put words on paper; to create for publication: 'She has to write a column every other day'; to enter matter into a computer

right-wing, right wing

right-wing *adj.* politically conservative

right wing *n.* the wing on the right side: 'The robin's right wing was broken'; the conservative part of a group

rigorous *See* vigorous

rime *See* rhyme

ring, wring

ring *n.* a circular band; a metal band worn on the finger; the sound made by a bell; a site or enclosure where boxing matches or bullfights are held

ring *v.* to produce a bell-like sound; to telephone someone: 'Give me a ring'; to put a band around; to draw a circle around; to possess a particular quality: 'Those remarks ring true'

wring *v.* to extort; to squeeze by twisting; to extract by force or threats: 'We will wring a confession from the robber'

rip-off, rip off

rip-off *n.* a theft; overpriced or defective goods; the charging of exorbitant prices

rip off *v.* to tear off; to steal or to pull a rip-off

rise, ryes, wrys

rise *n.* a small hill or slope; an increase; a response or stimulus: 'His poor performance gave rise to doubts about his ability'; a negative reaction: 'Her speech got a rise out of the audience'

rise *v.* to get up; to advance in status; to move upward; to stand up: 'Please rise to address the audience'; to become higher: 'The water level tends to rise dangerously during a hurricane'; to increase: 'Prices may rise over 10 percent during an inflationary surge'

ryes *n.* (pl.) grains used in making whiskey or the whiskey itself: 'I want two ryes and one scotch'

wrys *v.* 3d person, sing., present tense of wry, to twist or
    writhe

risible, visible

    risible *adj.* ludicrous, laughable

    visible *adj.* capable of being seen; in sight; obvious or
        apparent

risk, risqué

    risk *n.* a danger; a gamble; the policy or person covered by
        insurance

    risk *v.* to chance danger or injury: 'She had to risk her life to
        save the drowning child'

    risqué *[riss•kay']* *adj.* daring, bold; bordering on impropriety:
        'That comedian loves to tell risqué jokes'

rite *See* right

ritz, writs

    ritz *n.* an ostentatious or pretentious show

    ritz *v.* to snub: 'When he starts modeling he's sure to ritz his
        old friends'

    writs *n.* (pl.) court orders

road, rode, rowed

    road *n.* an open, public piece of ground that allows travel
        between places; a way or means of achieving something:
        'A college education is the best road to success'

    rode *v.* past tense of ride, to conduct a vehicle or horse; to sit
        in a moving vehicle; to depend: 'My hopes rode on a
        good presentation to my peers'

    rowed *[rode]* *v.* past tense of row, to propel a boat with oars

    rowed *[rhymes w.* loud*]* *v.* past tense of row, to quarrel: 'That
        couple rowed every night'

roam, roan, Rome

    roam *v.* to wander, to rove: 'Teenagers love to roam around
        shopping malls'

    roan *n.* a horse with a red and gray coat

    Rome *n.* the capital of Italy; the seat of the Vatican

roc, rock

roc *n.* a legendary bird of prey

rock *n.* a large or small stone; a solid foundation: 'My family's love is my rock'; contemporary pop music; a diamond (slang); crack cocaine (slang)

rock *v.* to move to and fro; to shake; to upset or disturb: 'Don't rock the boat with your criticism of the mayor'; to dance to rock music

rocked, rocket, rochet, rocquet

rocked *v.* past tense of rock, to move to and fro

rocket *n.* an engine that obtains its thrust from a backward jet of combustible gases and is used to propel a vehicle or missile

rocket *v.* to fly straight up: 'Prices will rocket if there's another oil crisis'

rochet *[roch'•it] n.* a religious vestment, a close-fitting garment worn by clerics, esp. by bishops

rocquet *[rock'•it] v.* in croquet, to strike another player's ball

rode *See* road

roe, row, rho

roe *n.* fish eggs

row *[roe] n.* a line of people or things

row *[rhymes w.* cow*] n.* a fight or dispute: 'They had a row over money'

row *[roe] v.* to propel a boat

rho *n.* a letter in the Greek alphabet

See also rouse

roger *See* rajah

roil, role, roll

roil *v.* to make water muddy by stirring up sediment; to upset or stir up others

role *n.* a part taken by an actor or actress; the position or function of an institution or person: 'The U.S. should no longer play the role of world policeman'

roll *n.* material, such as paper or cloth, wrapped up like a
cylinder or scroll; a very small bread: 'I'd like a roll with
my coffee'; a swaying movement; an official list: 'The
teacher called the roll'; a vibrating or deep sound: 'A roll
of thunder'

roll *v.* to form a cylinderlike wrapping; to rob someone
(slang); to turn over and over as if down a hill; to emit a
loud sound; to progress: 'The team should really roll
after this victory'; to turn around in odd movements: 'To
roll one's eyes'

Rome *See* roan

rondeau, rondo

rondeau *[ron'•doe] n.* a poem with a fixed form of verse

rondo *n.* a musical composition featuring repeated refrains

rood, rued, rude

rood *n.* a cross; a land measure

rued *v.* past tense of rue, to feel sorrow or regret

rude *adj.* offensively blunt

rookie, rooky

rookie *n.* a new recruit, a beginner, a novice

rooky *adj.* inhabited by rooks, crowlike birds

room *See* rheum

roomer, rummer, rumor

roomer *n.* a lodger

rummer *n.* a large-bowled drinking glass

rumor *n.* gossip, hearsay, an unverified report: 'We heard a
rumor that the president was ill even before the official
announcement'

root, rout, route

root *n.* the originating underground part of a plant or tree
which serves as anchor and provides nutrients; the part
of hair or teeth that is under the skin; the base of a
word, without affixes, that tells its meaning; the heart or
source: 'Money is the root of all evil'

root *v.* to establish solidly: 'He'll root his decisions firmly in the Constitution'; to support: 'She'll root for the Giants'; to search through objects looking for a specific item

rout *[rowt] n.* an overwhelming defeat; a mob; a riot

route *[root or rowt] n.* a road; a specific course; a way to reach a goal

rooter, router

rooter *n.* one who supports

router *n.* one who plans a specific course; a machine that cuts the surface of wood with a revolving spindle

rose, rows

rose *n.* a flower; a pink color

rose *v.* past tense of rise, to get up or increase

rows *[rose] n.* (pl.) lines of people or things

rows *[rose] v.* 3d person, sing., present tense of row, to propel a boat with oars or to move people on such a boat

See also rouse

rote, wrote

rote *adj.* relates to mechanical repetition: 'Too many students are engaged in rote learning'

wrote *v.* past tense of write, to put words on paper

rough, ruff

rough *n.* the tall, grassy border of a golf course; a hoodlum; a preliminary drawing: 'Has she shown you the rough of this plan yet?'

rough *adj.* having an uneven surface; approximate: 'At a rough guess, this is about 30 feet'; difficult: 'a rough time'

ruff *n.* a wheel-shaped stiff collar worn in the 16th and 17th centuries; a trumping of a card in the game of bridge

rouse, rows

rouse *v.* to wake someone up; to incite

rows *[rhymes w.* cows*] n.* (pl.) fights or quarrels: 'Their marriage was marred by daily rows'

See also rose

292

rout, route *See* root

router *See* rooter

roux, rue

roux *[roo] n.* a sauce thickener made of butter and flour

rue *n.* a plant; repentance or regret

rue *v.* to feel regret or to be sorry for

row *See* roe

rowan, rowen

rowan *n.* a tree, a mountain ash

rowen *n.* the second crop of grass in one season

rowed *See* road

rows *See* rose; rouse

rubber stamp, rubber-stamp

rubber stamp *n.* a die for making imprints

rubber-stamp *v.* to approve something as a matter of course: 'Busy officials usually rubber-stamp passports without even looking at the holder'

rubble, ruble

rubble *[rub'•bul] n.* a mass of bits of broken stone, rock, or masonry: 'The bombing reduced the city to rubble'

ruble *[rue'•bul] n.* the monetary unit of Russia

ruckus *See* raucous

rued, rude *See* rood

rue *See* roux

rues, ruse

rues *v.* 3d person, sing., present tense of rue, to regret

ruse *n.* a trick, an action intended to deceive: 'Their apparent agreement was a ruse to lull us into letting down our defenses'

ruff *See* rough

ruin, rune

ruin *n.* total destruction; the remains of something destroyed

rune *n.* a letter of an ancient Germanic alphabet, often linked to mystery or magic

rum *See* rhumb

rummer, rumor *See* roomer

runaround, run around

> runaround *n.* a deception used to delay a response: 'Every
> time I asked for my medical report, I got a runaround'
>
> run around *v.* to run by something or someone: 'The
> quarterback will run around the end on the next
> play'

rundown, run down, run-down

> rundown *n.* a summary: 'She gave me a quick rundown on
> our sales picture'; an action in baseball where a runner
> is caught off base
>
> run down *v.* to pursue: 'I'll run down that article we need'; to
> knock someone down while driving; to criticize; to lose
> power: 'Your battery will run down if you leave the lights
> on'
>
> run-down *adj.* to be weak and debilitated: 'After my illness, I
> was run-down for weeks'

rung, wrung

> rung *n.* a step on a ladder; a rank or level in an organization:
> 'You have to start at the bottom rung of the company'
>
> rung *v.* past participle of ring, to sound a bell; to call: 'I have
> rung her three times but she doesn't answer'
>
> wrung *v.* past participle of wring, to extort; to squeeze by
> twisting

run-in, run in

> run-in *n.* a quarrel or confrontation: 'He had a run-in with his
> supervisor'
>
> run in *v.* to stop by: 'I will run in tomorrow morning'; to take
> part in a race: 'I will run in the marathon'

ruse *See* rues

russel, rustle

> russel *n.* a type of cloth
>
> rustle *v.* to make small quick sounds, as with paper or dry
> leaves; to seek food; to steal cattle

rye, wry

    rye *n.* a grain; a whiskey made from grain

    wry *v.* to twist or writhe

    wry *adj.* bent to one side: 'She had a wry smile'; devious or
        ironic: 'She is noted for her wry humor'

ryes *See* rise

S

sabbat, sabbath

> sabbat *n.* a witches' or sorcerers' assembly

> sabbath *n.* a weekly religious day of rest

sac, sack, sacque

> sac *n.* a baglike pouch found in human and animal anatomies

> sack *n.* a big bag or pouch

> sack *v.* to fire someone; to destroy: 'Hitler threatened to sack Prague if his demands weren't met'

> sacque *n.* an infant's jacket

saccharin, saccharine

> saccharin *n.* a sugar substitute

> saccharine *adj.* overly sweet or sentimental: 'That love story was too saccharine'

sachet, sashay

> sachet [*sa•shay'*] *n.* a perfumed packet used to scent clothes

> sashay *n.* an excursion; a move in a square dance

> sashay *v.* to glide; to move in an ostentatious or conspicuous manner

safe, seif

> safe *n.* a container to hold valuables securely

> safe *adj.* secure, unhurt

> seif [*safe*] *n.* a sand dune

sail, sale

> sail *n.* a fabric used to catch wind on a boat; a boat ride: 'Let's go for a sail'

sail *v.* to ride on a boat; the boat's action: 'We sail at dawn'; to move quickly: 'Watch the ball sail over the fielder's head'

sale *n.* an offer of goods or services for purchase; such an offer at reduced prices: 'The stores seem to be running sales all the time'

sailer, sailor

sailer *n.* a special type of sailboat

sailor *n.* one who works on a boat; a member of the crew

sake, saki

sake *[sah•key] n.* Japanese rice wine

saki *[sah•key] n.* a South American monkey

salon, saloon, solon

salon *[sah•lahn'] n.* a drawing room; an asembly of distinguished prominent guests; a stylish business or shop

saloon *[sah•loon'] n.* a place where alcoholic drinks are sold and consumed

solon *[so'•lon] n.* a wise lawmaker; a member of a legislative body

salter *See* Psalter

salvage, selvage

salvage *v.* to save property from a damaged ship or building; to save something from a bad situation or loss: 'They should salvage some valuable lessons from their defeat'

selvage *n.* a border or edge of cloth, often made by a different weave

salve, salvo, save

salve *[rhymes w. have] n.* a medicinal, soothing ointment: 'She applied salve to her dried lips'

salve *[salv] v.* to rescue from loss; to salvage; to assuage: 'The rich salve their consciences by donating money'

salvo *n.* a multigun salute, usually in celebration

save *v.* to rescue: 'She can save him from drowning if she swims well'; to prevent; to keep: 'I will save a lot of money for a new house'; to avoid damage; to avoid loss or waste: 'We can save time by taking this shortcut'; to redeem from sin save *prep.* except for: 'All of us, save John, went boating'

salver, salvor

salver *n.* a metal tray to hold calling cards or food

salvor *n.* a person or ship taking part in a salvage operation

samba, sambar, somber

samba *n.* a Brazilian dance of African origin

sambar *n.* a large deer

somber *adj.* dark, gloomy, solemn

sane, seine, Seine

sane *adj.* of sound mind; rational

seine *[sane] n.* a fishing net held vertically with weights

Seine *[sane or sehn] n.* a major French river which flows through Paris

sank *See* cinque

sashay *See* sachet

Satan, sateen, satin

Satan *[say'•ten] n.* the devil, the adversary of God

sateen *[sa•teen'] n.* a smooth cotton fabric that looks like satin

satin *[sat'•in] n.* a silky, glossy material

satire, satyr

satire *[sa'•tire] n.* ridicule; humor, wit, or irony which exposes hypocrisy, foolishness, or vice; a creative work such as a play or book that uses ridicule or sarcasm: 'Swift wrote many articles of satire'

satyr *[sat•er or say•ter] n.* an ancient god with a human torso and head but ears and legs of a goat; an exceptionally lustful or lecherous person

saurel, sorrel

saurel *n.* a type of mackerel fish

sorrel *adj.* reddish brown

sorrel *n.* a horse of that color

save *See* salve

saver, savor

saver *n.* one who saves: 'Banks compete vigorously to attract each new saver' savor *v.* to taste, smell, or enjoy: 'They'll savor the victory, their first in weeks'

savior, Saviour

savior *n.* someone who saves or rescues people or institutions: 'George Washington was the savior of the revolution'

Saviour *n.* the name for Jesus Christ as rescuer of humankind

scallop, scalp

scallop *n.* a shellfish; an ornamental curved border on clothes or other items

scalp *v.* to remove the higher skin of the head in warfare; to sell tickets to sporting or theatrical events at greatly increased prices

scared, scarred

scared *v.* past tense of scare, to frighten

scarred *v.* past tense of scar, to leave a mark from a cut or other wound

scares, scarce, scars

scares *v.* 3d person, sing., present tense of scare, to frighten or become frightened: 'That strange noise in the attic scares me'

scarce *adj.* in short supply: 'Water is scarce in the desert'; hard to find: 'She made herself scarce after the show'

scars *v.* 3d person, sing., present tense of scar, to leave a mark by wounding; to suffer mental or emotional damage: 'He scars his children for life with his angry yelling'

scene, seen

scene *n.* a place where something happens; the locale; a fuss: 'She made a scene over his late hours'; one's surroundings: 'Those mountains make such a beautiful scene'; a picture of an area or activity: 'He paints alpine scenes'; a subdivision of a play or movie

seen *v.* past participle of see, to notice, observe, look

scent *See* cent

scenter *See* centaur

scents *See* cense

scepter, septum, septa

scepter *n.* a rod or staff; an emblem of authority

septum *n.* a biological partition or membrane, as in the nose: 'a deviated septum'

septa *n.* plural of septum

sceptic *See* skeptic

schist *See* cist

schmaltz, schmelz

schmaltz *n.* mushy, sentimental, or showy music or writing

schmelz *n.* decorative glass

scirrhus/scirrus/scirrhous *See* cerous

scissel/scissil, sizzle

scissel *or* scissil *[siss'•il] n.* metal scrap; remains of a strip from which coins have been cut

sizzle *v.* to scorch or sear with a hissing sound; to make a hissing sound

scissile, sessile, sisal

scissile *[sis'•il] adj.* capable of being easily split

sessile *[sess'•il] adj.* permanently attached; attached at the base

sisal *[sie'•sil] n.* a fiber used for twine

scissor, scissure, seizure

scissor *or* scissors *n.* a sharp, two-bladed cutting instrument

scissure *n.* a rupture; a cleft; a cutting

seizure *n.* the act of capturing or taking possession of; a sudden attack as from a disease

scrape, scrap

scrape *v.* to clean or remove by rubbing with an edged or rough object: 'Scrape the skin from the potatoes with this peeler'; to hurt oneself by scraping: 'You'll scrape your arms on the fence if you're not careful'; to do without in order to save: 'We'll scrape by until I get a job'; to make a harsh sound by rubbing scrap *v.* to get rid of something as garbage; to drop or abandon: 'They'll scrap their travel plans if one of them gets sick'; to fight or quarrel

scrip, script

scrip *n.* a certificate used as a money substitute in emergencies; a document entitling the holder to something

script *n.* the manuscript of a play or movie; a particular style of handwriting or printing

scull, skull

scull *n.* a small oar; a rowboat or shell propelled by a single oarsman

skull *n.* the skeleton of the head which holds and protects the brain

sculptor, sculpture

sculptor *[skulp' • ter] n.* an artist who shapes wood, stone, or metal forms

sculpture *[skulp' • chur] n.* what a sculptor produces: 'In his later years, Picasso turned his talent more and more toward sculpture'

sea, see, si

sea *n.* a large body of salt water, such as the ocean; a vast group: 'A sea of faces awaited the star'; seaside: 'We go to the sea for our vacation'

see *v.* to perceive or recognize with the eyes; to understand: 'I see what you mean'; to view: 'see a play'; to meet: 'I'm going to see her at 5 P.M.'; to accompany: 'I'll see you home after the party'; to find out or to discover: 'I see by the papers that the bill was passed'

see *n.* the seat or authority of a bishop

si *n.* in music, a variant of *te*, or the seventh tone in the diatonic scale

sea-born, seaborne

sea-born *adj.* produced by the sea: 'Aphrodite was sea-born' seaborne *adj.* carried on the sea: 'In WWII, troops in the Pacific were mainly seaborne'

seal *See* ceil

sealing *See* ceiling

seam, seem

seam *n.* a joining of the edges of materials: 'The seam on his pants split'; an underground layer of material: 'A coal seam'

seem *v.* to appear to be or do; to give an impression: 'They seem very bright'; to be probable: 'That calculation would seem to be right'

seaman, semen

seaman *n.* a sailor, usually of low rank; an enlisted person in the navy or marines

semen *n.* the fluid containing sperm secreted by male reproductive organs

sear *See* cere

sears *See* cerise

seas *See* cease

seasonal, seasonable

seasonal *adj.* periodical; pertaining to a season or a seasonal need: 'As a ski instructor, she had seasonal work'

seasonable *adj.* suitable to the season; timely: 'He made a seasonable proposal'

seat *See* cete

sebaceous *See* cetaceous

secondhand, second hand

secondhand *adj.* previously used; indirectly, not from a primary or direct source: 'She didn't tell me herself, I got the news secondhand'

second hand *n.* an indicator which measures seconds on a watch

sects, sex

sects *n.* (pl.) groups of people with dissenting religious beliefs; religious groups deemed heretical sex *n.* gender denoting male or female; the intimate physical or reproductive relation between a couple; intercourse; the feeling or desire relating to such relations: 'He was obsessed with sex'

Seder *See* cedar

see *See* sea

seed *See* cede

seeder *See* cedar

seek, Sikh

seek *v.* to search for: 'I seek the answer to life's riddles'; to try: 'I seek to improve my health through exercise'; to inquire: 'seek an opinion'

Sikh *[seek] n.* a member of a monotheistic Hindu religious sect

See also sic

seel *See* ceil

seem *See* seam

seen *See* scene

seep *See* cêpe

seer *See* cere

seers *See* cerise

sees *See* cease

seif *See* safe

seigneur, senior

seigneur *[sane•yer'] n.* a gentleman or lord

senior *n.* a student in the last year of school or college; an older person; one with a higher rank

senior *adj.* older: 'a senior citzen'; in a higher position or rank: 'Senior management gets the best perks'

seine, Seine *See* sane

seize *See* cease

seizure *See* scissor

sell *See* cell

seller *See* cellar

selvage *See* salvage

semen *See* seamen

seminar, seminary

seminar *n.* a class for advanced students; a meeting to discuss a specific subject: 'The doctor attended a seminar on AIDS'

seminary *n.* a school for candidates to the clergy

senate, sennet

senate *n.* the upper house of a bicameral legislature; a governing body of a university; the room in which such bodies meet

sennet *n.* a musical flourish of a trumpet to signal the entrance or exit of actors on a stage

senhor, señor, signor/signore, signorino

senhor *[sin•yoer']* *n.* the Portugese or Brazilian equivalent of Mr.

señor *[sane•yaw']* *n.* Spanish for Mr.

signor *or* signore *[seen•yor'•ay]* *n.* a conventional Italian title of respect for a man; the equivalent of Mr.

signorino *n.* Italian title of respect for a young man

senhora, señora, signora

senhora *n.* the Portuguese or Brazilian equivalent of Mrs.

señora *n.* the Spanish equivalent of Mrs.

signora *n.* the Italian equivalent of Mrs.

senhorita, señorita, signorina

senhorita *n.* the Portuguese or Brazilian equivalent of Miss

señorita *n.* the Spanish equivalent of Miss

signorina *n.* the Italian equivalent of Miss

senior *See* seigneur

sense *See* cense

senses *See* census

sensor *See* censer

sensual, sensuous

sensual *adj.* relating to material or fleshly gratification; worldly; lustful: 'He indulged his sensual pleasures of food, drink, and women to extremes'

sensuous *adj.* providing pleasure through the senses; as perceived through the senses or mind: 'Her sensuous poetry evoked rich images of nature's beauties'

sent *See* cent

septic, skeptic

    septic *adj.* infected with harmful organisms: 'a septic wound'; putrefying waste matter; 'a septic tank'

    skeptic *n.* one who habitually questions or doubts; an advocate of the doctrine that true knowledge in a specific area or religion is uncertain

sequence, sequins

    sequence *[see'•kwents] n.* the order in which things come, arrive, or act: 'You have to teach these items in the following sequence'; a series of movie or TV shots which make up one episode

    sequins *[see'•kwins] n.* (pl.) ornamental spangles made of shiny metal or plastic

sere *See* cere

serf, surf

    serf *n.* a peasant farmer on medieval manors

    surf *n.* the sea swell or white foam of breaking waves

serge, surge,

    serge *n.* a twill fabric

    surge *n.* an uprush; a sudden increase of power or other attributes: 'During the recovery, there was a surge in demand'

serial *See* cereal

series *See* cerise

serious *See* cereus

serous *See* cerous

sessile *See* scissile

session *See* cessation

setaceous *See* cetaceous

setback, set back

    setback *n.* a loss or delay: 'The storm caused a three-week setback to our project'; in architecture, a higher story set in from the edge of the lower story

    set back *v.* to force a change, delay, or retreat; to cost (slang): 'It set me back $30'; to turn back: 'Set back the clocks one hour'

settler, settlor

    settler *n.* one who moves and establishes himself in a new
        area

    settlor *n.* one who reaches a legal agreement

set-to, set to

    set-to *n.* a fight

    set to *v.* to start something with energy or enthusiasm: 'They
        set to work and finished the job in two days'

setup, set up

    setup *n.* a plan that fixes blame on another person: 'The
        setup involved planting stolen papers in his office'
        (slang); an arrangement: 'I like this setup, and think
        I'll enjoy this job'; a camera's position for shooting;
        liquids and utensils that go with liquor; a phony sports
        match

    set up *v.* to arrange something; to be put in a satisfactory
        position: 'That loan set me up for life'; to erect; to
        establish or found

sever, severe

    sever *v.* to end or cut off: 'After the divorce, she'll surely
        sever all ties with her husband and his friends'

    severe *adj.* extreme or strict: 'The judge was severe with him
        because of his repeated crimes'; simple or austere: 'He
        was dressed in a severe style'; of a great degree: 'a severe
        wound'

sew, so, sough, sow

    sew *v.* to fasten with stitches using a needle and thread

    so *adv.* very, to a certain degree or extent: 'That movie was so
        good'; then or therefore: 'We got married, so we lived
        happily ever after'; as a summary: 'So it wasn't the butler
        who did it'

    so *conj* also: 'If you move, so will we'

    sough *[rhymes w. cow]* *n.* a sighing of the wind

    sow *[rhymes w. cow]* *n.* a female pig

    sow *[so]* *v.* to plant seed

sewer, sower, suer

> sewer *[soo'•er] n.* a drain or conduit to carry off waste
>
> sewer *[soh'•er] n.* one who sews clothes
>
> sower *[soh'•er] n.* one who plants seeds
>
> suer *[soo'•er] n.* one who initiates legal proceedings

sex *See* sects

shagreen *See* chagrin

shanty *See* chantey

shape-up, shape up

> shape-up *n.* a hiring system in which workers are chosen
> each day for that day or shift: 'There is a shape-up for
> longshoremen every day'
>
> shape up *v.* to get fit by exercising; to improve performance
> on a job or elsewhere to a higher level: 'The new
> employees better shape up'

sharif, sheriff

> sharif *[shu•reef'] n.* a descendant of Muhammed; a member
> of Islamic nobility
>
> sheriff *n.* a local law officer; an official with judicial duties

shear, sheer

> shear *v.* to cut the hair from: 'The army barber will shear the
> new recruits'
>
> sheer *v.* to suddenly change direction, to veer or swerve
>
> sheer *adj.* steep or vertical; thin, transparent, as of a fabric;
> utter or complete: 'That remark is sheer nonsense!'

sheik/sheikh *See* cheek

shier/shyer, shire

> shier *or* shyer *adj.* comparative of shy, timid, bashful
>
> shire *n.* a county

shirk, shriek, shrike

> shirk *v.* to evade responsibility or work: 'If he continues to
> shirk his duties, he'll be fired'; to sneak around
>
> shriek *v.* to utter a high-pitched cry of anger, terror, or
> laughter: 'The whole house can hear her shriek at her
> husband'

shrike *n.* a bird with a hooked beak

shirt *See* chert

shirt-sleeve, shirt sleeve

shirt-sleeve *adj.* being informal by removing one's jacket:
'He's known as a shirt-sleeve executive'

shirt sleeve *n.* the portion of a shirt that covers one's arms

shoe *See* chou

shone, shown

shone *v.* past tense of shine, to light up; to polish; to excel:
'Their debating team shone at all state competitions'

shown *v.* past participle of show, to display or to indicate:
'Our loss of the Japanese market is clearly shown on this
graph'; to teach: 'The students were shown how to use a
computer'; to present or put on; to make an appearance:
'They have not shown up yet'

shoo *See* chou

shoot *See* chute

shot, shote/shoat

shot *n.* the act of firing a weapon or the bullets used in firing;
a move in sports: 'That was a great shot: it hit the basket
from 40 feet'; a photo or a single film moment; a guess;
an opportunity: 'I had a good shot at that job'; a drink of
liquor

shot *v.* past tense of shoot, to fire a weapon; to film; to make
a move in sports

shote *or* shoat *n.* a young hog

show-off, show off

show-off *n.* someone who tries too hard to impresss others;
an exhibitionist

show off *v.* to display: 'He was eager to show off his new car'

shriek, shrike *See* shirk

shudder, shutter

shudder *v.* to shake badly due to fear or cold: 'You could see
him shudder when he heard footsteps in the hall'; to
shiver

shutter *n.* a hinged cover for a window; a device that allows a camera to take a picture by uncovering an opening, exposing the film

shut-in, shut in

shut-in *n.* someone who is forced to stay in, as in a hospital; someone who prefers solitude or isolation

shut in *v.* to confine a person or animal: 'They always shut these patients in their rooms, so they lose interest in life'

shutout, shut out

shutout *n.* a game, such as baseball, where one team does not score

shut out *v.* to keep someone or something out of a place or situation: 'They shut me out of their key meetings'

shyer *See* shier

si *See* sea

sic, sick

sic *v.* to command a dog to attack; the command itself, meaning 'chase, attack'

sic *adv.* a printing instruction to spell something exactly as it is shown, even if deliberately misspelled; intentionally so written

sick *adj.* ill; disgusted; angry; bored: 'I'm sick of fancy dinners'; mentally or emotionally unsound: 'That frequent violence is sick behavior'; macabre or sadistic: 'sick jokes'

See also seek

sics, six

sics *v.* 3d person, sing., present tense of sic: 'That man sics his dog on intruders'

six *n.* the number between five and seven, 6

sigher, sire

sigher *n.* one who sighs or takes audible breaths

sire *n.* a male parent

sire *v.* to beget or originate

sight *See* cite

sign, sine

sign *n.* a symbol that represents a word, an idea, or an action and is often displayed on a board: 'a traffic sign'; a trace or evidence: 'There was no sign of movement'; a gesture

sign *v.* to write your name: 'Sign this letter'; to join or support: 'Sign me up'; to hire: 'They propose to sign that college star for $1 million'; to signal using sign language

sine *n.* a trigonometric function

signet *See* cygnet

signor/signore, signorino *See* senhor

signora *See* senhora

signorina *See* senhorita

Sikh *See* seek

silicon, silicone

silicon *n.* an element that occurs in sand and is used in electronics: 'a silicon chip'; 'Silicon Valley'

silicone *n.* an organic compound containing silicon, used in lubricants and cosmetics, and at one time used in breast implants

simile, smile

simile *n.* a figure of speech that uses *like* or *as* to compare two different things: for example, 'He's as happy as a lark'; 'She swam like a fish'

smile *n.* a happy or derisive facial expression

simulate, stimulate

simulate *v.* to show or act out a representation of an object or process: 'They should simulate that new production line'; to feign a feeling or belief: 'We expect them to simulate sorrow, even though we know they're pleased with the outcome'

stimulate *v.* to arouse: 'That exciting teacher can stimulate anyone's interest in acting'; to energize or animate: 'Coffee stimulates my best thinking'

since, sins

since *[sins]* adv. before the present time: 'She's been long
since gone'; from that time until now: 'They were
married in 1980, and have stayed married ever since';
after a time in the past: 'He has since lost all that weight'

since *prep.* after, from the time of: 'It's been hot since the
beginning of August'

since *conj.* at or from a time in the past: 'She has moved four
times since she left home'; the reason for: 'Since you
were late, we started without you'

sins *[sinz]* n.(pl.) violations of a moral or religious code

sine *See* sign

singeing, singing

singeing *[sin•jing]* v. present participle of singe, to burn
slightly, to scorch; to remove fuzz or hair by passing
quickly over flame

singing *[seeng•ing]* v. present participle of sing, to produce
music vocally; to praise in poetry or song: 'They are
singing of their glorious victories in battle'; to produce a
ringing or whistling sound: 'The kettle is singing'; to
inform or squeal on a criminal partner (slang): 'He is
singing to the police'

single *See* cingle

singular *See* cingular

sink, sync/synch

sink *n.* a kitchen basin; a corrupt place

sink *v.* to go under water; to decline in level or value: 'The
dollar will sink against the franc for the second straight
week'; to deteriorate physically; 'Without surgery, he'll
sink fast'; to dig: 'sink a well'; to score in golf or
basketball; to defeat: 'Notre Dame will sink Navy in
football'

sync *or* synch *n.* in a state of agreement: 'Those two people
are always in sync'

sync *or* synch *v.* to synchronize, to cause to agree in rate or
speed, or to adjust so that two things coincide

sin tax *See* syntax

Sioux *See* sou

sip *See* cyp

sire *See* sigher

sisal *See* scissile

siss *See* cis

sissed *See* cist

Sistine *See* cysteine

sit-down, sit down

sit-down *n.* a form of strike in which workers halt operations
but remain inside the plant or office

sit down *v.* to take a seat

site *See* cite

sit-in, sit in

sit-in *n.* a peaceful form of protest: 'They held a sit-in at the
restaurant until a public apology was made'

sit in *v.* to take part in or attend anything, such as a concert:
'He likes to sit in with the band when he is free'

six *See* sics

sizzle *See* scissel/scissil

skull *See* scull

slated, slatted

slated *v.* past tense of slate, to choose; to schedule: 'The move
was slated for January'; to cover with slate, a light rock
material

slatted *v.* past tense of slat, to use a thin strip of metal or
wood in furniture or building

Slav, slave

Slav *n.* a member of any of several Eastern European ethnic
groups

slave *n.* one held in servitude by another as chattel; one
controlled by a person or habit: 'a slave to drink'; a
mechanism controlled by another device; a very hard
worker

slay, sleigh

slay *v.* to kill; to extinguish; to overwhelm (slang): 'Those comedians slay me'

sleigh *n.* a sled, a vehicle on runners which travel over snow and ice: 'a one-horse sleigh'

sleight, slight

sleight *[slight] n.* dexterity, deceit, or craftiness

slight *v.* to ignore in an insulting manner; to treat with indifference: 'I knew her before she became famous; now she likes to slight her old friends'; to pay little attention to or treat as unimportant: 'If you slight your studies, you'll be dropped'

slight *adj.* slender; very little; meager: 'There was only a slight increase in sales this month'

slew, slough, slue

slew *n.* a great number: 'A slew of people came to the party'

slew *v.* past tense of slay, to kill

slough *[sloo] n.* a swamp; a hole full of mire, or a mud hole

slough *[rhymes w.* cow] *n.* a state of despair

slue *v.* to swing around a mast on its own axis

See also slough

slews, sluice

slews *v.* 3d person, sing., present tense of slew, to turn a ship's mast on its axis; to turn something on its side

sluice *n.* a floodgate or valve for regulating water flow in rivers or ponds; an artificial stream

sloe, slow

sloe *n.* a plumlike, sour fruit used as the chief flavoring of sloe gin

slow *v.* to reduce speed: 'Please slow down when you drive near schools'; to delay or retard: 'His absences will slow his progress at school'

slow *adj.* not fast; dull mentally; behind: 'The clock was slow'; not hasty: 'slow to anger'; boring: 'What a slow party'; backward or conservative: 'a slow town'

sloped, slopped

sloped *v.* past tense of slope, to move in an oblique or slanted manner; to form something at an angle: 'They sloped the embankment to encourage the runoff of the rain'

slopped *v.* past tense of slop, to spill things clumsily: 'The waiter slopped the food all over my new suit'; to feed pigs slop; to walk through water

slough, sluff

slough *[rhymes w. tough] n.* a snake's shed skin; anything that is thrown off; a swamp

slough *v.* to cast off; to shed; to get rid of: 'He'll slough off his drinking habit'

sluff *v.* to discard a playing card

See also slew

slowdown, slow down

slowdown *n.* a protest by workers by reducing their work tempo

slow down *v.* to go less fast: 'Slow down, you're driving too fast'

slue *See* slew

smile *See* simile

smuggle, snuggle

smuggle *v.* to import or export goods or people illegally: 'They smuggle dope through Miami'

snuggle *v.* to cuddle or cozy up: 'Honey, snuggle closer to me, it's cold out there'

sniped, snipped, snippet

sniped *[sny•pt'] v.* past tense of snipe, to fire from a hidden position; to criticize maliciously and anonymously

snipped *[sni•pt'] v.* past tense of snip, to cut something with short strokes; to trim one's hair

snippet *[snip'•it] n.* a small piece or part; a little bit of news or only a partial story: 'The news only gave us a snippet of what really happened'

so *See* sew

soar, sore

soar *v.* to glide or fly at a very great height; to increase dramatically: 'Prices will soar this spring'

sore *n.* a wound, infection, abscess; a cause of pain or irritation

sore *adj.* painful; annoying; mentally distressing; angry: 'She was sore because he failed to call as promised'

soared, sord, sword

soared *v.* past tense of soar, to rise very high

sord *n.* a flock of mallards

sword *n.* a weapon with a long blade; war or violence; a symbol of military force or authority: 'The pen is mightier than the sword'

sodality, solidarity, Solidarity, solidity

sodality *n.* a fellowship; a close-knit organization; a Catholic lay society

solidarity *n.* unity based on close ties, strong support, and mutual interests: 'the solidarity of the union movement'

Solidarity *n.* the Polish trade union movement

solidity *n.* the condition of being solid or strong in finances or character: 'That firm stresses its solidity'

sodden, Sudan, sudden

sodden *adj.* very wet, lumpy; listless or sluggish; dull from overindulgence in alcoholic beverages

Sudan *n.* a nation in Africa

sudden *adj.* unexpected; abrupt; rash: 'That was a sudden decision to marry'

Soho, SoHo

Soho *n.* a London district with many restaurants and night clubs

SoHo *n.* a New York City district with many galleries and restaurants

sol, sole, soul

sol *n.* a note on a musical scale

sole *n.* the bottom of the foot or of a shoe or sock; a flat fish

sole *adj.* only, solitary, independent: 'She's the sole proprietor of this business'

soul *n.* the spiritual or moral aspect of humans; the spirit; the emotions; an individual: 'Not a soul survived the wreck'; the exemplification, personification: 'Martin Luther King, Jr., was the soul of the civil rights cause'; the cultural and emotional fervor of the African-American movement: 'soul food'; 'soul music'

sold, soled

sold *v.* past tense of sell, to offer goods or services for money: 'I sold that ugly lamp!'

soled *v.* past tense of sole, to put soles on shoes

solder, soldier

solder *[sod' • er] n.* a soft metal alloy used to join other metals under heat

solder *v.* to unite or join firmly

soldier *n.* a member of the armed forces

solidarity/Solidarity *See* sodality

solidity *See* sodality

solon *See* salon

somber *See* samba

some, sum

some *adj.* an indefinite quantity: 'some fruit'; 'some people'; a lot: 'some centuries ago'; remarkable or exceptional: 'That was some concert'

some *adv.* to an extent, somewhat: 'We conferred some about this matter'

some *pron.* an unspecified quantity different from others: 'some came home'

sum *n.* a total of two or more numbers; the essence of a matter; an amount of money: 'You can buy this for the sum of $500'

sum *v.* to find the total of a set of numbers; to summarize

sometime, some time, sometimes

sometime *adj.* former: 'his sometime friend'

sometime *adv.* a future time: 'We'll come sometime next
week'; 'Let's have lunch sometime'; an unspecified or
indefinite point: 'He called sometime last week'

some time *n.* 'I need some time to make a decision'

sometimes *adv.* occasionally, from time to time: 'He
sometimes comes to visit his mother, but not often'

son, sun

son *n.* a male child or descendant

sun *n.* the bright star which is the source of light and heat for
our planetary system and around which the earth
revolves; other bright stars in other solar systems or
galaxies; one resembling the sun's splendor or radiance:
'He's the sun, moon, and stars to his fans'

soot, sot, suit

soot *[rhymes w.* foot*] n.* a black powder resulting from fire
lining a chimney

sot *[rhymes w.* pot*] n.* a drunk

suit *n.* a clothing set made up of a jacket and pants or a skirt;
a legal action in a court; a set of playing cards with the
same symbol

sora *See* psora

sord *See* soared

sordid, sorted

sordid *adj.* base, vile: 'The press revealed the sordid details of
the crime'; filthy, depressing: 'People in slums live in
sordid conditions'

sorted *v.* past tense of sort, to organize things by size or some
other specification: 'He sorted the towels by color'

sore *See* soar

sorrel *See* saurel

sou, sue, Sioux

sou *n.* a French coin; a 5-cent piece.

sue *v.* to seek legal redress for harm or injustice

Sioux *[sue] n.* a Native American tribe of the plains

sough *See* sew

soul *See* sole

sow *See* sew

sower *See* sewer

spacious, specious

> spacious *adj.* roomy, vast: 'America's spacious plains'
>
> specious *adj.* having a false sound or look of truthfulness or genuineness; deceptively attractive: 'They rejected his specious defense of Star Wars'
>
> *See also* specie

spade, spayed

> spade *n.* a long-handled digging tool; a playing card suit
>
> spayed *v.* past participle of spay, to remove the ovaries of a female animal

spars, sparse

> spars *v.* 3d person, sing., present tense of spar, to practice boxing with light gloves or without striking
>
> spars *n.* (pl.) masts or booms of a ship; stout poles
>
> sparse *adj.* thin; lightly distributed, meager: 'The budget provided sparse funding for the homeless'

specie, species

> specie *[spee'•she] n.* coins, gold or silver, not paper money
>
> species *[spee'•sheez] n.* a class of individual animals or plants that have common characteristics; the symbol for bread and wine in the Eucharistic church service
>
> *See also* spacious

spilt, spilth, split

> spilt *v.* past participle of spill, to pour or drop accidentally: 'The milk was spilt on the ground by the children'; to spread out of bounds: 'The audience spilt onto the stage'; to shed or flow: 'Nobody wants to see any more blood spilt in wars'; to divulge: 'She has always spilt my secrets'
>
> spilth *n.* a fall; a spilling
>
> split *n.* a piece broken off; a sharp difference between groups: 'the split between rich and poor'; an organization's rupture: 'There was a split between the two union factions'; an ice cream dish made with fruit: 'a banana split'

split *v.* to break or tear into parts; to become torn: 'I split my pants at the seams'; to take off (slang): 'My boyfriend just split and left me broke'

spits, spitz

spits *v.* 3d person, sing., present tense of spit, to eject saliva

spitz *v.* a type of dog

spoor, spore

spoor *n.* an animal's trail or scent, enabling one to track it

spore *n.* a reproductive cell of many organisms

staff, staph

staff *n.* a long stick or rod often used for support; a group of assistants or personnel; the lines and spaces on which music is written

staph *n.* short for staphylococcus, a parasitic bacteria:'He caught a staph infection while in the hospital'

staid, stayed

staid *adj.* grave, sedate; old-fashioned: 'The old senator retained his staid manner'

stayed *v.* past tense of stay, to continue; to remain: 'The guests stayed at our home too long'; to endure: 'Despite the attacks leveled at her, she stayed the course and continued her race for office'

stair, stare

stair *n.* a series or group of steps that you climb or descend

stare *v.* to look intently with one's eyes open: 'People stare at him in astonishment because of his bizarre clothing'

stake, steak

stake *n.* a pointed stick or post placed in the ground as part of a fence or plant support; a bet; a share or major interest in a business or any venture; a vertical post used in punishment: 'Joan of Arc was burned at the stake'

stake *v.* to risk something on the outcome of a venture: 'I'll stake my reputation on that man's honesty'; to give someone money: 'stake him to a meal'; to mark with a stake, or to secure or fasten to a stake

steak *n.* a slice of beef or large fish cut thick for broiling or
   frying

stanch, staunch, stench

stanch *v.* to stop the flow of blood or other liquids; to stop
   any excessive loss: 'They'll stanch the outflow of gold by
   buying more at home'

staunch *adj.* strong or steadfastly loyal: 'Liberals were his
   staunch supporters in the election'

stench *n.* a very bad odor

standby, stand by

standby *n.* a substitute announcer or actor, used when a
   regular performer can't make it; a traveler without a
   reservation waiting for a last-minute seat; a supporter of
   a cause or person; something on which one relies: 'That
   old umbrella is still my standby'

stand by *v.* to support; to wait; to stick to one's views: 'I stand
   by my previously stated position'

stand-in, stand in

stand-in *n.* a person who fills in for a movie actor while the
   scene is being set up; any substitute for another person:
   'I'm a stand-in for the professor tonight'

stand in *v.* refers to one's good standing with another: 'I stand
   in good stead with these business people'; the act of
   substituting: 'If the star remains ill, the understudy will
   have to stand in for her'

standoff, stand off

standoff *n.* a tie in sports: 'The game was a standoff, 0-0, and
   was called after 20 innings'

stand off *v.* to move away; to stay at a distance: 'He tends to
   stand off from the main group at the party'; to avoid or
   repel: 'They hoped to stand off the enemy for years if
   necessary'

standout, stand out

standout *n.* a superior or outstanding person: 'That rookie is
   a standout in his class'

stand out *v.* to stick out or project physically: 'The proposed balcony would stand out from the main entrance'; to be noteworthy: 'That woman's stature makes her stand out from the rest of the crowd'

stare *See* stair

starlet, starlit

starlet *n.* a young movie actress; a starfish

starlit *adj.* lighted by stars: 'the starlit sky'

stater, stator

stater *n.* an ancient gold or silver coin

stator *n.* a stationary motor part around which a rotor turns

stationary, stationery

stationary *adj.* immobile; still, either physically or figuratively: 'The building was stationary even in the hurricane'; 'Prices remained stationary even after wages rose'

stationery *n.* writing materials and implements such as pens, pencils, and paper: 'That store carries a complete line of stationery'; writing paper with matching envelopes

statue, stature, statute

statue *n.* a carved, cast, or molded depiction of a person, animal, thing, or abstraction

stature *n.* the height of any body or object; status or quality gained by achievement: 'Her stature as a writer is undiminished by this latest work'

statute *n.* a law or a regulation

staunch *See* stanch

stayed *See* staid

steak *See* stake

steal, steel, stele

steal *v.* to take something, such as money, property, or ideas, from someone wrongfully and without permission; in baseball, a base runner's advance to another base before the ball has been hit; to look quickly: 'steal a glance'; to move very quietly: 'She tried to steal up the stairs at 2 A.M. so her parents wouldn't hear her'

steel *n.* processed iron: 'Cars are made of steel'; great
  strength: 'His nerves are made of steel'
stele *[steel'•ee] n.* a monument; a tablet on the side of a building
stele *[steel] n.* a cylinder in plant roots and stems

steep, step, steppe

steep *v.* to soak in liquid: 'steep the tea bag'; to fill or
  saturate: 'She'll steep her screenplay in sex and violence'
steep *adj.* sharply angled: 'That's a steep hill'; big or great:
  'You're asking for a steep pay increase at 20 percent';
  expensive: 'Those prices are steep for used cars'
step *n.* the movement of the feet for advancing; a stride; a
  general movement in a direction: 'One small step for
  man, one giant step for mankind'; a stage in a
  development or process: 'This is the first step toward
  freedom'; one unit of a set of stairs: 'Go up one step at a
  time'; a move or style in dancing: 'I know that step'
steppe *n.* a vast treeless expanse with extreme temperatures
  and arid soil, usually referring to Russia and Siberia

steer, stere

steer *n.* a castrated ox raised for beef; a piece of advice: 'He
  gave me a bum steer on that stock'
steer *v.* to guide: 'steer the car'; to direct: 'They'll steer me to
  the right restaurant'
stere *n.* a timber measure, a cubic meter

stele *See* steal
stench *See* stanch
stile, style

stile *n.* a step or rung used to scale a wall or fence that holds
  sheep or cattle; an upright panel used to frame furniture
  pieces; a turnstile
style *n.* a characteristic or distinctive manner, appearance,
  action, or way of life; 'The house was built in a postmodern
  style'; an artistic method: 'She paints in a realistic style'
style *v.* to design something distinctive: 'We'll style your hair
  like that actress's'; to use a name or designation: 'They
  style themselves freedom fighters'

stimulate *See* simulate

stoic, Stoic, stoke

stoic *adj.* calm, uncomplaining, impassive; not showing
passion or feeling: 'They were stoic about the hurricane'

Stoic *n.* the ancient Greek philosophy that teaches passive
acceptance of one's fate and that one should remain
unmoved by passions, joy, or grief

stoke *n.* a unit in physics that measures fluids

stoke *v.* to poke a fire's coals; to feed coal to a fire or steam
engine; to stir up trouble: 'He'll stoke discontent with his
speeches'

stolen, stollen, stolon

stolen *v.* past participle of steal, to wrongfully take

stollen *[shtoh'•lin] n.* a sweet bread containing fruit and nuts

stolon *n.* in botany, an underground stem; in zoology, a bud

stoop, stop, stoup, stupe

stoop *n.* a small series of steps leading to the entrance of a
house; a porch or veranda

stoop *v.* to bend over, mainly with the head and shoulders; to
lower oneself in behavior, to debase: 'Don't stoop to
argue with him, he's so bigoted'

stop *n.* the act of stopping or being halted: 'You'd better put a
stop to your behavior or else'; a place where vehicles
halt: 'a bus stop' 'a train stop'; an end

stoup *[stoop] n.* a basin for holy water in a church

stupe *n.* a wet medicated cloth used as a skin counterirritant

straight, strait

straight *adj.* not curved or bent: 'A straight line is the shortest
distance between two points'; direct or frank: 'He's
straight, you can believe what he says'; off drugs or no
longer engaged in criminal activity; heterosexual;
conventional: 'Those people are very straight: they don't
party or stay up late'; complete, wholehearted: 'They vote
the straight party ticket'; clean or put in the proper
position: 'Make the room straight'; without elaboration:
'Tell the story straight'

straight *adv.* directly: 'Go straight home'

strait *n.* a narrow passageway connecting two larger bodies of water; a position of difficulty or distress (often used in plural): 'dire straits'

stricter, stricture, structure

stricter *adj.* comparative of strict, more demanding of performance or behavior, more severe: 'This school was stricter than that one, insisting on higher grades'; more exact

stricture *n.* restriction or something that limits: 'moral stricture'; an adverse criticism: 'The writer made a major stricture on the play'

structure *n.* a building or something that is constructed; the way something is organized and developed: 'the structure of a play'; 'the city's political structure'

structure *v.* to organize: 'They'll structure the meeting to allow for a few short speeches'

strikeout, strike out

strikeout *n.* a baseball term for someone who is out after three strikes

strike out *v.* to fail at any endeavor; to cross out: 'Strike out those extra words'; to get started: 'We'll strike out for the mountain top directly after breakfast'

strong-arm, strong arm

strong-arm *v.* to apply undue pressure to someone, threatening the use of force: 'Some landlords strong-arm their tenants to get them to leave so the building can bring in higher rents'

strong arm *n.* an arm with muscular strength: 'Someone who excercises regularly will develop a strong arm'

studded, studied

studded *v.* past tense of stud, to decorate with small nailheads; to cluster (something) thickly: 'The queen's crown was studded with jewels' studied *v.* past tense of study, to learn by reading or thinking; to go to school; to observe closely; to consider: 'He studied his options carefully before deciding'

stupe *See* stoop

style *See* stile

subside, subsidy

subside *v.* to become less, in activity, arousal, or response, often to below normal level: 'An audience's applause tends to subside after two to three minutes'; to abate: 'After a minute, my anger should subside'

subsidy *n.* a special monetary award or government aid to support the operations of a private firm or industrial enterprise whose work is deemed advantageous to the public

suburb, superb

suburb *n.* a residential area surrounding a city

superb *adj.* outstanding, marvelous: 'The musician gave a superb performance of the Beethoven concerto'

succah, Succoth

succah *[sook'•uh] n.* a temporary building made of branches and leaves used to celebrate the Jewish Festival of Tabernacles

Succoth *[soo'•koth] n.* a Jewish harvest festival which commemorates the temporary shelters erected by Hebrew tribes following their exodus from Egypt

success, succus, succuss

success *n.* the favorable result; the attainment of wealth or influence; a person who has attained such standing

succus *[sook'•is] n.* a medicinal juice

succuss *[suh•kuss'] v.* to shake up

succor, sucker

succor *[sucker] n.* help or relief: 'The UN's refugee aid provides succor to millions throughout the world'

sucker *n.* someone who can be easily cheated: ' "Never give a sucker an even break" '(W. C. Fields); a lollipop;

someone who is attracted to something: 'I'm a sucker for talk shows'

Sudan *See* sodden

sudden *See* sodden

sue *See* sou

suede, swayed

suede *[swayed] n.* the rough or napped underside of tanned leather

swayed *v.* past tense of sway, to swing from side to side: 'The couple swayed to the music'; to influence: 'His views were swayed by the mass protests'

suer *See* sewer

suit *See* soot

suite, sweet

suite *[sweet] n.* a set of furniture; a group of adjoining rooms: 'We rented a suite in a fancy hotel'; a group of attendants, a retinue: 'The rock star was always accompanied by a suite of helpers'; a short musical piece

sweet *adj.* sugary; cloying: 'She is just too, too sweet for words'; dear

sum *See* some

summa, summer

summa *[soo'•muh] n.* with the highest honors or distinction: 'Summa cum laude is a degree reflecting the highest possible grades'; a massive philosophical work

summer *n.* the season between spring and fall

summary, summery

summary *n.* a brief account of a longer document or statement: 'I need a 1-page summary of this 26-page report by tonight'

summary *adj.* brief; prompt; quickly executed without formality: 'a summary trial'; comprehensive

summery *adj.* like the summer; very hot

sun *See* son

superb *See* suburb

surf *See* serf

surge *See* serge

surplice, surplus

surplice *[ser'•plis] n.* a knee-length religious garment

surplus *[ser'•pluss] n.* the amount over one's needs; the amount of the net worth of a corporation greater than its capital

swayed *See* suede

sweet *See* suite

sword *See* soared

sycosis *See* psychosis

symbol *See* cymbal

symmetry *See* cemetery

sync/synch *See* sink

synopsis, synopses

synopsis *n.* a brief outline or summary of a longer document; an abstract

synopses *n.* plural of synopsis

syntax, sin tax

syntax *n.* the way or order in which different parts of speech are put together to make sense; the branch of grammar dealing with this; the rules of ordering parts of speech

sin tax *n.* a tax on items deemed harmful or immoral, such as liquor and cigarettes

synthesis, syntheses, synthesize

synthesis *n.* the pulling together of different ideas, styles, or parts to make a whole; the combination of elements to form a whole; the chemical action combining different substances to form a new one; the creation of music via electronic means

syntheses *n.* plural of synthesis

synthesize *v.* to create a synthesis; to produce by synthesis

T

tablespoonsful, tablespoons full

tablespoonsful *n.* (pl.) one tablespoon filled more than once: 'She swallowed three tablespoonsful of the cough medicine'

tablespoons full *n.* (pl.) individual tablespoons: 'I want three tablespoons full of cough medicine to serve three patients'

tacked, tact

tacked *v.* past tense of tack, to attach something with a tack or a pin; to add on

tact *n.* sensitivity to another's feelings; the ability to know the right thing to say in order to avoid offense: 'He used tact in criticizing employees gently'

tacks, tax

tacks *v.* 3d person, sing., present tense of tack, to attach something with a tack

tax *v.* to assess or impose a compulsory payment to a government: 'We will tax! tax! tax! spend! spend! spend!'; to make serious demands: 'That will tax my resolve'; to accuse or censure: 'They might tax him with a charge of malfeasance'

tai *See* tie

tail, tael, tale, taille

tail *n.* the flexible appendage of an animal; the reverse side of a coin: 'heads or tails'; in the plural, a man's dress suit:

'He wore white tie and tails'; the rear section of an airplane; the bottom or last of anything; a person who has another under surveillance and secretly tracks his or her movements; the buttocks (slang)

tail *v.* to follow, to shadow

tael *[tale] n.* a weight or coin

tale *n.* a story, a piece of gossip; a lie: 'Mark Twain loved a tall tale'

taille *[tah'•yuh] n.* a feudal tax

tailer, tailor

tailer *n.* one who follows someone secretly

tailor *n.* one who makes or repairs clothes

takeoff, take off

takeoff *n.* a departure; an ascent in an airplane: 'The takeoff of the airplane was faultless'; mimicry: 'His takeoff of the mayor was hilarious'

take off *v.* to remove: 'Please take off your hat'; to deduct: 'They'll take 30 percent off your bill this week'; to depart: 'They'll take off from JFK at 9 P.M.'; to become very popular: 'That record will take off fast and become number one on the charts'; to stay away from work: 'I plan to take off every Monday this summer'

takeout, take out

takeout *adj.* refers to prepared food sold for consumption at home, not in a restaurant: 'That was a good takeout Chinese meal'

take out *v.* to go out with someone socially: 'He will take her out for the first time on New Year's Eve'; to obtain insurance or a license: 'Before the wedding, they'll have to take out a marriage license'; to remove: 'The dentist will take out my molar at my next visit'; to kill (slang): 'They would take out the rival drug ring if they could'

takeover, take over

takeover *n.* a political or business seizure of control: 'His takeover of the cereal company cost $17 million' take over *v.* to assume leadership or control: 'She will take over the reins of the company at the beginning of next year'

talc, talk, torque/torc

talc *[talk] n.* a fine powder

talk *[tawk] n.* a conversation; speech; a dialogue; a lecture: 'I loved the author's talk last night'; a special conference: 'peace talk'; rumor or gossip: 'There's talk that he's quitting his job'; slang: 'street talk'; empty speech: 'You're all talk and no action'

torque *or* torc *[tawrk] n.* a force that produces rotation; the mechanical ability to overcome resistance to turning

tale *See* tail

tall, tole, toll

tall *adj.* having above average height: 'Most basketball players are very tall'; relating to one's height: 'She's five feet, four inches tall'; large; extreme; exaggerated: 'a tall tale'

tole *n.* metal enamelware

toll *n.* a fee paid to use a highway or other public facility; the loss from a disaster: 'The earthquake's death toll rose to 500'; the cost incurred by hard work: 'That campaign took its toll; he's been out of it since then'; the sound of a ringing bell

tamper, temper

tamper *n.* someone who tamps or packs down tightly; a part in an atomic bomb

tamper *v.* to alter for dishonest purposes: 'The burglar tried to tamper with the lock'; to try to influence illegally: 'The lawyers tried to tamper with the jury'

temper *n.* one's disposition; a tendency to anger: 'She has a bad temper'; strength given to metals by special heat treatment

temper *v.* to moderate: 'They all temper their ideologies with practical policies'; to harden, as with metals; to mix materials to achieve a consistent output

tankard, tanker

> tankard *n.* a large silver or pewter drinking cup, usually lidded
>
> tanker *n.* a vehicle, like a ship, plane, or truck, designed to carry liquids or gases: 'an oil tanker'

tannage, tonnage/tunnage

> tannage *n.* the act of tanning; something that is tanned
>
> tonnage *or* tunnage *n.* the capacity of a ship or the weight of the goods it carries; the total capacity of a port

tantara/tarantara, tarantella, tarantula

> tantara *or* tarantara *n.* the sound of a trumpet
>
> tarantella *n.* a fast Italian folk dance marked by showy movements and rapid turns
>
> tarantula *n.* a large hairy spider; a wolf spider

taper, tapir

> taper *n.* a thin candle; a long candle wick; the gradually reduced thickness of an item; one who records on magnetic tape
>
> taper *v.* to reduce or lessen gradually: 'Their interest in camping will taper off when they see how much work is involved'
>
> tapir *[taper] n.* a South American short-legged animal

tare, tear

> tare *n.* a deduction from the gross weight of a product's container and its contents to allow for the weight of the container; a noxious weed
>
> tear *[rhymes w. ware] v.* to pull something away violently: 'He will tear the watch from my hand'; to move forcefully or quickly: 'That hurricane wind will tear through the orchard'; to leave reluctantly: 'It was hard to tear myself away from the party'; to cause to have a rip; to force one to make tough choices: 'Choosing between his career and love will tear him apart'
>
> *See also* tear

tarmac *See* ptarmic

taro, tarot

taro *[tah'•ro] n.* a plant widely cultivated in the Pacific for its edible root

tarot *[ta'•ro] n.* a set of cards used in fortune telling

Tatar/Tartar, tartar

Tatar *or* Tartar *n.* a people of central Asia, descendants of Mongolian tribes that conquered eastern Europe in the 13th century

tartar *n.* an encrustation on the teeth: 'If you don't brush and floss your teeth regularly they will accumulate tartar'; a formidable opponent or one with a savage temper; a creamy substance derived from grape juice, used as a dressing for foods: 'tartar sauce'

tau, taw

tau *[rhymes w.* ow] *n.* a letter of the Greek alphabet

taw *n.* a letter of the Hebrew alphabet; a playing marble; a shooting marble

taw *v.* to dress raw material such as animal skins

taught, taut

taught *v.* past tense of teach: 'He taught school for twelve years'

taut *adj.* stretched tight: 'The rope was taut'

See also tort

taupe, tope, toupee

taupe *[rhymes w.* hope] *n.* a brownish gray color

tope *n.* a species of small shark; a grove; a Buddhist dome for relics

tope *v.* to drink excessively

toupee *[too•pay'] n.* a hair piece or wig (usually for men)

tax *See* tacks

taxes, taxis

taxes *n.* (pl.) more than one tax, a compulsory payment

taxis *n.* (pl.) taximeter cabs, cars that carry passengers for a charge

tea, tee, ti

> tea *n.* a drink made from the leaves of the tea plant; an afternoon social at which tea is served
>
> tee *n.* the letter T; a small wooden peg used to hold a golf ball
>
> tee *v.* to place a golf ball on a tee
>
> ti *[tee] n.* the seventh musical syllable; a small Pacific tree

teal, teel/til, teil

> teal *n.* a species of duck
>
> teel or til *n.* sesame
>
> teil *[teel] n.* a linden tree

team, teem

> team *n.* a group of people playing a sport: 'The team lined up on the right side of the field'; a working collaboration: 'They're a good team'; two animals, such as horses, used to pull farm machinery or vehicles: 'Hitch up the team for a ride into town'
>
> team *v.* to work or join together: 'I'll team with him to speed up the work'; to drive a team of draft animals
>
> teem *v.* to be full to overflowing: 'The place will teem with birds in a few weeks'; to pour out: 'It will teem outside, so wear a raincoat'

tear, tier, Tyr

> tear *[rhymes w. fear] n.* a saline drop secreted by the eye: 'A tear rolled down his cheek'; any small drop of liquid
>
> tier *[rhymes w. fear] n.* a row or layer of something: 'We sat in the twelfth tier of the stadium'
>
> Tyr *n.* the Norse god of war
>
> *See also* tare

teas, tease, tees

> teas *n.* plural of tea, a drink
>
> tease *v.* to annoy or irritate with jokes or insults; to comb hair by pushing toward the scalp; to comb wool
>
> tees *n.* plural of tee, a small wooden peg used in golf

tee *See* tea

teel *See* teal

teem *See* team

teeter, tether, tetter, titer, titter

>teeter *v.* to walk unsteadily, to waver: 'Watch her teeter on her spike heels'; to waver: 'The candidates teeter on the edge of a decision'; to be at a danger point: 'They teeter on the brink of a depression'

>tether *n.* a rope fastened to an animal to limit its range; the limit of one's ability, resources, or patience: 'I'm at the end of my tether'

>tetter *n.* a skin disease

>titer *n.* the concentration of a substance in a solution

>titter *n.* a nervous laugh

teeth, teethe

>teeth *n.* plural of tooth, a bonelike structure set in the jaws

>teethe *v.* to develop teeth: 'The baby should teethe in about six weeks'

teil *See* teal

temper *See* tamper

tempera, tempura

>tempera *[tem'•pur•a] n.* a painting medium in which pigment is mixed with egg yolk

>tempura *[tem•por'•a] n.* a Japanese dish of battered, deep-fried seafood or vegetables

tenace, tennis, tenuis

>tenace *n.* a combination of playing cards

>tennis *n.* a game played on a court with a ball, rackets, and a net

>tenuis *[ten'•yuh•wis] n.* a voiceless consonant

tenant, tenent, tenet

>tenant *n.* one who lives in a residence but doesn't own it: 'A tenant in the building is thinking of buying into a co-op'

tenent *adj.* a biological term: the ability of certain insects to hang by hairs, feet, etc.

tenet *n.* an opinion, belief, or dogma especially one held by a group: 'A tenet of his church calls for tithing'

tenor, tenure, tenner

tenor *n.* a high male voice; a singer with such a voice: 'Caruso was a great operatic tenor'; the meaning or tone of speech or actions: 'I will never forget the tenor of her farewell letter'

tenure *n.* the right to keep a job, protected from dismissal, after a trial period (often used with teachers): 'He will receive tenure in three years'; occupying an office or owning property

tenner *n.* a ten-pound note or ten-dollar bill (slang)

tense, tents

tense *n.* a verbal form or inflection which conveys the time of an action

tense *adj.* tight or taut; marked by strain or suspense; showing nervous tension: 'He's always tense when talking to the boss'; unable to relax

tents *n.* (pl.) temporary canvas or nylon shelters used in camping and by the military

terce, terse

terce *n.* the third canonical hour

terse *adj.* abrupt; concise: 'That was a very terse report'

termer, tremor

termer, *n.* someone serving for a period of time, such as a prisoner or a student: 'a first termer'

tremor *n.* a shaking or trembling: 'an earth tremor of 6.6 on the Richter scale'; 'People reveal certain illnesses via a tremor of the hands'

tern, terne, turn

tern *n.* a bird; a schooner

terne *n.* an alloy of lead and tin

turn *n.* a change of direction: 'Make a right turn at the light'; a rotation; the beginning of a new time period: 'the turn of the century'; a period of duty or a shift: 'It's your turn to do the dishes'; a shift in events or circumstances: 'Business took a turn for the worse'; a twist or injury: 'He gave his ankle a nasty turn when he fell'; a special deed or act: 'One good turn deserves another'; a short trip out and back: 'a turn in the park'; a shock: 'News of his illness gave me quite a turn'

terrain, terrane, terrene, terrine, tureen

terrain *n.* the physical features of an area of land: 'The commander surveyed the terrain'

terrane *n.* a rock formation

terrene *adj.* earthly, mundane

terrine *n.* an earthenware jar or pot in which foods are cooked and served; a type of stew

tureen *n.* a deep covered dish, usually used for serving soups

testis, testes

testis *n.* a testicle, a male reproductive gland

testes *n.* (pl.) more than one testicle

tether, tetter *See* teeter

tew *See* to

Thai *See* tie

than, then

than *conj.* introduces the second part of a comparison: 'His sister is older than he'; 'She writes more often than he'; shows greater or lesser quantities: 'There are more than 10,000 people at this demonstration'

then *n.* a specific time: 'Until then, don't do anything about it'

then *adj.* belonging to a specified time: 'The then president was highly regarded'

then *adv.* at a certain time: 'Will you be there then?'; the next action or next in order: 'We'll eat, then we'll go to the movies'; therefore, as the second part of a logical clause or as a consequence: 'If you have a problem, then we'll talk'

their, there, they're

their *adj.* possessive case of the pronoun they: 'their jobs'; 'their home'

there *n.* that point or stage: 'He'll take the matter from there'

there *adv.* at that place, as opposed to *here*: 'We will go there for dinner'; available: 'That computer is there for everyone'; in existence: 'That obstacle was not meant to be there'

there *pron.* something that exists, used to introduce a clause: 'There are 8 million people in this city'; 'There is too much crime here'

they're *contr.* they are: 'They're going to the movies'

theirs, there's

theirs *pron.* belonging to them (there is no need for a noun to follow *theirs* as there is with *their*): 'The car is theirs'

there's *contr.* there is: 'There's plenty of room in the front of the theater'

thesis, theses

thesis *n.* a long dissertation involving original research required of certain students for an academic degree; an argument or position: 'His thesis was that all life is cyclical in nature'

theses *n.* (pl.) more than one thesis

thigh, thy

thigh *n.* the upper leg of a person or animal

thy *adj.* possessive case of the pronoun thee: 'thy kingdom come'

thrash, thresh

thrash *v.* to flog, to whip: 'The warden will thrash the prisoners'; to defeat badly in competition; to flail or swing about wildly and violently

thresh *v.* to beat ripened grain to separate seeds from the husk: 'The farmhands will thresh the wheat after the harvest'

thread, threat

thread *n.* a thin, long piece of textile fiber like cotton or wool used in sewing; a long piece of any substance; the thin, fine line of a discussion, argument, or train of thought: 'I have long since lost the thread of his thesis'; the spiral part of a screw

thread *v.* to put thread through the eye of a needle; adapted in sports to a very fine move: 'Jordan can thread his way through the opposition with ease'; to insert some type of roll, as of film: 'thread the film in the camera'

threat *n.* a statement of intent to harm someone; a dangerous person or object: 'That man's a threat to society'

threw, through

threw *v.* past tense of throw, to hurl or propel: 'The pitcher threw a knuckle ball'; to block, frustrate, or overcome: 'The heavy burden nearly threw her'; to put on or remove quickly: 'I threw on the first shirt I saw'; to indulge in: 'She threw a tantrum when he lied'; to lose a game intentionally: 'The gamblers made money when the team threw the game'

through *prep.* in one end and out the other: 'I went through the open door'; from one time period consecutively to and including another: 'I work Monday through Friday'; by means of: 'I earned my promotion through hard work'; completed or used up: 'I went through the paper in ten minutes'

through *adj.* finished: 'I'm through with this course.'

through *adv.* completion or accomplishment: 'see this job through'; completely: 'I'm soaked through'

throes, throws

throes *n.* (pl.) pains: 'She is going through the throes of childbirth'; a hard or difficult struggle: 'in the throes of painting'

throws *v.* 3d person, sing., present tense of throw, to hurl through the air; to confuse

throne, thrown

throne *n.* a royal chair or its occupant; royal power: 'A
speech from the throne carries special weight'; toilet
(slang)

thrown *v.* past participle of throw, to toss or propel: 'The ball
was thrown by the quarterback'

thy *See* thigh

thyme, time

thyme *[time] n.* an herbal leaf used in cooking

time *n.* a measure of when or how long something takes,
exists, or lasts, measured in seconds, minutes, hours,
days, years, etc.; an age or era: 'The time of the Kennedy
presidency'; a season: 'It's hot for this time of year'; an
appointed hour: 'Be there on time'; conditions during a
certain period: 'We had a hard time during the
depression'; the moment or period when something
happens: 'They eat dinner at a fixed time'

ti *See* tea

tic, tick

tic *n.* a twitching, an involuntary spasm in the face or limbs

tick *n.* the sound made by a clock or watch; a mark used to
check off something; a bloodsucking arachnid; the
covering of a mattress

ticks, tix

ticks *n.* plural of tick: a clock's or watch's sound; check marks

ticks *v.* 3d person, sing., present tense of tick, to make
repeated clicking sounds: 'The clock ticks too loudly'

tix *n.* tickets (slang)

tide, tied

tide *n.* the rise and fall of ocean waters; anything that rises
and falls: 'the tide of public opinion'

tide *v.* to move with the tide

tied *v.* past tense of tie, to attach with a cord or similar object;
in sports, to make the same score

tie, Thai, tai, tye

tie *n.* a necktie; a bond or connecting link: 'His tie to his family was always strong'; a rope or cord used to fasten or attach something; an equal score in sports competitions: 'The game's 5-5 tie lasted into the ninth inning'

tie *v.* to bind with a cord, wire, or other object; to make the knot in a necktie; to fasten; to bind, oblige, or restrict; to make the same score in a contest

Thai *[tie] n.* a native of Thailand

tai *[tie] n.* a Japanese fish

tye *n.* a trough for washing ores

tie-in, tie in

tie-in *n.* a connection or association: 'The advertiser arranged a promotional tie-in between its automobile client and the movie'

tie in *v.* to be consistent: 'Her story will tie in with his'

tier *See* tear

tie-up, tie up

tie-up *n.* a temporary halt: 'The traffic tie-up lasted for hours'

tie up *v.* to fasten: 'He will tie up the package'; to delay: 'That accident will tie up train traffic for hours'

tigress, Tigris

tigress *n.* a female tiger

Tigris *n.* a river in Iraq

timber, timbre

timber *n.* cut wood ready for use; a group of trees grown for wood; material or qualification for a particular position: 'I always felt she was presidential timber'

timbre *[tam' ber] n.* the quality of sound or resonance made by a person or an instrument: 'His voice had a beautiful timbre'

time *See* thyme

tinge, tingle, twinge

tinge *n.* a touch or trace of a color or other quality: 'His voice had a tinge of sadness'

tingle *n*. the feeling of prickles or slight shakes due to
excitement, anticipation, cold, or illness

twinge *n*. a slight touch of pain or tingling, physical or
emotional: 'He had a slight twinge of regret at her
leaving, but it passed'

tinned, tint

tinned *v*. past tense of tin, to put a coat of tin on a substance:
'They tinned the roof to add protection against rain'

tint *n*. a hue; a variation of color; a slight touch of another
color added to a main color; a pale color; a hair dye

tinny, tiny

tinny *[tin'•nee]. adj.* having a weak metallic sound; not solid
or strong

tiny *[tie'•nee] adj.* very small: 'just a tiny bit of milk in my
coffee'

titan, titian

titan *n*. a giant in accomplishment, size, or power:
'Rockefeller was a titan of the oil industry'

titian *n*. an orange brown color

titer *See* teeter

titillate, titivate

titillate *v*. to cause an exciting or pleasant sensation: 'That
lecture is sure to titillate you'; to stimulate sexually

titivate *v*. to dress up or spruce up

titter *See* teeter

tix *See* ticks

to, too, tew, two

to *prep*. shows direction: 'We're going to the movies.';
indicates the receiver of an action: 'Give this to her'; 'I
talked to him'; to a certain extent: 'We'll fight to the last
man'; in grammar, to indicate the infinitive of a verb: 'to
go', 'to run', 'to see'

to *adv*. in one direction; toward a position: 'Push the door to';
into consciousness: 'After five minutes, he came to';
alternating this way and that: 'He ran to and fro'

too *adv.* in addition: 'She is beautiful, and smart, too'; more than enough: 'You're too much'

tew *n.* worry; anxiety

two *n.* the sum of one and one; 2; a pair, or a couple: 'two houses'

two *adj.* amounts to two: 'This song is a two parter'

toad, toed, towed

toad *n.* a froglike animal

toed *v.* past tense of toe, to touch with one's toes; to conform: 'He toed the mark after that scolding'

toed *adj.* having a number or type of toes: 'She was pigeontoed'

towed *v.* past tense of tow, to haul

toady, toddy, tody

toady *n.* a sycophant, a yes-man

toddy *n.* a hot, spiced rum-based drink

tody *n.* a West Indian bird

tocsin, toxin

tocsin *n.* an alarm

toxin *n.* a poisonous compound

to-do, to do

to-do *n.* a fuss, confusion: 'What's all the to-do about?'

to do *v.* to perform, to accomplish: 'We have much to do today'

toe, tow

toe *n.* one of the extensions or appendages at the end of a foot; the tip of a shoe, sock, or stocking

toe *v.* to touch with one's toes; to obey: 'You'd better toe the line on this issue, or else'

tow *n.* the act of being pulled; under control or guidance: 'I went to California with my children in tow'; short fibers used in making yarn; a rope or cable used to pull something; 'a ski tow'

toed *See* toad

toiled, told, tolled

toiled *v.* past tense of toil, to work hard and long: 'They toiled for six months to fix the road'

told *v.* past tense of tell, to let someone know; to reveal; to say or write; to command: 'I told you to clean your room'; to have an effect: 'In my work as an editor, every error told'

tolled *v.* past tense of toll, to ring a bell: 'They tolled the church bells at his funeral'; to have taxed or exacted a toll or charge

toilet, toilette

toilet *[toy'•let] n.* a bathroom; a fixture or bowl for urination or defecation; the act of dressing

toilette *[twa•let'] n.* the act of grooming oneself; one's style of dress

toke, toque

toke *n.* a puff on a marijuana cigarette (slang)

toque *n.* a woman's small, round, brimless hat

told *See* toiled

tole, toll *See* tall

tolled *See* toiled

tomb, tome

tomb *[toom] n.* a burial place; a grave, a large burial vault, a monument: 'Who's buried in Grant's tomb?'

tome *[rhymes w. home] n.* a big, heavy book; a volume in a series

ton, tone, tun, tune

ton *n.* a measure of weight (2,240 pounds); a large amount: 'We donated a ton of money and materials for earthquake relief'

tone *n.* a musical sound; a vocal pitch that conveys meaning; a style or manner of writing: 'This piece has an optimistic tone'; bodily health: 'Exercise produces good muscle tone'; a general quality or characteristic: 'That house gives this area a nice tone'; color quality

tun *n.* a large wine or beer cask

tune *n.* a musical melody; the right musical pitch; agreement: 'I'm in tune with what you're doing'; a state of harmony or fit: 'He's never in tune with his times'

tune *v.* to adjust a radio, TV, musical instrument, or mechanical device: 'To tune a motor is as difficult as to tune a piano'

tongs, tongues

tongs *[tahngs] n.* tools used for holding or picking up: 'fireplace tongs'; Chinese secret societies

tongues *[tungs] n.* plural of tongue, the organ in the mouth that has taste buds and is used for licking, tasting, swallowing, and speaking; languages; manner of speech: 'sharp tongues'; thin pieces of an area: 'Tongues of land off the island'; flaps of shoes beneath the laces

tonnage/tunnage *See* tannage

too *See* to

tool, tule, tulle

tool *n.* a device, machine, or implement used by hand to make or fix something; any useful thing: 'This word collection is a useful tool'; an exploited person: 'He was a tool in the hands of his supervisors'

tool *v.* to create or decorate with a tool; to drive in a leisurely manner

tule *[too'•lee] n.* a bulrush, a plant that grows in wetlands

tulle *[tool] n.* a fine, gauzy material used in veils or costumes

tope *See* taupe

topography, typography

topography *n.* the physical features of a place; the relation of natural and manmade features of a place; a graphic representation of an area; the art or practice of graphic representation of an area

typography *n.* the art of printing types and styles

toque *See* toke

torque/torc *See* talk

tort, torte

tort *n.* a wrong for which a civil suit can be brought

torte *n.* a rich cake

See also taught

tortious, tortuous, torturous

tortious *[tor'•shus] adj.* relating to a tort or a civil wrong

tortuous *[torch'•oo•us] adj.* twisting or winding: 'a tortuous road'; complicated or devious: 'They planned a tortuous story to tell the district attorney'

torturous *adj.* cruelly painful; causing agony

touch, touché

touch *n.* the act of touching; a light stroke; a small quantity: 'Put just a touch of paint on the wall'; a hint or indication: 'I have a touch of the flu'; a stroke of art: 'She has a wonderful touch on the saxophone'

touch *v.* to contact; to equal or rival in quantity: 'He doesn't touch her writing ability'; to eat: 'She didn't touch her food'; to affect or concern: 'Homelessness should touch all of us'; to treat or address: 'His speech failed to touch on the issue of housing'

touché *[too•shay'] interj.* from the French, in fencing, used to acknowledge a hit, now acknowledges a successful point in an argument, accusation, or a witty remark

tough, tuff

tough *n.* a violent person: 'He's a young tough who always hangs around that corner'

tough *v.* to endure or to stand firm (slang): 'tough it out'

tough *adj.* hard to break or eat: 'That meat is very tough'; strong: 'He can take it, he's tough'; severe: 'a tough summer'; difficult: 'That's a tough job'; great (slang)

tuff *n.* a rock composed of fine volcanic fragments

toughed, tuft

toughed *v.* past tense of tough, to stand firm or endure; to withstand pressure or difficulty: 'She toughed out the first year on a difficult job' tuft *n.* short strands of hair, grass, or similar matter emerging from a common base

tuft *v.* to sew or stitch a mattress tightly in order to keep its stuffing intact

toupee *See* taupe

towed *See* toad

toxin *See* tocsin

tracked, tract

tracked *v.* past tense of track, to trail, to follow: 'He tracked the wild bears'; to keep tabs on: 'They tracked the Venus spacecraft for millions of miles'

tract *n.* an area or stretch of land; a piece of printed propaganda; a bodily system: 'digestive tract'

trade-in, trade in

trade-in *n.* an exchange: 'The dealer took the old car as a trade-in for the new one'

trade in *v.* to buy or sell goods, stocks, or commodities: 'He can trade in gold on the commodities exchange'

trade-off, trade off

trade-off *n.* a compromise, an even exchange: 'Their union agreement was a trade-off of pay for production'

trade off *v.* to get rid of by exchange or trading: 'I think I will trade off my old Edsel'

trail, trial

trail *n.* a narrow or worn path, especially in a forest; an indication or mark that someone or something has gone by: 'The scouts left a trail of yellow markers behind them'

trail *v.* to follow someone: 'The private detective plans to trail her'; to be losing in competition: 'John and Karen trail Jack and Cindy in the tennis tournament'

trial *n.* a formal court hearing to judge guilt or innocence; something that tests one's patience and ability to cope: 'That hyperactive child is a trial to his parents'; a test of a process or product to see if and how it will work: 'New computers are always run through a severe trial'

trial *adj.* pertaining to a test: 'The new subway cars were put through dozens of trial runs'

travail, travel

travail *n.* toil, heavy labor, suffering

travail *v.* to toil or exert oneself

travel *v.* to journey; to move from place to place; to go on a trip; to go on the road; in basketball, to take illegal steps

tray, très, trey

tray *n.* a small carrying receptacle used mainly for food; an office receptacle for mail or other papers

très *[tray] adj.* French for *very*, as in 'très chic' (very elegant)

trey *n.* the side of a dice or domino that has three spots on it; a card numbered three

treasure, treasury, Treasury

treasure *n.* valued or dear objects such as precious metals or gems; a well-loved or valued object or person: 'That child's a treasure'

treasury *n.* a place that stores items of great value or interest: 'This library is a treasury of information'; a place where business or government funds are kept; the funds or income of firms

Treasury *n.* a central government's money manager

treaties, treatise

treaties *n.* (pl.) formal agreements between countries: 'After 40 years of war, Japan still has not signed any treaties with Russia or China'; any other formal agreements

treatise *[tree'•tiss] n.* a formal and systematic piece of writing about some subject including a methodical discussion of facts and conclusions: 'He wrote a treatise on Egyptian hieroglyphics'

tremor *See* termer

très, trey *See* tray

triad, tried

triad *n.* a set of three; a common chord in music

tried *v.* past tense of try, to attempt: 'He tried to find the right word in the dictionary'; to test: 'He tried the new recipe'; to conduct a legal case in court; to subject to stress or annoyance: 'That pupil tried the teacher's patience'

trial *See* trail

tricky, tricksy

tricky *adj.* difficult or complicated: 'Fixing a computer can be tricky'; deceitful: 'Watch that man, he's very tricky'

tricksy *adj.* playful, mischievous

trip, tripe

trip *n.* a voyage; the act of stumbling or falling; any error or slip; a visit or course: 'My trip to the bank'; 'My monthly trip to the doctor'; a reaction to certain hallucinogenic drugs (slang)

trip *v.* to walk lightly; to fall or stumble from hitting something with one's feet; to make a mistake or stumble in articulation: 'He may trip over the premier's name when introducing him'; to release a part that operates a mechanism

tripe *n.* part of the stomach of sheep or oxen used as a food; something worthless; a falsehood

trivia, trivial

trivia *n.* minor matters or items: 'The trivia contest tests your knowledge of little known facts'

trivial *adj.* not important: 'Don't bother me with trivial matters'

troche, trochee

troche *[troh'•kee] n.* a medicinal lozenge

trochee *[troh'•kee] n.* in poetry, a metrical foot consisting of an accented and an unaccented syllable

troop, trope, troupe

troop *n.* a group of soldiers: 'a troop of cavalry'; a group of people, animals, or insects assembled or moving together

trope *n.* the use of a word in a nonliteral sense, such as a metaphor or simile; a figure of speech troupe *[troop] n.* a company of theatrical performers

trooper, trouper

trooper *n.* a mounted policeman; a private soldier

trouper *n.* an experienced or veteran actor; a loyal worker or anyone loyal to an undertaking: 'She's a real trouper'

trussed, trust

trussed *v.* past tense of truss, to tie up; to tie up parts of fowl in cooking; to support with a truss or beam

trust *n.* reliance on or confidence in a person or thing; 'I put my trust in you to keep your promise'; business credit: 'sell goods on trust'; a property interest held by one person for the benefit of another person; a combination of several companies formed by a legal agreement

trustee, trusty

trustee *n.* one who holds property in trust; a member of a board which manages a college, church, or corporation; a nation that administers a trust territory

trusty *n.* a trusted person, often a convict who is given special privileges

trusty *adj.* trustworthy

tryout, try out

tryout *n.* a test of ability: 'He was given a tryout for the lead in the play'

try out *v.* to compete 'I think I will try out for the chorus'

tuff *See* tough

tuft *See* toughed

tuille *See* twill

tule, tulle *See* tool

tun, tune *See* ton

tune-up, tune up

tune-up *n.* an adjustment to a motor.: 'After the tune-up, the car ran beautifully'

tune up *v.* to bring musical instruments to a proper pitch: 'The orchestra will tune up'; to make adjustments to a motor

tunnage *See* tannage

turban, turbine

> turban *n.* a close-fitting head covering made of wound cloth and worn in Eastern countries; a woman's hat resembling a turban: 'Carmen Miranda wore a fruit-covered turban'
>
> turbine *[ter'•bin] n.* a machine with a rotor and blades, driven by pressure of fluid, steam, or gas

tureen *See* terrain

turn *See* tern

turnout, turn out

> turnout *n.* a gathering of people for a specific purpose: 'The turnout at the rally was impressive'; 'Heavy voter turnout'
>
> turn out *v.* to get rid of; to switch off: 'Turn out the lights, please'; to produce: 'The company will turn out toasters and microwaves this year'

turnover, turn over

> turnover *n.* the speed at which goods are sold and replaced; a shift in personnel or the rate at which workers leave and are replaced: 'Our staff turnover falls when conditions are bad'; a small pastry pie: 'I bought an apple turnover in the bakery'; change or movement of people in, out, and through a place: 'The restaurant had a lively turnover'
>
> turn over *v.* to pass something on: 'Turn over that old car to me'; to change to an opposite position: 'Turn over on your stomach'; to meditate on

twill, tuille

> twill *n.* a weave of cloth with a diagonally ribbed pattern
>
> tuille *[tweel] n.* plate armor covering the thigh

twinge *See* tinge

two *See* to

tye *See* tie

typography *See* topography

U

udder, utter

> udder *n.* an organ consisting of two or more milk-secreting
> mammary glands and nipples in a single pouch,
> especially in a cow

> utter *v.* to vocalize, to express: 'She did not utter a sound'

> utter *adj.* absolute, to the highest degree: 'The honeymooners
> were in a state of utter happiness'

ugli, ugly

> ugli *[ugly] n.* a fruit, the result of a cross between a
> grapefruit, a tangerine, and an orange

> ugly *adj.* repulsive, vile: 'ugly rumors'; unsightly: 'He received
> an ugly gash'

umbles *See* humbles

umpire *See* empire

unable *See* enable

unapt *See* inapt

unaware, unawares

> unaware *adj.* not aware; not knowing: 'He was unaware of the
> impending divorce.'

> unawares *adv.* without preparation, suddenly: 'The divorce
> proceedings caught him completely unawares'

underlay, underlie

> underlay *n.* something inserted under another item: 'The felt
> padding was an underlay for the carpet'

underlie *v.* to lie below or under; to be the basis for an idea or action: 'Deregulation was said to underlie the widespread S&L corruption'

undo, undue

undo *v.* to reverse: 'That decision will undo 100 years of constitutional law'; to open by releasing a fastening; to ruin someone's reputation

undue *adj.* excessive: 'He is under undue pressure'

unexceptionable, unexceptional

unexceptionable *adj.* lacking any weakness or fault, beyond reproach: 'Her performance in school is unexceptionable'

unexceptional *adj.* ordinary or average: 'He is an unexceptional student with a C average'

union *See* onion

unique *See* eunuch

unit, unite

unit *n.* a single person or thing, alone or as part of a group or process: 'The accounting unit is too slow'; a part of a school course with a theme: 'A history unit on South Africa'

unite *v.* to come together; to marry; to combine with a common objective

unreal, unreel

unreal *adj.* not genuine; fanciful, imaginary, fantastic: 'Her expectations were unreal'

unreel *v.* to unwind: 'In order to free his line, the fisherman had to unreel his spinner'

unrooted, unrouted, uprooted

unrooted *adj.* not uprooted: 'The tree remained unrooted in spite of the severe storm'; without roots: 'He's unrooted—can't settle down'

unrouted *adj.* not charted: 'Gorbachev had taken the Soviet Union down an unrouted path' uprooted *adj.* torn up by the roots: 'The storm uprooted many trees'; forcibly removed from one's location: 'The population was uprooted by the war'

unsewn, unsown

unsewn *adj.* not sewed: 'The dress patterns were cut, but still unsewn'

unsown *adj.* not sowed: 'The fields were left unsown to increase their fertility'

unwanted, unwonted

unwanted *adj.* not desired: 'She resisted his unwanted attention'

unwonted *adj.* unusual, infrequent, rare: 'He had an unwonted feeling of being at ease with the world'

urban, urbane

urban *[ur'•bin] adj.* characteristic of a city: 'New York City reflects the nation's urban problems'

urbane *[ur•bane'] adj.* sophisticated, elegant, refined: 'He moves in a very urbane circle of theatergoers and writers'

urn *See* earn

use, yews

use *[yooz] v.* to put into service: 'I'll use the small car to pick him up'; to exploit: 'They'll use her for their own selfish purpose'

use *[yoos] n.* the state of being used or put into service

yews *n.* (pl.) evergreen trees

utter *See* udder

uvula, uvular

uvula *n.* the fleshy protuberance hanging above the back of the tongue

uvular *adj.* pertaining to the uvula; articulated with the back of the tongue held close to the uvula

V

vacation, vocation

    vacation *n.* a holiday

    vocation *n.* a regular occupation; a calling: 'His vocation was
        medicine'

vail, vale, veil

    vail *v.* to lower oneself as an act of deference

    vale *n.* a valley: 'Over hill, over vale'

    veil *n.* a length of cloth often used as a face covering; a nun's
        vocation; something that conceals

vain, vane, vein

    vain *adj.* proud; conceited: 'Because of his good looks, he is
        extremely vain'; fruitless: 'We made a vain attempt to
        complete the job by six'

    vane *n.* a blade of a windmill; a weathervane

    vein *n.* a blood vessel

    vein *v.* to streak or branch out in the manner of blood vessels

valance, valence

    valance *n.* a short drapery hung along the upper edge of a
        window, altar, bed, or table; a wood or metal piece hung
        along the upper edge of a window or canopy

    valence *n.* in physics, the ability of elements to combine; the
        degree to which elements can combine; the appeal of an
        activity as a goal to which one aspires

vary, very

    vary *v.* to modify, change, or alter: 'Candidates always vary
        their political platforms in different regions'

very *adv.* much, a great deal: 'I'm very sorry'

very *adj.* actual, plain, real: 'The very heart of the system is the mainframe computer'; same: 'My very thought'

veil *See* vail

vein *See* vain

vellum, velum

vellum *n.* a fine parchment

velum *[vee'•lum] n.* the soft palate

venal, venial

venal *adj.* ready to sell principle or honor; open to corruption, especially bribery: 'A venal judge is the bane of the criminal justice system'

venial *adj.* excusable, easily pardonable: 'That is a venial sin, not a mortal one'

veneer, venire

veneer *n.* a thin layer of material or facing; a superficial quality or manner: 'He has a veneer of learning, but really knows little'

venire *[vuh•nie'•ree] n.* a prospective panel in the courts from which a jury is drawn

venerable, vulnerable

venerable *adj.* deserving to be revered: 'a venerable judge'; conveying an impression of aged goodness and benevolence

vulnerable *adj.* exposed to something harmful or detrimental: 'His errors made him vulnerable too attacks'; capable of being attacked

veracity, voracity

veracity *n.* truthfulness: 'I doubt his veracity'

voracity *n.* greediness, rapaciousness

verses, versus

verses *n.* (pl.) more than one verse or line of metrical writing or stanza in poetry; the numbered paragraphs in the Bible

versus *prep.* against: 'Columbia versus Princeton'; in contrast to: 'high tariffs versus free trade'

vertical, verticil

vertical *n.* an upright position; perpendicular to the horizontal plane

verticil *[ver'•ti•sil] n.* an arrangement around an axis, such as leaves, flowers, or hairs

very *See* vary

vial, vile, viol

vial *n.* a small bottle

vile *adj.* despicable or loathsome; foul tasting or smelling: 'a vile odor'; repulsive or utterly bad: 'their vile lives in the slums'; morally repugnant

viol *n.* one of a family of stringed instruments

See also file

vice, vise

vice *n.* a moral fault or shortcoming; an immoral or depraved habit: 'Crack use is a dangerous vice'

vise *[vice] n.* a device with two movable jaws that clamp together: 'Some vices possess you like a vise'

vigorous, vigorish, rigorous

vigorous *adj.* robust, full of strength: 'For a man of 68, he was hale, hearty, and vigorous'; done with vigor or force: 'a vigorous workout'

vigorish *n.* excessive interest or fees charged by a loan shark

rigorous *adj.* precise, severe, or strict: 'The training at the parachute school was rigorous and hard'

vile *See* vial

villain, villein

villain *n.* a malevolent, wicked person, the "bad guy" in a movie or play; a scoundrel or criminal

villein *[vil'•en or vil•ayne'] n.* a feudal serf; a free villager or peasant in a low-ranking feudal class

villous/villose, villus

villous *or* villose *adj.* covered with long, soft hair

villus *n.* a soft, long hair covering parts of certain plants; a hairlike structure on certain membranes that often aids in absorption

viol *See* vial

virus, virous

virus *n.* an ultramicroscopic infective agent; an agent of contagious disease: 'It is believed that AIDS is caused by HIV, human immunodeficiency virus'; a disease caused by a virus: 'a stomach virus'

virous *adj.* caused by a virus

viscose, viscous

viscose *n.* a chemical substance used in making nylon and rayon

viscous *adj.* sticky; a special quality of fluids that makes them thick and hard to pour

vise *See* vice

visible *See* risible

vocation *See* vacation

voracity *See* veracity

vulnerable *See* venerable

W

wad, wade, weighed

wad *[rhymes w.* pod*] n.* soft or small masses of material used as filler in many applications: clothing, cars, guns: 'a wad of gum'; a lot of money (slang): 'He's carrying a big wad'

wade *v.* to walk through shallow water; to work one's way through a hard task: 'Wade through those term papers'

weighed *v.* past tense of weigh, to measure the heaviness of something

waddy, wadi

waddy *n.* a native Australian club; a walking stick; a cowboy

wadi *n.* a dry river bed; a gully

wail, wale, whale

wail *n.* a lamentation or prolonged cry of grief; a high pitched sound: 'The wail of the police sirens awakened the neighborhood'

wale *n.* a welt; a ridge or rib on cloth: 'wide wale corduroy'; a ship's plank

whale *n.* a giant sea mammal; any big item or accomplishment: 'That's a whale of a job'

wain, wan, wane

wain *[rhymes w.* main*] n.* a wagon; a heavy farm vehicle

wan *[rhymes w.* on*] adj.* pale, melancholy, sickly, feeble

wane *n.* a gradual decrease; a decrease in intensity: 'The full moon is on the wane'

waist, waste

waist *n.* the part of the human body that narrows between the ribs and the hips; a garment that covers the waist; the middle, narrower part of an object

waste *n.* garbage or trash; a loss; destruction; the squandering of ability or resources: 'a waste of her talents'

waste *v.* to squander time, money, or objects; to ruin or destroy; to become gradually worn or weak: 'AIDS will waste his body'; to use inefficiently: 'He will waste the opportunity to double his income'; to kill (slang): 'He boasted that he would waste all his rivals'

wait, weight

wait *v.* to stay ready for something to occur: 'I'll wait for hours to get into that disco'; to postpone: 'That trip will have to wait'; to work as a waiter or server: 'She'll wait on tables until she gets an acting job'

weight *n.* the amount or degree of heaviness of an item or person: 'It had a weight of 20 pounds'; a load or a burden: 'carry weight'; 'pull one's weight'; importance or influence: 'throw one's weight about'

waive, wave

waive *v.* to relinquish: 'He will waive all claim to the inheritance'; to refrain; to postpone; in sports, to drop a player from one's team

wave *n.* a moving ridge in a body of water: 'That's a good surfing wave'; an up-and-down or back-and-forth movement of the arms as a greeting; a social action or movement: 'a wave of protest about repression'; a high point or peak: 'A wave of selling hit Wall Street'; an electrical oscillation

wave *v.* to flutter, to shake back and forth lightly: 'The flags wave with the breeze'; to signal: 'wave farewell'; to put curls into hair

waiver, waver

waiver *n.* in law, a voluntary relinquishment of a right or advantage or the legal proof of such relinquishment

waver *n.* one who waves or performs the act of fluttering the
hands and arms

waver *v.* to vacillate or hesitate: 'His determination didn't
waver in spite of the carnage'; to tremble or move
unsteadily: 'His hands waver when he speaks of the
accident'; to fluctuate: 'Stock prices waver rapidly on
major news breaks'

wale *See* wail

walk-in, walk in

walk-in *n.* a room that can be entered directly; an apartment
that can be entered directly from the street rather than
through the lobby; a person who enters a place such as a
doctor's office without an appointment

walk-in *adj.* large, permitting direct entrance: 'a walk-in
closet'

walk in *v.* to proceed with one's feet: 'I take a walk in the
park every day'; to enter in; to move around in

walk-on, walk on

walk-on *n.* a minor role in a theatrical production

walk on *v.* to move on foot on something: 'I told him not to
walk on the new rug with his muddy boots'

walkout, walk out

walkout *n.* a strike or protest

walk out *v.* to leave: 'I will walk out of the restaurant if I'm
not served immediately'

walk-up, walk up

walk-up *n.* an apartment house without an elevator

walk up *v.* to approach on foot: 'I will walk up to her and
comfort her'

wall, waul/wawl

wall *n.* an upright enclosure; a partition; an item or situation
that's hard or impossible to penetrate: 'We're up against
a wall and can't solve this problem'

waul *or* wawl *v.* to wail or howl like an infant or kitten

wan *See* one; wain

wander, wonder

wander *v.* to roam about aimlessly; to ramble; to meander

wonder *n.* a feeling of doubt; astonishment; admiration; a miracle: 'It's a wonder that you don't collapse from overexertion'

wonder *v.* to speculate: 'I wonder who's kissing you now'; to be astonished: 'I wonder at your calm in this hurricane'

wane *See* wain

wangle, wrangle

wangle *v.* to obtain through trickery, to finagle: 'He'll wangle money from his mother with another phony tale'

wrangle *v.* to quarrel bitterly or noisily: 'They wrangle over his efforts to wangle money from his mother'; to herd livestock on a range

want, wont, won't

want *v.* to desire: 'I want a new car'; to need; to lack: 'He won't want knowledge of science'; to be poor or destitute: 'I won't allow my children to want'; to seek to arrest: 'The police want him for armed robbery'; like: 'Say what you want, I like him'

wont *n.* habit: 'It's my wont to exercise two hours a day'

wont *adj.* accustomed: 'I am wont to nap at three'

won't *contr.* will not: 'I won't come to the movies; I'm too tired'

wanton, wonton

wanton *[wahn'•tun] adj.* sexually loose: 'a wanton woman'; senseless or unjustified: 'wanton destruction'; 'wanton cruelty'; extravagant: 'wanton spending'

wonton *[wahn•tahn] n.* a Chinese dumpling

war, wore

war *n.* an armed or other major open and declared conflict or struggle: 'the War Between the States'; 'the war on poverty'

wore *v.* past tense of wear, to be clothed in: 'She wore a blue
ribbon in her hair'; to show or exhibit: 'She always wore
a smile'; to damage gradually: 'The sleeves wore out
before the rest of the shirt'; to last: 'That hotel's
architecture wore well'

ward, warred

ward *n.* a unit in a hospital, prison, or city; a minor or
incompetent who is under someone else's legal control;
a person or thing under guard or protection

ward *v.* to fend off or to turn aside, to deflect: 'By taking the
injection, she hoped to ward off the disease'; to guard

warred *v.* past tense of war, to carry on armed or other
serious conflict or struggle

ware, wear, where

ware *n.* goods, merchandise; goods of fired clay

wear *n.* clothing for a particular use: 'Summer wear is selling
well'; the result of usage: 'wear and tear'; durability

wear *v.* to have on one's body: 'She'll wear pants to the
luncheon'; to have a particular look: 'She'll never fails to
wear a smile'; to damage by heavy use: 'You'll soon wear
out that suit'; to weary or tire: 'This work will soon wear
me down'; to retain the quality or vitality: 'This suit
should wear well'

where *adv.* refers to what place or location, modifies a verb:
'Where did she go?'; 'Where does she live?'; what
position or direction: 'Where do you stand on abortion?'

where *pron.* acts independently as a noun, meaning which
place: 'Where did she come from?'; the point at which
something exists or happens: 'That's where we will build
our new house'

where *conj.* in what place: 'See where she lives'; wherever:
'Put on the sunscreen where you're exposed'; any place:
'She will go where I go'

See also weir

warm-up, warm up

warm-up *n.* preparation for a performance, as in the loosening of a baseball pitcher's arm

warm up *v.* to heat or reheat: 'He will warm up the soup when he gets home'; to exercise mildly before heavier exercise; to become friendly: 'I sense that he'll warm up to me in time'

warn, worn

warn *v.* to alert to a potential harm or danger; to give notice of impending danger: 'She tried to warn him never to call again'

worn *v.* past participle of wear, to have on: 'I have worn the same suit every day'

worn *adj.* showing the effects of use: 'She donates her worn clothes to charity'

warrantee, warranty

warrantee *n.* a person to whom a warranty is given

warranty *n.* a guarantee of performance: 'The air conditioner is still under warranty, therefore the manufacturer will fix it'

warred *See* ward

wart, wort

wart *n.* a small hard excrescence on the skin caused by a virus

wort *n.* an herb; unfermented malt

wasp, WASP

wasp *n.* an insect

WASP *n.* a White Anglo-Saxon Protestant: 'A horde of WASPs were at the Newport ball'

waste *See* waist

watt, what

watt *n.* a unit of electrical power

what *adj.* used in a question about an amount, kind, or number: 'What time is it?'; which: 'What kind of eggs would you like?'; expresses how great or bad: 'What silliness!'

what *pron.* which specific thing: 'What are we having for supper?'; that which: 'See what I've done to this room'; used with a request for particular information: 'What are you doing?'; to learn identity or origin: 'What are these flowers?'; how much: 'What does this cost?'

what *adv.* how: 'What do you care?'; to what extent: 'What does it matter?'

waul/wawl *See* wall

wave *See* waive

waver *See* waiver

wavey, wavy

wavey *n.* a snow goose

wavy *adj.* having waves; rolling as with waves

wax, whacks

wax *n.* a malleable substance produced by bees to make a honeycomb; a chemical or physical imitation of that substance used as a polish, a coating, or a seal; anything that can be easily shaped or molded

wax *v.* to grow larger or more numerous, to increase in intensity, as the moon; to become: 'wax sentimental'; to treat or rub with wax, as wood

whacks *v.* 3d person, sing., present tense of whack, to administer a blow

way, weigh, whey

way *n.* a path, route, or direction: 'What's the best way to get to Washington?'; one's preferred style or moves: 'I like this done my way'; one's capability: 'She has a way with children'; condition: 'I'm in a bad way'; distance: 'That's a long way off'; a location: 'When you're down my way, drop in'; a plan: 'find a way to cut costs'; custom: 'I like the old way of doing things'; feature: 'In no way does she look like him'; possibility: 'No two ways about it'

way *adv.* away: 'Go way'; to a great extent: 'That job is way too hard' weigh *v.* to measure the heaviness of a person or object: 'He'll soon weigh 200 pounds'; to think about: 'He'll weigh the matter carefully'

whey *[hway] n.* the watery part of milk, separated from the curd

we, wee, whee

we *pron.* plural of I, you and I and others: 'We are going to the movies'; or of people in general: 'We're going to win the war against poverty'

wee *adj.* very small: 'a wee child'; very early: 'In the wee hours of the morning'

whee *interj.* an exclamation of joy or relief

weak, week

weak *adj.* without strength or force, feeble: 'I have weak muscles'; inadequate, ineffective, impotent: 'He's a weak president'; diluted: 'Bring me weak coffee'; deficient or lacking proficiency: 'He's weak in math; she's weak in spelling'

week *n.* a period of seven days

weakly, weekly

weakly *adj.* feeble, sick, frail

weakly *adv.* in a weak manner: 'She reprimanded him weakly'

weekly *n.* a newspaper or magazine published once a week

weekly *adj.* occurring or done once a week or every week: 'He received his weekly paycheck on Fridays'

weekly *adv.* every week once a week: 'She meets him for lunch weekly'

weal, we'll, wheal/weal, wheel

weal *n.* well-being or welfare: 'The public weal requires that we pass this legislation'

we'll *contr.* we will, we shall: 'We'll go to the movies tomorrow'

wheal *or* weal *n.* a welt; a raised ridge on the skin

wheel *n.* a revolving circular frame: 'the wheel of a car'

wheel *v.* to move an object with wheels: 'She'll wheel her bicycle to the store'; to move in a circular manner; to turn quickly in place: 'The sudden noise made him wheel around'

wear *See* ware

weather, wether, whether

weather *n.* the atmospheric conditions of temperature, wind velocity, precipitation, etc.: 'They listen to his forecast of the weather at 11 o'clock every night'

weather *v.* to withstand: 'They will weather the period of unemployment and come out fine'; to wear out or to become discolored by exposure to air and the elements

wether *n.* a castrated ram

whether *conj.* introducing the first of two alternatives: 'I don't know whether or not I'll take a vacation this year'

weave, we've

weave *v.* to make a fabric on a loom by interlacing threads; to combine elements in any operation, particularly a creative one: 'She strives to weave elements of her personal life into her poetry'; to contrive; to spin, as a web

we've *contr.* we have: 'We've been there before'

weaver, weever

weaver *n.* a person who makes a fabric on a loom

weever *n.* a genus of fish

we'd, weed

we'd *contr.* we had, we should, we could, we would: 'We'd go to Paris if we had the money'

weed *n.* an undesired plant that often grows rampantly and tends to choke other plants; marijuana (slang)

wedgie, wedgy

wedgie *n.* a shoe with a wedge heel that creates a continuous flat sole

wedgy *adj.* shaped or used like a wedge

wee *See* we

weed *See* we'd

week *See* weak

weekly *See* weakly

weever *See* weaver

weigh *See* way

weighed *See* wad

weight *See* wait

weir, we're

weir *[weer] n.* a low dam; a fence set to divert flow or to take
fish; an obstruction

we're *contr.* we are: 'We're happy to see you again'

See also ware

we'll *See* weal

wen, when

wen *n.* a cyst formed by an obstruction in a sebaceous gland

when *n.* the time of any event: 'The when and why of
recessions'

when *pron.* at what time: 'Since when have you been
waiting?'

when *adv.* at what time: 'When will we arrive?'; at what point,
under which conditions: 'When is it proper to call on
them?'

when *conj.* as soon as: 'I'll see you when you return'; while:
'When she was old, she sat in her garden'; after which:
'We had just gone out when it began to rain'; whenever:
'When she eats pasta she falls asleep'

wench, winch

wench *[rhymes w.* bench*] n.* a girl or young woman; a
prostitute

winch *[rhymes w.* pinch*] n.* a crank for hoisting or pulling

we're *See* weir

wet, whet

wet *n.* moisture; rain; one who is in favor of legalizing the
sale of liquor

367

wet *adj.* covered with water or liquid: 'The ground is wet
from rain'; still moist: 'wet paint'; rainy: 'Seattle has a wet
climate'; wrong: 'You're all wet'

whet *v.* to sharpen or hone; to stimulate: 'The smell of that
cooking will whet my appetite'

wether *See* weather

we've *See* weave

whacks *See* wax

whale *See* wail

what *See* watt

wheal *See* weal

whee *See* we

wheel *See* weal

when *See* wen

whence *See* hence

where *See* ware

whet *See* wet

whether *See* weather

whetstone, wet stone

whetstone *n.* an abrasive stone used for sharpening tools

wet stone *n.* a stone covered with water

whew *See* ewe

whey *See* way

which, witch

which *adj.* what one of a group: 'Which shirt should I wear?';
introduces a clause that refers to a word or concept in a
preceding clause: 'The game was postponed for an hour,
during which time the players received a deserved
rest'—'which' refers to 'an hour'

which *pron.* what particular one or ones: 'Which of these jobs
do you prefer?'; in grammar, to introduce a relative
clause: 'The tide, which is heavy in the morning, is not
good for swimming'

witch *n.* a woman with malignant supernatural powers; a
sorceress; a hag; a seductive woman

whicker, wicker

whicker *n.* a neigh or a whinny

wicker *n.* a pliant twig; something, usually furniture, made of wicker

Whig, wig

Whig *n.* a British person seeking to limit royal authority and increase parliamentary power; an early American form of the Republican party; a conservative

wig *n.* a false hair covering for the head

while, wile

while *n.* a short time: 'Rest for a while'

while *v.* to pass time pleasantly: 'We'll while away the day doing nothing'

while *conj.* during that time, at the same time: 'Watch the kids while I go shopping'; although: 'While we are friends, we don't see one another often'

wile *n.* a sly trick

whine, wine

whine *v.* to complain; to make a high, unpleasant cry: 'He can whine all he wants, we won't give him candy'

wine *n.* an alcoholic beverage made from fermented grapes

whirl, whorl

whirl *v.* to turn rapidly or swiftly

whorl *n.* a ridge of a fingerprint; anything shaped like a coil; an arrangement of like parts around a point on an axis

whit, wit

whit *n.* the least bit: 'not a whit the wiser'

wit *n.* clever humor; high intelligence

whitewash, white wash

whitewash *n.* a mixture for whitening walls or another structure; an effort to exonerate by concealing the truth: 'The investigation was a complete whitewash'

white wash *n.* a laundry that is white: 'He did a white wash and a dark wash at the laundromat'

whither, wither
>   whither *conj.* to which place: 'Whither thou goest, I will go'
>   wither *v.* to dry up; to wilt; to weaken: 'The plant will wither
>   in the sun'

whoa, woe
>   whoa *[wo] interj.* stop, halt, often used with horses
>   woe *n.* great suffering or trouble

whole *See* hole

wholly *See* holey

whoop *See* hoop

whore, who're *See* hoar

whored *See* hoard

whores *See* hoars

whorl *See* whirl

whose, who's
>   whose *pron.* that which belongs to who(m): 'Whose hat is this?'
>   who's *contr.* who is: 'If you don't know who's in this year,
>   you will never get invited to any of the parties'

wicker *See* whicker

width, with, withe
>   width *n.* size in terms of the distance from side to side, breadth:
>   'The width of the football field was shorter than its length'
>   with *prep.* alongside, near, accompanied by: 'I'll walk with
>   you'; in favor of, for: 'I'm with you'; by way of: 'He won
>   the election with a massive TV campaign'; using or
>   showing: 'He sang with glee'; against or in opposition:
>   'She fought with her brother over the vacation plans'
>   withe *n.* a slender, flexible branch or twig

wig *See* Whig

wile *See* while

winch *See* wench

windlass, windless
>   windlass *n.* a winding device consisting of a barrel set
>   between two posts and turned by a crank which rolls the
>   rope on the barrel

windless *adj.* devoid of wind

windup, wind up

> windup *n.* the conclusion or end: 'The windup of the convention resulted in greater unity'; in baseball, the preliminary motion of a pitcher
>
> wind up *v.* to set: 'I will wind up the clock before it runs down'; to settle or conclude: 'They hope to wind up the negotiations today'

wine *See* whine

wipeout, wipe out

> wipeout *n.* a fall from a skateboard, surfboard, or skis; a complete failure or disaster: 'The party was a wipeout'
>
> wipe out *v.* to obliterate, annihilate, or abolish

wit *See* whit

witch *See* which

with, withe *See* width

wither *See* whither

woe *See* whoa

won *See* one

wonder *See* wander

wont, won't *See* want

wonton *See* wanton

wood, would

> wood *n.* the fibrous substance that makes up trees and branches; a dense area where trees grow; a golf club with a wooden head or a similarly shaped head made of metal
>
> would *v.* past tense of will, used to express desire, choice, or willingness: 'He would sit there and dream for hours'; used mostly as an auxiliary verb meaning to wish, to want, or to intend: 'I would do that if I could'

wore *See* war

workout, work out

> workout *n.* a session of exercises; strenuous exercise or work

work out *v.* to make its way out, as from being embedded: 'The splinter will work itself out in time'; to solve: 'We'll work this out without anyone's help'; to exercise or practice: 'They will work out in the gym all day'

worn *See* warn

worst, wurst

worst *adj.* superlative of bad, the most unpleasant, dangerous, or unsuccessful: 'He is the worst student in the class'; evil or harmful in the highest degree: 'He's the worst crook in the S&L scandals'

worst *v.* to defeat; to get the better of

wurst *n.* a sausage

wort *See* wart

worthless, worth less

worthless *adj.* lacking worth or value; lacking honor; useless; contemptible

worth less *v.* of less value: 'My stock seems to be worth less and less each day'

would *See* wood

wrack *See* rack

wraith *See* rath

wrangle *See* wangle

wrap *See* rap

wrapped *See* rapped

wrapper *See* rapper

wrasse *See* rasse

wrath *See* rath

wreak *See* reek

wreath, wreathe

wreath *[rhymes w.* teeth*] n.* a twisted band of flowers or leaves; a garland

wreathe *[rhymes w.* seethe*] v.* (usually used in the past tense) to entwine or coil so as to make a wreath; to decorate with wreaths; to envelop: 'Her face was wreathed in smiles'

wreck *See* reck
wrest *See* rest
wretch *See* retch
wright *See* right
wring *See* ring
wrist *See* rest
write *See* right
write-in, write in

> write-in *n.* a name a voter writes in on a ballot, not one officially listed
>
> write in *v.* to place words or other marks in an object such as a book: 'Please don't write in the book'; to enter a name that is not officially listed on a ballot

writs *See* ritz
wrote *See* rote
wrung *See* rung
wry *See* rye
wrys *See* rise
wurst *See* worst

Y

yawl, yowl

> yawl *n.* a sailboat
>
> yowl *v.* to cry mournfully; to wail

yew *See* ewe

yews *See* use

Yoga, yoga, yogi

> Yoga *n.* a Hindu philosophy teaching suppression of activity to achieve liberation of the self
>
> yoga *n.* a system of exercises for attaining bodily and mental control
>
> yogi *n.* one who practices yoga; a mystical or reflective person

yoke, yolk

> yoke *n.* a wooden frame used to couple two draft animals; a device to carry two pails; a crushing burden, servitude, or bondage: 'They suffered under the yoke of the tyrant'
>
> yolk *n.* the yellow portion of an egg

yore, your, you're

> yore *n.* time past and long past: 'in days of yore'
>
> your *pron.* possessive, belonging to you: 'I respect your smarts'
>
> you're *contr.* you are: 'You're very smart'
>
> *See also* ewer

you *See* ewe

yu *See* ewe